SATHER CLASSICAL LECTURES

Volume Forty-three

THE ANCIENT ECONOMY

THE
ANCIENT
ECONOMY

by M. I. FINLEY

Updated Edition
With a Foreword by Ian Morris

UNIVERSITY OF CALIFORNIA PRESS
Berkeley · Los Angeles · London

University of California Press
Berkeley and Los Angeles, California

University of California Press, Ltd.
London, England

Second Edition 1985, Updated Edition 1999

Library of Congress Catalog Card Number 86-672785

ISBN 978-0-520-21946-5 (pbk.)

Printed in the United States of America

14   13   12   11   10   09   08   07   06
     12   11   10   9   8   7   6   5   4

The paper used in this publication is both acid-free and
totally chlorine-free (TCF). It meets the minimum
requirements of ANSI/NISO Z39.48-1992
(R 1997) (*Permanence of Paper*). ∞

To the

FACULTY OF CLASSICS
UNIVERSITY OF CAMBRIDGE

and the

DEPARTMENT OF CLASSICS
UNIVERSITY OF CALIFORNIA, BERKELEY

Contents

Foreword

Introduction

HISTORIANS LOVE an anniversary. Twenty-five years have now passed since the University of California Press published Moses Finley's *The Ancient Economy*, which is based on the forty-third series of Sather lectures that he gave at Berkeley in 1972. No book this century has had such a great influence on the study of Greek and Roman economic history, and so it is only fitting that the Press should reissue this classic for a new generation of readers. In this foreword, I want to introduce new readers to this book by giving a sense of its intellectual roots, how it advanced the study of the ancient economy, and how its arguments stand up after a quarter century of scrutiny.

Ancient economic history is a relatively young field. August Böckh published a monumental study of Athenian political economy as long ago as 1817, but economic questions only entered the mainstream of classical scholarship much later. In 1893, Karl Bücher, applying an influential general theory of economic evolution to European history, suggested that Greece and Rome were characterized by very simple, small-scale, closed household economies aimed at self-sufficiency and engaged only in very limited exchanges with other households. The Middle Ages saw the rise of larger city economies, and the sixteenth century the emergence of integrated national economies. Some professional ancient historians, most notably Eduard Meyer, were outraged by this theory and insisted that Bücher had it all wrong: ancient economies were in fact much like those of the modern world, just rather smaller. Meyer claimed that "in the history of Greece, the seventh and sixth centuries B.C. correspond to the fourteenth and fifteenth in the modern world, the fifth corresponds to the sixteenth."[1]

Scholarly debate can only take place when academics agree on which questions they should be asking. It is not a criticism of the scholars involved in the primitivist-modernist debate, as it came to be known, to point out that it narrowed the discussion down to the single issue of where to place Greece and Rome along a continuum from self-sufficient households to contemporary industrial nations. In the 1890s, this struck German classicists as a real and important issue, and in the first half of the twentieth century, scholars from other countries joined in. On the whole, they concluded (1) that this was indeed the most important question to ask, and (2) that the modernists had the better of it. In 1933, Mikhail Rostovtzeff, a Russian writing in America and the greatest ancient economic historian of his age, even echoed Meyer in stating that "by the Hellenistic period the economy of the ancient world was only quantitatively, not qualitatively, different from that of modern times." And there things stayed until the 1950s.[2]

Scholarship tends to change direction not through the gradual accumulation of details in well-established frameworks but in sudden spurts. Like all research programs, the primitivist-modernist debate ignored a wide range of phenomena. Historians of scholarship have found that revolutions in thought tend to happen when scholars (often newcomers to the field or those on its margins) start to feel that the anomalies that "normal science" does not explain have accumulated to such an extent that the conventional models do more harm than good. Some scholars respond not by offering new answers to the old questions but by throwing out the old questions altogether in favor of new ones that seem more compelling—what Thomas Kuhn christened a "paradigm shift."[3]

Such shifts are rarely, if ever, the result of an individual genius confronting a misguided world. Usually it begins with a group of scholars. If their concerns are valid and they present them well enough, they will communicate their sense of unease with the prevailing wisdom to others. If the revolution takes off, there will be a rush to map out new research programs that answer the questions now deemed important. The old agenda may simply be forgotten. Finley, at first very much a marginal figure, worked with like-minded scholars in the 1950s (particularly Karl Polanyi at Columbia and A. H. M. Jones at Cambridge) to establish new questions. He did not create the "Finley model" out of nothing; but by the 1970s he was the central figure in rethinking ancient social and economic history, and *The Ancient Economy* cemented the new structure. In essence it redefined the terms of the debate.

Finley's Ancient History

Finley came to ancient history in an odd way.[4] Something of a prodigy, he earned an M.A. in public law in 1929 at the tender age of seventeen. This was a period when classical historians learned their craft through training in philology, but after gaining his law degree, Finley entered the field by serving as a research assistant in Roman law at Columbia University. He then enrolled as a graduate student in Columbia's history department. He was deeply involved in the intense intellectual life of 1930s New York. He held part-time jobs working for the *Encyclopedia of the Social Sciences* and the Frankfurt School's Institut für Sozialforschung, where he cut his teeth as a historian on the German exiles' critiques of Hegel, Marx, and Weber.

Like those of so many of his generation, Finley's career plans were derailed by the Second World War. Finley worked for war relief agencies before returning to ancient history in 1947. His social-scientific interests made him eccentric in classical circles, as he was well aware,[5] but in 1948 he found a position at Rutgers University. He had still not finished his Ph.D., but teaching in New Jersey meant that he could keep his ties to Columbia. For the next five years he was a regular member of Karl Polanyi's economic history seminar there.

Polanyi was a Hungarian émigré who had gained sudden prominence in 1944 with the publication of *The Great Transformation*. As interested in economics, sociology, and anthropology as he was in history, he did not fit easily into established university departments, and upon his appointment at Columbia in 1946 created an interdisciplinary group that explored some of the implications of his arguments. In *The Great Transformation*, Polanyi proposed that capitalism and communism were not the only ways to run a complex modern economy. Neo-classical economic theory did not produce immutable laws; rather, its generalizations applied only to a particular type of modern society, which, he believed, could be replaced by an ethically preferable system that combined the principles of socialism and Christianity.[6]

Polanyi argued that before around 1800 in western Europe (and long after in much of the rest of the world), economic activity had not been an independent sphere of life governed by its own rules. Instead, production and exchange had been embedded in other institutions and attitudes. Polanyi never denied that the profit motive had been strong in earlier societies, but he insisted that profit had been a means to other ends and not an end in itself. He argued that goods and services had circulated through mechanisms of reciprocity and redistribution rather than through impersonal markets. Social relationships, not abstract laws of supply and demand, fixed values; and these relationships made the rational choices of the maximizing isolated actor of economic theory irrelevant in most societies. He called his model *substantivism*, as distinct from conventional economic *formalism*, the belief that an economic sphere always exists outside and independent of social relations.

Polanyi created the Columbia group because he saw that his political agenda depended on historical and anthropological arguments. He suggested that because disembedded, price-setting markets were a relatively recent development in world history, it ought to be possible to re-embed economic markets in other social relationships, subordinating profit to more humane concerns. He accepted that "more than once in the course of human history have markets played a significant part in integrating the economy," even suggesting that Athens in the age of Aristotle was one such case.[7] But the most important point was that early markets, even in Athens, "never [operated] on a territorial scale, nor with a comprehensiveness even faintly comparable to that of the nineteenth-century West."[8] While Athens was only one of many historical examples Polanyi explored, it was an important one for him, because most ancient historians since the 1890s had assumed that the classical Athenian economy ran along much the same lines as modern economies, even if on a smaller scale. Against the modernists, Polanyi asserted that the Greek economy had little in common with modern capitalism, but against the primitivists he asserted that this was because economic interests were subordinated to or absorbed within concerns with politics, honor, and war and *not* because of the scale of economic activity. From this perspective, the primitivist-modernist debate about where the ancient economy fell on the continuum from simple to complex was going nowhere.

Finley had serious reservations about Polanyi's interpretation of Greece,[9] although we can hardly doubt that the discussions at the Columbia seminar greatly influenced his thinking. But ancient historians sometimes allow Polanyi's influence to overshadow the ways in which both Polanyi and Finley drew on the ideas of Max Weber, the founding father of modern sociology. Polanyi rarely cited Weber, but Finley referred to him as early as 1935 and cited Weber's "Agrarverhältnisse im Altertum" (but none of Polanyi's work) in the bibliography of his dissertation. In his later works he made his debt to Weber very clear.[10]

Weber and Polanyi had very different political views,[11] but they agreed on some of the main questions. Weber thought sociology should be about understanding modernity, and like Polanyi, placed the historical roots of modernity's economic institutions and thought at the forefront. Polanyi and Weber also agreed on the need for comparative work. Weber wrote about China, India, Reformation Europe, and the Roman empire; Polanyi wrote about Dahomey, the ancient Near East, and classical Athens. And the conclusions they reached were not dissimilar. For Weber, the most important category for analyzing nonmodern societies was *status*. He explained that

> "Status" (*ständische Lage*) shall mean an effective claim to social esteem in terms of positive or negative privileges; it is typically founded on
>
> a) style of life, hence
> b) formal education, which may be[:]

α) empirical training or

β) rational instruction, and the corresponding forms of
behavior,

c) hereditary or occupational prestige.

In practice, it expresses itself through

α) conubium,

β) commensality, possibly

γ) monopolistic appropriation of privileged modes of
acquisition or the abhorrence of certain kinds of acquisition,

δ) status conventions (traditions) of other kinds.

Status *may* rest on class position of a distinct or an ambiguous
kind. However, it is not solely determined by it: Money and an
entrepreneurial position are not in themselves status qualifications, although they may lead to them; and the lack of property
is not in itself a status disqualification, although this may be a
reason for it . . .

A "status group" means a plurality of persons who, within a
larger group, successfully claim

a) a special social esteem, and possibly also

b) status monopolies.

Status groups may come into being:

a) in the first instance, by virtue of their own style of life,
particularly the type of vocation: "self-styled" or occupational status groups.

b) in the second instance, through hereditary charisma, by
virtue of successful claims to higher-ranking descent:
hereditary status groups, or

c) through monopolistic appropriation of political or hierocratic powers: political or hierocratic status groups.[12]

Status groups are by their nature fluid, open to challenge and reinterpretation. They are what sociologists nowadays would call contested categories. New groups are constantly created and old ones
redefined in a competitive process, and Weber observed that "in
this case stratification is purely conventional and rests largely on
usurpation." However, he went on, "the road to legal privilege, pos-

itive or negative, is easily traveled as soon as a certain stratification of the social order has in fact been 'lived in' and has achieved stability by virtue of a stable distribution of economic power."[13] In Athens and Rome, male citizens made the transition from "self-styled" status group to a legally defined order with important privileges, such as exclusive intermarriage with one another's daughters, control of the land, monopolies on political rights, legal defenses against exploitation (particularly debt bondage), and occasionally commensality. In doing so, they created other orders defined largely by their negative privileges—particularly the women they considered their dependents, chattel slaves, freedmen, and resident aliens.

Ancient man, Weber felt, was a *homo politicus*, interested in economics and profits chiefly as ways of promoting the political/military success of his city-state, conceived as a "guild of warriors," and his own ability to take a leading role in it. Modern man is a *homo oeconomicus*, pursuing gain wherever it might lead him.[14] What made Greece and Rome interesting was how they differed from medieval Europe. For good or for evil, the status structures of the latter created the spaces within which *homo oeconomicus* grew up; those of the former did not. That demanded explanation.

Weber contrasted status groups to class groups, explaining that

> In our terminology, "classes" [unlike "status groups"] are not communities; they merely represent possible, and frequent, bases for social action. We may speak of a "class" when (1) a number of people have in common a specific causal component of their life chances, insofar as (2) this component is represented exclusively by economic interests in the possession of goods and opportunities for income, and (3) is represented under the conditions of the commodity or labor markets. This is "class situation."[15]

He filled out this typology by saying that

> always this is the generic connotation of the concept of class: that the kind of chance in the *market* is the decisive moment

which presents a common condition for the individual's fate.
Class situation is, in this sense, ultimately market situation . . .
According to our terminology, the factor that creates "class" is
unambiguously economic interest, and indeed, only those interests involved in the existence of the market.[16]

Weber concluded that

As to the general *effect* of the status order, only one consequence
can be stated, but it is a very important one: the hindrance of
the free development of the market . . . The market is restricted, and the power of naked property *per se*, which gives its
stamp to class formation, is pushed into the background . . .
where stratification by status permeates a community as strongly
as was the case in all political communities of Antiquity and the
Middle Ages, one can never speak of a genuinely free market
competition as we understand it today.[17]

Weber suggested that market relationships, with their characteristic
forms of modern rationality, came to dominate some parts of Europe in the nineteenth century, making class more important than
status and creating situations in which class-based action was a constant possibility. Like Polanyi, he believed that the market and class
had not played the same roles in earlier societies.

Weber had effectively discredited the primitivist-modernist debate by the time of the First World War, but ancient historians simply did not read him. The exception that proves the rule is Johannes Hasebroek, whose two books on the Greek economy were
summarily dismissed.[18] To a great extent, the paradigm shift that
Finley spearheaded between the 1950s and the 1970s could be
called a neo-Weberian revival.

In *Studies in Land and Credit in Ancient Athens*, Finley—like Weber,
Hasebroek, and Polanyi—suggested that although the Athenian
economy had been large and complex, it could not be called a market economy. To prove his point, he collected the evidence of the
horoi, or inscribed mortgage stones. Whenever a stone recorded the

reasons for the mortgage, it was always for consumption rather than production: Athenians mortgaged land to pay for weddings and funerals, not to create capital for investment. As such, their economic activities were driven by status concerns, and there was little trace of the rationalistic, economizing mentality that Weber and Polanyi saw as a precondition for capitalist relations. Finley suggested that there was no genuine land market in Athens, just some rich men raising money for conspicuous consumption. Nor, he concluded, was there a proper credit market. The characteristic way for Athenians to raise cash was through *eranos* loans, contracted through groups of *philoi*, or "friends," not normally involving interest payments. A good citizen should help out his friends and should never under any circumstances profit from another citizen's misfortunes. Athenians wanted to be rich, but status considerations always dominated market concerns. Although Finley did not use this terminology, his vision of the Athenian economy was consistent with Polanyi's redistributive model.[19]

By 1953, Finley perhaps felt that he had provided an adequate account of the nonmarket workings of the Athenian economy, for he then turned to trying to explain where this social system had come from. He quickly wrote a second book, the classic *The World of Odysseus*, in which he explicitly took over Polanyi's categories. He suggested that after the collapse of redistributive Mycenaean economies around 1200 B.C., heroic gift economies emerged. As in the classical Athenian system, reciprocity was the basis of interactions, but instead of creating a unified, homogeneous male citizen body, in Homeric times (which Finley put around 900 B.C.), gift exchange was competitive and functioned to create hierarchy. The heroes were calculating supermen struggling against common enemies and against one another in a Hobbesian war of all-against-all, forming complex webs of political alliances, gifts, counter-gifts, and marriages, where might was right and the price of weakness was destruction.[20]

By 1954 Finley was under considerable pressure at Rutgers for his and his wife's political connections with radicals. As a serious student of Weberian sociology, Finley would have made a strange communist, but he and his wife, Mary, decided to emigrate to Britain. There he found a post at Cambridge among a group of classical scholars headed by Jones, who took social history, and even Marxism, seriously. In this more sympathetic setting, Finley confronted the new problem that his interpretation of Homer had raised: how did Greek society move from the hierarchical reciprocity of the heroic age to the egalitarian reciprocity of the classical citizen polis? In 1959, he published the first of a series of essays giving his answer: slavery.[21]

Weber had suggested that crises over debt were among the few situations in which genuine class conflicts could emerge in antiquity.[22] Finley followed this view, suggesting that archaic social revolutions triggered by resistance to debt bondage, like that leading to Solon's reforms at Athens in 594, had swept away the Homeric system of graded statuses. Through violence or its threat, the poor refused to be reduced by debt to dependency on the households of the great and created the idea of the city-state as a community of equal men. Men (women are conspicuously absent from Finley's story) were polarized into two groups, one of free citizens practicing reciprocal exchange, alienating exploitation onto the other, of imported chattel slaves. The parameters of economics were set by status considerations: only reputable sources of wealth were acceptable, which ruled out direct exploitation of fellow citizens and inhibited the development of price-setting markets in land, labor, or credit. Only outsiders should be exploited, in the extreme but common case through commoditizing their very bodies as chattel slaves.

As Weber, Hasebroek, and Polanyi had seen, ancient economic history was thus a subject for the historical sociologist, not the economist. Finley followed Weber in seeing the history of the ancient world as the history of the construction of status groups. He suggested that we could sum up the whole period from 1000 B.C. though A.D. 500 in terms of

> [a] highly schematic model of the history of ancient society. It moved from a society in which status ran along a continuum towards one in which statuses were bunched at the two ends,

the slave and the free—a movement which was most nearly completed in the societies which most attract our attention for obvious reasons. And then, under the Roman Empire, the movement was reversed; ancient society gradually returned to a continuum of statuses and was transformed into what we call the medieval world.[23]

Nine years later, *The Ancient Economy* provided a book-length exposition of this model.

The Ancient Economy

The Ancient Economy is quintessentially Finleyan. The prose style is discursive: it reads well and draws the reader in. Finley does not wear his learning, whether it be substantive or comparative, on his sleeve; he chooses his ancient examples carefully and eschews extended theoretical discussions. For readers used to either conventional classical scholarship, with its mass of references to secondary literature and detailed discussion of specific passages in ancient texts, or for those coming from the social sciences, where explicitly stated propositions are the norm, this can indeed be (as Shaw and Saller put it) "unconventional, puzzling, and even disconcerting."[24] It is notoriously difficult to find a sentence or two in Finley's articles and books that serve to sum up his whole argument. There are such passages in *The Ancient Economy*, but they rarely leap out at first-time readers from the overall smoothness of the text.

The core thesis of Finley's book is that we can build a coherent model of a single ancient economy, which sums up the important features of the whole Graeco-Roman Mediterranean from 1000 B.C. through A.D. 500, but excludes the ancient Near East, at least until its incorporation into Macedonian kingdoms and then the Roman empire. Finley recognized the diversity of economic arrangements within this huge slice of time and space, but as in all his work, insisted that "we must concentrate on the dominant types, the characteristic modes of behaviour" (page 29). The model had to be qualitative not quantitative, because the ancients kept no usable statistics; but that fact in itself is significant. Their failure to collect systematic numerical data is not just an empirical problem for us, or evidence of their intellectual shortcomings, but a sign that the ancients did not see economic activity as a distinct element of life. In short, the ancient economy was embedded.

The analytical heart of Finley's model is status. In chapter 2 he explains why we should prefer order and status to class as conceptual categories. His definition of status is typically low-key. In a discussion of wealthy slaves and freedmen in the Roman empire, he says that "for such distinctions I suggest the word 'status', an admirably vague word with a considerable psychological element" and adds that Greeks and Romans "were, in the nature of things, members of criss-crossing categories" (page 51). Throughout the book he uses these ideas in the Weberian sense, but he prefers to let the sense he gives them emerge gradually, from the examples he gives, over presenting a formal sociological typology. Much of chapter 2 is taken up with Cicero's thought about status and wealth, which neatly illustrates Finley's method. At the end of the chapter Finley explains that "I chose Ciceronian Rome for special analysis precisely because that was the period when the status-based model appeared to be nearest to a break-down. It did not break, however, it bent, it adapted, by extending the choices in some directions, not in all; in directions, furthermore, which can be seen to have followed logically from the very values that were being threatened and defended" (page 61). And what we learn is very Weberian: in both Athens and Rome, "the citizen-élite were not prepared, *in sufficient numbers*, to carry on those branches of the economy without which neither they nor their communities could live at the level to which they were accustomed . . . They lacked the will; that is to say, they were inhibited, as a group (whatever the responses of a minority), by over-riding values" (page 60).

In the rest of the book he elaborates on three key areas in his model: first, rural life (divided into chapters on unfree labor and the peasantry), then the place of cities, and finally the place of the economy in politics. Finley's vision comes through very clearly in these chapters. Ancient social and economic history is above all rural history, the history of peasants, although in two vital cases—beginning in Greece around 600 B.C. and Italy around 200 B.C. and ending in both after A.D. 200—the creation of "true" slave economies made free citizenries possible. This was a world in which family came first and nearly everyone aimed for economic self-sufficiency. Trade generally took place on a small scale and was conducted over short distances. Most fortunes were made from rents and control of the machinery of taxation. Only rarely did traders or industrialists make good, and when they did, they were eager to invest their gains in land. There were economic changes—in particular, the steady concentration of land in fewer and fewer hands in the Roman empire, and with it the blurring of the boundary between free and slave—but there was little economic growth to speak of. There were, of course, exceptions, such as the super-cities like Rome, Alexandria, and Antioch, or, in a smaller way, classical Athens. These cities needed permanent grain imports to feed their citizens and housed substantial nonagricultural groups. But they remained exceptions: even in the high Roman empire, the truly urban population was never more than one-twentieth of the rural. It would be a mistake to call Graeco-Roman civilization urban, although its ruling classes certainly were. They showed little interest in the countryside so long as they could get enough food from it, and there was rarely (if ever) anything we could call state economic policy.

This model does nothing to help us with the older questions of the primitivist-modernist debate. We cannot place Greece and Rome on a continuum from simple to complex economies, because their economies do not belong on such a continuum. They were qualitatively different. As Weber had foreseen, the ancient economy, unlike the medieval, did not contain the seeds from which *homo oeconomicus* could grow: contrary to Polanyi's somewhat confused account of Athens, there were no forces acting to disembed the economy, to allow class and the market to override status. Finley's ancient economy was a functioning, coherent system, which came to an end not because of its internal contradictions but because of the interaction between Roman social structures and the exogenous force of increasing pressure on the frontiers: "There, if one wishes, is an economic explanation of the end of the ancient world" (page 176).

When one reads *The Ancient Economy* alongside Finley's other writings, five consequences of the ancient civic status structure seem to loom large. First, for Finley, as for Weber, the most important thing about Graeco-Roman concepts of status was the way they acted as a brake on the development of markets in land, labor, and capital and therefore on technology and trade. Demosthenes and Cicero's conceptions of appropriate behavior were different, but both sets of attitudes functioned to embed economic activity in a broader network of social relationships. Neither the Athenian nor the Roman orator was comfortable with admitting to lending at interest, investing heavily in profitable long-distance trade, or defining their identities in terms of wealth-producing activities. In one essay Finley collected a whole group of stories about ancient failures to exploit the commercial potential of technological developments and suggested that the status structure was once again responsible.[25]

Second, the triumph of citizen status severely limited the opportunities for the rich to persuade poor citizens to provide labor power, leading to "the advance, hand in hand, of freedom *and* slavery."[26] Finley argued that when three social facts coincided—the existence of concentrations of land in private hands, the existence of external markets for the produce of the land, and the unavailability of an internal labor supply—the conditions were ripe for the creation by the rich of large-scale chattel slavery. He saw the social struggles of archaic Greece and Rome as fulfilling the third (negative) condition, so that the ancient economy was the world's first true slave economy.[27]

Third, the status concerns of citizens tended to push even profitable activities to the margins of society. Foreigners, women, and slaves were unusually prominent in trade and finance. Some rich citizens generated their wealth from selling agricultural staples grown mainly by slaves on their estates or from selling their shares in crops grown by dependents or rents paid in kind, but they would try to have noncitizen agents carry out the actual transactions.

Fourth, Greeks and Romans tended to pursue wealth through legal and political channels rather than through what we would call economic avenues. Finley suggested that ancient cities were consumer rather than producer cities, exploiting the countryside through taxes, tribute, and rent rather than by selling urban goods to rural consumers.[28]

Fifth, the need to push exploitation outside the citizen community and the preference for political solutions may have given Graeco-Roman society a particularly powerful socioeconomic motive for war and imperialism, making these natural ways to acquire wealth. In his final book, Finley showed that despite the many studies of wars, hardly any ancient historians have treated war as a structural feature of ancient societies.[29]

The Ancient Economy After Twenty-Five Years

Thomas Kuhn insisted that the humanities and social sciences do not experience the same kind of paradigm shifts as do the natural sciences. In the latter, once a new framework gains acceptance, rival ways of seeing things are quickly driven from the field by being denied access to funds and therefore students. There is no room for the old-fashioned in science. But in the former fields, the champions of older models, secure in their positions, do not go away. Their influence can remain strong for decades, with the result that we normally speak of "schools of thought" rather than of "paradigms."

The influence of Finley's work took root gradually. Not surprisingly, it was felt most strongly in Cambridge. Even before Finley's arrival there, Jones was making the economy central to a particularly Cambridge approach to ancient history, and many of the students they taught between the 1950s and 1980s went on to champion this approach. But outside Cambridge, Finley's impact on English-language scholarship developed more slowly. British scholars like to joke that the journey from Cambridge to Oxford is longer than that from Cambridge to anywhere else in the world, and at first Finley stimulated the most interest on the European continent. He had more interest in and contact with eastern European Marxist scholars than did most Westerners, and continental classicists ranging from Dutch social historians to French and Italian neo-Marxists found his Weberianism reasonably consistent with their own interests.[30]

What is more surprising is that for some years his ideas had more of an impact on Romanists, sociologists, and anthropologists than on Hellenists, among whom they generated not so much resistance as studied neglect.[31] This had changed by the time of Finley's death in 1986, and as early as 1983, Keith Hopkins was already speaking of "a new orthodoxy . . . masterminded by A. H. M. Jones and Sir Moses Finley."[32] In the last ten years there have been more books and articles exploring and expanding Finley's insights than I could possibly list here.

But a quarter of a century is a long time in historical scholarship. As Finley came of age as a historian in the 1930s, American "New Historians" like Charles Beard and James Harvey Robinson and French Annalistes like Lucien Febvre and Marc Bloch were, for the first time in a century, challenging the idea that proper history was about political narratives. These historians wanted to analyze social structures and economic forces and even to borrow the methods of the social sciences. When Finley delivered the Sather lectures in 1972, this approach was positively mainstream in modern history—so much so that in the 1980s social and economic history came under attack from a movement of "new cultural historians." This group drew much of their inspiration from literary criticism. In introducing a collection of essays called simply *The New Cultural History*, Lynn Hunt explained that for these historians, "Economic and social relations are not prior to or determining of cultural ones; they are themselves fields of cultural practice and cultural production—which cannot be explained deductively by reference to an extracultural dimension of experience."[33] By the 1990s, many social and economic historians feel themselves under siege as the materialist consensus of the 1970s crumbles.

Ancient historiography has developed differently. Ancient historians are still found chiefly outside university history departments, in classics departments in north America, or in ancient history departments in Europe. They tend to go to different conferences than the ones attended by modern historians, to publish in different journals, and almost to speak a different language. As late as the 1970s, the vision of historiography as the handmaiden of philology still dominated the field. In engaging with Weber, Marx, and functionalist social science, Finley had been in a distinct minority since his graduate school days. The growing influence of *The Ancient Economy* did more than anything else to put the questions he had been asking for thirty years on the agenda for the main body of ancient historians. But paradoxically, by the time this was happening in the 1980s, those ancient historians whose interests lay closest to literary criticism were already picking up on the new cultural history.

Ancient historians effectively skipped the stage in the development of modern historiography when social and economic questions dominated the agenda and moved straight from philology and politics to cultural poetics. Most history departments contain a substantial group of (now aging) radical economic and social historians hired in the 1970s and early 1980s who defend their turf against the cultural historians. The slow spread of ancient economic and social history, the small scale of most ancient history programs, and the demographic structure of the profession—which made the 1970s and 1980s lean years for new appointments—combined to create a situation in which very few classics departments hired in social and economic history.

One result of this dearth of social and economic historians is that the shift toward cultural history in classical studies has been defined not against social and economic history but against more traditional philological scholarship.[34] If anything, there has been more interest in social and economic history in the late 1990s than at any other time. This development may have much to do with ancient historians' continuing interest in *The Ancient Economy* and in its twenty-fifth anniversary. There have been conferences and seminar series devoted to it in Cambridge, Leiden, Liverpool, Paris, and Stanford, all destined for publication.[35] It is hard to imagine that American historians will respond in this way to the twenty-fifth anniversary of a classic such as Fogel and Engerman's *Time on the*

Cross, due out in 1999, let alone that they will want the book reissued.[36] Just when economic and cultural historians' inability to communicate is causing alarm among modernists, more ancient historians than ever are confronting Finley's arguments.

The price (indeed, the clearest sign) of success is criticism, and in the 1990s Finley's model came under sustained attack.[37] In his last book, Finley observed that "ideologies change, and so the writing of history undergoes constant 'transformation,'"[38] so this would not have surprised him. We might break the responses down into three broad types. The first is the *empiricist*, which has many continuities from the pre-Finleyan philological history. Its champions try to show that Finley's general model of the ancient economy cannot account for the details of particular parts of the Graeco-Roman world between 1000 B.C. and A.D. 500 or even that in trying to make his model work, Finley committed factual errors.[39] Empiricist studies tend to foreground details at the expense of formal argument and methodological exposition, drawing attention to the richness, variety, and irreducible uniqueness of individuals, institutions, and states in the ancient world.

Although these critiques are valuable, they tend to be undertheorized. As Weber explained, there is always an inverse relationship between the general applicability of a model and its ability to accommodate reality: "The more sharply and precisely the ideal type has been constructed, thus the more abstract and unrealistic in this sense it is, the better it is able to perform its functions in formulating terminology, classifications, and hypotheses."[40] The best ideal types work to highlight certain features of reality and allow us to simplify and make sense of vast quantities of empirical detail. We need different models for different jobs. Finley and Polanyi, driven by radical political agendas, wanted very high-level models that would help them think about the differences among ancient, medieval, and modern European economies. Most ancient historians seem happier with low-level models of one period, region, or town. Their models are likely to be more realistic, in the sense that they account for more data and are contradicted by fewer facts, but they are also less likely to interest the large communities of social scientists and comparativists that Finley, Polanyi, and Weber reached. Decisions about appropriate levels of generalization are driven by what we think ancient history is *for*: they are philosophical, aesthetic, and ultimately political. Mid-nineteenth-century historians like Grote and Marx were happy to talk about these questions, but historians of our own day generally are not.

The philosopher of science Richard Levins suggests that "there is no single, best all-purpose model . . . it is not possible to maximize simultaneously generality, reality, and precision."[41] The failure to recognize this vitiates many of the empiricist critiques of *The Ancient Economy*. But that being said, there certainly are empirical grounds for evaluating models within a community of historians who more or less agree on the appropriate level of generalization. We should judge a model by how helpful it is in making sense of the data. At a certain point, which some historians reach sooner than others, the number of cases that cannot be accommodated within a model reaches a level at which the model clearly does more harm than good. Finley had harsh words for the practitioners of local histories, what he called the "tell all you know about X" school of historiography,[42] but they become important for Finley's own questions when they start to suggest that he, like Hasebroek in the 1920s, was guilty of systematic omissions or errors. The most common argument has been that Finley consistently underestimated the scale of ancient trade, industry, banking, and other nonagricultural economic activity, so that his substantivism, the idea that economic activities were embedded in other social relations, in fact slid over into crude primitivism, the belief that ancient economies were basically household economies.[43] The issue is muddied by the way some critics are unable to tell the two concepts apart, but it is a serious problem, bringing us to the next category of criticism.

I take my second and third categories of critiques from the sociologist Mark Granovetter's discussion of Polanyi. Granovetter suggests that discussions of Polanyi's work can be divided into two types, those that see it as "oversocialized" and those that see it as "undersocialized."[44] The *oversocialization critics* hold that Weber and his intellectual heirs exaggerate the amount of sociological "friction" that status generates and consequently also exaggerate the extent to which noneconomic considerations, however defined, can suppress market relationships. Finley could then be accused of taking the ancient sources too much at face value: Cicero may talk as if what Romans really cared about was status, but this may be mere ideology (in the sense of false consciousness) masking deeper economic realities. Rather than starting from what the ancients say, we might do better to construct formal economic models, or models that seem rational in light of cross-cultural comparisons. We could then explore why what ancient writers say in their texts fails to match these models and we could also read the sources against the grain to find places where economic realities peep through the masks of culture.[45]

Those historians who think that Finley underestimated the scale of the ancient economy tend to accuse him of oversocialization. This argument is particularly common among Romanists. Keith Hopkins, for instance, drawing much more heavily on formal economic thought than Finley ever did, and testing his conclusions against archaeological evidence from shipwrecks for the scale of long-distance trade, argued that there was significant economic growth in the empire between 200 B.C. and A.D. 200. David Mattingly reached much the same conclusion after conducting a survey of rock-cut oil presses in Roman North Africa. He argued that oil production happened on a scale far larger than what the local population needed, which could only be explained by assuming that farmers were heavily tied to an export market. It now seems to be generally accepted that the vast market in food, wine, oil, lumber, bricks, and so forth created by the growth of Rome to a population of about one million by the first century B.C. stimulated production and went some way toward disembedding economic activity.[46]

Oversocialization critiques have made less headway among Greek historians but have nonetheless raised important issues. The most significant is Edward Cohen's discussion of how Greek orators distinguished between a visible (*phaneros*) and an invisible (*aphanes*) economy, with banking and other financial activities falling into the latter. Rich men tried to conceal their involvement in the invisible economy, which was—contrary to Finley's interpretations—very large. Cohen argues that rich Athenians made a considerable part of their fortunes like this, and that in this sphere economics were disembedded from conventional status concerns, with foreigners, women, and slaves playing large roles.[47]

As with the Romanists, archaeology has also played a part. Since the 1970s, intensive surface surveys in the Greek countryside have been indicating a change in settlement patterns in the fifth and fourth centuries. In an effort to explain this, and also to account for how so many people made their living off such small territories, historians and archaeologists have begun to sketch a "new model" of classical agriculture, which involved far more production for the market than Finley's vision would have it.[48] This model remains highly speculative, given the quality of the surface remains, but it would explain much of the data.

Whether Hellenists or Romanists, archaeologists or close readers of texts, the oversocialization critics try to read through the evidence to reach underlying economic structures. Whatever the sources may say, we know (within certain parameters) that Rome would have needed a certain amount of grain each day, and Athenian aristocrats would have needed to generate a certain amount of cash. Given this information we can move beyond the texts.

Finally, Finley's model also has its *undersocialization critics.* This line of thought draws much of its inspiration from the new cultural history of more modern periods and focuses on the hegemonic discourses in ancient literature and the complexities involved in the construction of ideology. Rather than beginning from sociological categories and looking at how they structured ancient literature, the critics claim that we should instead look for how such categories were created and contested in the discursive practices of knowledgeable actors.[49]

This approach to the ancient economy is largely restricted to Hellenists[50] and to literary scholars. Sitta von Reden, for example, has criticized Finley for "his complete elimination of the ideological negotiations about the meaning and limits of the institutions he analyzed—such as slavery, landownership, citizenship and credit."[51]

To some extent, Finley would have sympathized with this, even though he would have resisted the implications von Reden draws from it. Weber had insisted that "for a science which is concerned with the subjective meaning of action, explanation requires a grasp of the complex of meaning in which an actual course of under-standable action thus interpreted belongs."[52] In the same vein, Finley suggests that "My justification for speaking of 'the ancient economy' lies ... in the common cultural-psychological framework" (page 34). He devoted much of *The Ancient Economy* to arguing that Greeks and Romans imagined "the economic" as a dimension of status relations rather than as a separate sphere of life. But the new cultural historians take things much further. Finley, like Weber, always explained economic discourse in terms of nondiscursive re-alities of social stratification, exploitation through tax, rent, and slavery, agricultural technology, or military issues. Greek economic discourse was part of a larger sociological picture. The new cultural historians, however, bring discourse itself to the fore in their analy-ses, so that extracultural dimensions of experience begin to disap-pear altogether.

For example, in *Mass and Elite in Democratic Athens*, Josiah Ober fol-lowed Finley to a large extent in identifying the most important questions to ask about Athenian democracy as how did it avoid sta-sis for two centuries and how did it function without a ruling elite. Ober, however, came up with very different answers. He passed quickly over imperialism and slavery, which Finley had emphasized, and instead focused on political discourse. He argued that in fourth-century Athens, "public rhetoric not only *revealed* social ten-sion, it was a primary vehicle for *resolving* tension."[53] Generalizing from this, he suggested that in classical Athens, "discourse is an as-pect of social practice, and, as such, not only reflects beliefs, but brings into being social and political realities."[54] Rhetoric was "the most important form of ongoing communication between ordinary and elite Athenians" and "the demos ruled, not so much because of its 'sovereignty', as because of its control over significant aspects of the symbolic universe of the Athenian community."[55]

Ober argued that the generally wealthy litigants who dramatized their feuds in front of the generally poor jurors exposed themselves to many dangers. As a result, the men who wrote our texts did not simply distort realities; they constructed alternative, context-dependent realities. Litigants tried to draw their audiences into shared fictions so that speakers could forge bonds of identity with the jurors. They did not just tinker with details: they stepped into dramatic personae in much the same way as actors do. Ober suggested that "theater-going citizen 'learned' to suspend disbelief... This 'training' helped jurors to accept elite litigants' fictional representations of their own circumstances and their relationship to the Athenian masses. The complicity of speaker and audience to create and accept dramatic fictions regarding social status was an important factor in the maintenance of Athenian social equilibrium."[56] We can identify conflicts of belief and values within Athenian culture, but it would be a great mistake to assume that we can read away the rhetorical construction of reality to figure out how the economy "really" worked. In more recent studies, some Greek historians/literary critics (the boundary rapidly blurs) extend these arguments even to the most supposedly "economic" of categories, such as coinage and food, reinterpreting them as elements in the struggles over meaning through which the Greeks created their city-states.[57]

Conclusion

A quarter of a century after it was published, *The Ancient Economy* is still squarely at the center of debate. Finley showed decisively that philological/empiricist history could not make sense of ancient economic phenomena. A great deal of very good work is still being done in this style, but on the whole it has more to say about the debates of the 1890s than about the new orthodoxy. *The Ancient Economy* stands midway between deterministic, economistic approaches and postmodern literary explorations. Both undersocialization and oversocialization critics must engage seriously with Finley's work if they are to make any headway.

Weber believed that true sociological understanding called for two kinds of research, one oriented toward formulating abstract ideal types and the other toward contrasting these with the evidence for people's actual behavior and beliefs.[58] Ideally, the same person would conduct both activities at different moments. The result would be a constant tacking back and forth between generalized structures and the experiences of individual actors, which is precisely what Finley does in *The Ancient Economy*. Inevitably, newer studies mean that we need to modify many of Finley's conclusions, such as those on the scale of Athenian banking, the location of the market in the Roman economy, and economic growth in antiquity, but *The Ancient Economy*'s humane vision of the Greek and Roman past will remain at the center of our arguments for the foreseeable future. Any informed discussion of these phenomena has to start with Finley's model of the centrality of the egalitarian citizen group and its interrelations with large-scale chattel slavery. For many of us who came to ancient history in the 1970s and 1980s, reading *The Ancient Economy* was a formative experience. This new edition extends the same opportunity to a new generation of students.

Ian Morris
Stanford University
September 1998

NOTES TO FOREWORD

1. Quoted from Michel Austin and Pierre Vidal-Naquet, *Economic and Social History of Ancient Greece* (rev. ed., London 1977) p. 5. Their first chapter provides the best summary of the history of the scholarship.

2. The original essays are available in Moses Finley, ed., *The Bücher-Meyer Controversy* (New York 1980). Rostovtzeff is quoted in S. C. Humphreys, *Anthropology and the Greeks* (London 1978) p. 42.

3. Thomas Kuhn, *The Structure of Scientific Revolutions* (2nd ed., Chicago 1970).

4. This section owes much to Brent Shaw and Richard Saller, "Editors' Introduction," in Moses Finley, *Economy and Society in Ancient Greece* (London 1981) pp. ix–xxvi.

5. As Finley reveals in a letter of December 11, 1947, to Fritz Heichelheim,

published in Brent Shaw, "The Early Development of M. I. Finley's Thought: The Heichelheim Dossier," *Athenaeum* 81 (1993) 183–84.

6. Karl Polanyi, *The Great Transformation* (Boston 1944) p. 234. S. C. Humphreys, *Anthropology and the Greeks* (n. 2 above) 31–75 gives a perceptive discussion of Polanyi's work and its influence on ancient historians.

7. Karl Polanyi, "Aristotle Discovers the Economy," in *Trade and Market in the Early Empires*, ed. Karl Polanyi, Conrad Arensberg, and Harry Pearson (Glencoe, Ill., 1957) 64–97.

8. Karl Polanyi, *The Livelihood of Man*, ed. Harry Pearson (New York 1977) 43. This flawed manuscript, dated May 1951, was published posthumously. Finley tried to persuade Pearson to omit the Greek material; see David Tandy and Walter Neale, "Karl Polanyi's Distinctive Approach to Social Analysis and the Case of Ancient Greece: Ideas, Criticisms, Consequences," in *From Political Economy to Anthropology: Situating Economic Life in Past Societies*, ed. David Tandy and Colin Duncan (Montreal 1994) 25 n. 6.

9. Moses Finley, "Aristotle and Economic Analysis," *Past and Present* 47 (1970) 3–25, reprinted in *Studies in Ancient Society*, ed. Finley (London 1974); also *The Use and Abuse of History* (London 1975) 117.

10. Polanyi, *Great Transformation* (n. 6 above), 45–46; Finley, "*Emporos, naukleros*, and *kapelos*: Prolegomena to the Study of Athenian Trade," *Classical Philology* 30 (1935) 320–36. Finley completed his dissertation in 1951 and published it as *Studies in Land and Credit in Ancient Athens, 500–200 B.C.* (New Brunswick, NJ, 1952; reprinted New York 1979; New Brunswick 1985). The bibliography of significant works is on pp. 304–8. Later comments on Weber: "The Ancient City: From Fustel de Coulanges to Max Weber and Beyond," *Comparative Studies in Society and History* 19 (1977) 305–27, reprinted in Finley, *Economy and Society* (n. 4 above) pp. 3–23; *Ancient History: Evidence and Models* (London 1985) pp. 3, 52, 60–61, 88–108. In a conversation in February 1984, he told me that he thought that Weber had been the single greatest influence on his thought and that he planned to reread all Weber's major works in the next few years.

11. The best accounts of Weber remain H. H. Gerth and C. Wright Mills, "Introduction: The Man and His Works," in their *From Max Weber: Essays in Sociology* (New York 1946) pp. 3–74; Reinhard Bendix, *Max Weber: An Intellectual Portrait* (New York 1960), and Guenther Roth, "Introduction," in Max Weber, *Economy and Society*, ed. Guenther Roth and Claus Wittich (2 vols., New York 1968, reissued Berkeley 1978; translated from German original of 1922, collecting many of Weber's earlier writings) pp. xxxiii–cx.

12. Weber, *Economy and Society* (n. 11 above), pp. 305–6.

13. *Ibid.*, p. 933.

14. *Ibid.*, pp. 1354, 1359.

15. *Ibid.*, p. 927.

16. *Ibid.*, p. 928.

17. *Ibid.*, p. 937.

18. Johannes Hasebroek, *Die imperialistische Gedanke im Altertum* (Stuttgart 1926); *Trade and Politics in Ancient Greece*, transl. L. M. Fraser and D. C. MacGregor (London 1933, from German original of 1928). On the dismissal of Hasebroek, see Paul Cartledge, "'Trade and Politics' Revisited: Archaic Greece," in *Trade in the*

Ancient Economy, ed. Peter Garnsey, Keith Hopkins, and C. R. Whittaker (Cambridge 1983) pp. 2–5.

19. Finley, *Studies in Land and Credit* (n. 10 above); "Land, Debt, and the Man of Property in Classical Athens," *Political Science Quarterly* 68 (1953) 249–68, reprinted in Finley, *Economy and Society* (n. 4 above), pp. 62–76.

20. Finley, *The World of Odysseus* (New York 1954; rev. ed. 1979).

21. Finley, "Was Greek Civilisation Based on Slave Labour?," *Historia* 8 (1959) 145–64; "The Servile Statuses of Ancient Greece," *Revue internationale des droits de l'antiquité,* 3rd ser., 7 (1960) 165–89; "Between slavery and freedom," *Comparative Studies in Society and History* 6 (1964) 233–49; "La servitude pour dettes," *Revue historique de droit français et étranger,* 4th ser., 43 (1965) 159–84. The papers are reprinted in Finley, *Economy and Society* (n. 4 above), pp. 97–166.

22. Weber, *Economy and Society* (n. 11 above), pp. 303–4, 931.

23. Finley, "Between Slavery and Freedom" (n. 21 above), 249 (*Economy and Society,* p. 132).

24. Shaw and Saller, "Editors' Introduction" (n. 4 above), p. xviii.

25. Finley, "Technical Innovation and Economic Progress in the Ancient World," *Economic History Review,* 2nd ser., 18 (1965) 29–45 (*Economy and Society,* pp. 176–95).

26. Finley, "Was Greek Civilisation Based on Slave Labour?" (n. 21 above), 164 (*Economy and Society,* p. 115).

27. Finley, "Slavery," *International Encyclopedia of the Social Sciences* (New York 1968) 14: 307–13; *Ancient Slavery and Modern Ideology* (London 1980) pp. 11–92; and pp. 62–94 below.

28. Finley, "Ancient City" (n. 10 above).

29. Finley, *Ancient History* (n. 10 above) pp. 67–87.

30. E.g., Harry Pleket, "Economic History of the Ancient World and Epigraphy," *Akten des VI. Internationalen Kongresses für griechische und lateinische Epigraphik* (Munich 1972) pp. 243–57; Willem Jongman, *The Economy and Society of Pompeii* (Amsterdam 1988); Pierre Vidal-Naquet, "Économie et société dans la Grèce ancienne: l'oeuvre de Moses I. Finley," *Archives européenes de sociologie* 6 (1965) 111–48; and the general discussions of Finley's work in the Italian journal *Opus* vols. 1 (1982) and 6–8 (1987–89). Finley's account of the International Historical Congress at Stockholm in 1960 in *Ancient Slavery and Modern Ideology* (n. 27 above) pp. 60–62 is very informative.

31. I single out particularly Peter Garnsey and Richard Saller, *The Roman Empire* (London 1987); Dominic Rathbone, *Economic Rationalism and Rural Society in Third-Century A.D. Egypt* (Cambridge 1991); C. R. Whittaker, *Land, City and Trade in the Roman Empire* (Aldershot 1993); Peter Garnsey, *Famine and Food Supply in the Graeco-Roman World* (Cambridge 1988); *Cities, Peasants and Food in Classical Antiquity* (Cambridge 1998). For the social scientists, see Orlando Patterson, *Slavery and Social Death* (Cambridge, Mass., 1982); Maurice Godelier, *The Mental and the Material* (London 1986, translated from French original of 1984).

32. Keith Hopkins, "Introduction," in *Trade in the Ancient Economy,* ed. Garnsey et al. (n. 18 above), p. xi.

33. Lynn Hunt, "Introduction," in *The New Cultural History,* ed. Hunt (Berkeley 1989) p. 7.

34. See particularly Carol Dougherty and Leslie Kurke, "Introduction," in *Cultural Poetics in Archaic Greece,* ed. Dougherty and Kurke (Cambridge 1993) pp. 1–12.

35. The Paris papers have already appeared, in *Annales Histoire Sciences Sociales* 50 (1995) 947–89.

36. Robert W. Fogel and Stanley Engerman, *Time on the Cross: The Economics of American Negro Slavery* (2 vols., Boston 1974). Stanley Elkins, in *Slavery: A Problem in American Institutional and Intellectual Life* (3rd ed., Chicago 1976) pp. 267–302, gives an excellent account of the shift from social and economic to cultural questions in American slave studies.

37. Finley responded to criticisms of *The Ancient Economy* published up to 1984 in a postscript to the book's second edition (pp. 177–207).

38. Finley, *Ancient History* (n. 10 above), p. 5.

39. The best-known example is Martin Frederiksen, "Theory, Evidence and the Ancient Economy," *Journal of Roman Studies* 65 (1975) 164–71.

40. Weber, *Economy and Society* (n. 11 above), p. 21. Cf. Finley, *Ancient History* (n. 10 above), pp. 60–1.

41. Richard Levins, *Evolution in Changing Environments* (Princeton 1968) p. 7.

42. Finley, *Ancient History* (n. 10 above) p. 61.

43. See Edmund Burke, "The Economy of Athens in the Classical Period: Some Adjustments to the Primitivist Model," *Transactions of the American Philological Association* 122 (1992) 199–226.

44. Mark Granovetter, "Economic Action and Social Structure: The Problem of Embeddedness," *American Journal of Sociology* 91 (1985) 481–510.

45. Thomas Rawski explains this in more detail in his essays in *Economics and the Historian,* ed. Rawski (Berkeley 1996) pp. 1–59.

46. Keith Hopkins, "Economic Growth and Towns in Classical Antiquity," in *Towns in Societies,* ed. P. Abrams and E. A. Wrigley (Cambridge 1978) pp. 35–79; "Taxes and Trade in the Roman Empire," *Journal of Roman Studies* 70 (1980) 101–25; "Models, Ships and Staples," in *Trade and Famine in Classical Antiquity,* ed. Peter Garnsey and C. R. Whittaker, *Proceedings of the Cambridge Philological Society,* supp. vol. 8 (Cambridge 1983) 84–109. Hopkins's incisive summary of the Jones-Finley orthodoxy at pp. xi–xii of his introduction to *Trade in the Ancient Economy,* ed. Garnsey et al. (n. 18 above), concentrates almost entirely on what he calls "the cellular self-sufficiency of the ancient economy" rather than on Finley's substantivism. David Mattingly, *Tripolitania* (Oxford 1995). For the new consensus, see William Harris, ed., *The Inscribed Economy, Journal of Roman Archaeology,* supp. vol. 6 (Ann Arbor 1993); Nigel Morley, *Metropolis and Hinterland* (Cambridge 1996).

47. Edward Cohen, *Athenian Economy and Society: A Banking Perspective* (Princeton 1992).

48. Particularly Paul Halstead, "Traditional and Ancient Rural Economies in Mediterranean Europe: Plus ça change?," *Journal of Hellenic Studies* 107 (1987) 77–87; Stephen Hodkinson, "Animal Husbandry in the Greek Polis," in *Pastoral Economies in Classical Antiquity,* ed. C. R. Whittaker, *Proceedings of the Cambridge Philological Society,* supp. vol. 14 (Cambridge 1988) pp. 35–74; "Imperialist Democracy and Market-Oriented Pastoral Production in Classical Athens," *Anthropozoologica* 16 (1992) 53–60; John Cherry, Jack Davis, and Eleni Mantzourani, *Landscape Archaeology as Long-Term History* (Los Angeles 1991) pp. 333–46; Michael Jameson,

Curtis Runnels, and Tjeerd van Andel, *A Greek Countryside* (Stanford 1994) pp. 383–94; Victor Hanson, *The Other Greeks* (New York 1995).

49. Roger Charter, *Cultural History: Between Practices and Representations* (Ithaca 1988) is a particularly good introduction to this line of thought in modern French history.

50. There are some important equivalent studies of Rome, however, such as Catharine Edwards, *The Politics of Immorality in Ancient Rome* (Cambridge 1993) and *Writing Rome* (Cambridge 1996), and Emily Gowers, *The Loaded Table* (Oxford 1994).

51. Sitta von Reden, *Exchange in Ancient Greece* (London 1995) p. 5.

52. Weber, *Economy and Society* (n. 11 above), p. 9.

53. Josiah Ober, *Mass and Elite in Democratic Athens* (Princeton 1989) p. 308; Finley, *Democracy Ancient and Modern* (London 1973; 2nd ed., London 1985).

54. Josiah Ober, *The Athenian Revolution* (Princeton 1996) p. 8.

55. Ober, *Mass and Elite* (n. 53 above), pp. 45, 338.

56. *Ibid.*, 153–4.

57. Sitta von Reden, "Money, Law and Exchange: Coinage in the Greek Polis," *Journal of Hellenic Studies* 117 (1997) 154–76; James Davidson, *Courtesans and Fishcakes: The Consuming Passions of Classical Athens* (New York 1997); Leslie Kurke, *Coins, Bodies, Games, and Gold: The Politics of Meaning in Archaic Greece* (Princeton, forthcoming).

58. Weber, *Economy and Society* (n. 11 above), pp. 20–1.

Preface

THE TITLE of this volume is precise. Although change and variation are constant preoccupations, and there are many chronological indications, it is not a book one would call an "economic history". I have preserved the form and substance of the Sather Classical Lectures, which I had the honour to give in Berkeley during the Winter Quarter of 1972, adding the annotation and making the considerable changes and amplifications that a year's further work and reflection suggested.

It is nearly forty years since I published my first article on an ancient economic subject. In the intervening years I have accumulated a large stock of debts to other scholars, some of which are acknowledged in the notes. Here I shall restrict myself to thanking friends and colleagues who were immediately helpful in the preparation of this book: Michael Crawford, Peter Garnsey and particularly Peter Brunt, who read the complete manuscript and were most generous with their suggestions and criticisms; Jean Andreau, John Crook, Geoffrey de Ste. Croix, Richard Duncan-Jones, Yvon Garlan, Philip Grierson, Keith Hopkins, Leo Rivet, Ronald Stroud and Charles Wilson, who read portions, discussed specific problems with me, or made available unpublished work of their own; Jacqueline Garlan, who provided me with translations of Russian articles; and my wife, for her continuing patience and helpfulness.

Finally I have the pleasure of expressing thanks, on behalf of my wife and myself, for the warm Berkeley hospitality, so graciously offered by the doyen of the Department of Classics, W. K. Pritchett, the other members of the Sather Committee, W. S. Anderson, T. G. Rosenmeyer, R. S. Stroud, and their wives, and by colleagues in other departments and universities.

Jesus College, Cambridge   M. I. F.
20 January 1973

Preface
to the Second Edition

For this edition I have written a substantial new chapter of "further thoughts", and I have made some seventy-five small corrections and alterations in the original text and notes.

It is slightly more than eleven years since I completed writing the first edition. In that relatively short period the volume of publication on ancient economic history has grown so rapidly as to be almost unmanageable, and I like to think that this book is in part responsible. The new work is also on the whole more advanced, more sophisticated methodologically and conceptually. I have tried to take account of the more important publications, but I have still been fairly selective in my citations and references. Since my basic approach is not much changed, the selection necessarily reflects that, both in what I have explicitly rejected and in what I agree requires correction or adjustment of my earlier statements.

Darwin College, Cambridge   M.I.F.
May 1984

Some Dates for Orientation

SOME ROMAN EMPERORS

81–96	Domitian
98–117	Trajan
117–138	Hadrian
138–161	Antoninus Pius
161–180	Marcus Aurelius
180–192	Commodus
212–217	Caracalla
284–305	Diocletian
306–337	Constantine
360–363	Julian
408–450	Theodosius II
527–565	Justinian

THE ROMAN EMPIRE IN THE
SECOND CENTURY A.D.

EDGAR HOLLOWAY

Olbia

DACIA
um

BLACK   SEA   CAUCASUS

O E S I A

THRACIA   ARMENIA

Byzantium   Sinope
Nicomedia

BITHYNIA ET PONTUS

GALATIA   PARTHIA

D   Ankara

Pergamum   CAPPADOCIA

ASIA   ASSYRIA

DONIA

ium   Ephesus   LYCIA

Athens   Miletus   ET   CILICIA   MESOPOTAMIA

Delos   PAMPHYLIA

AEGEAN
SEA

Rhodes   Tarsus   Antioch   Euphrates

SYRIA   Tigris

CRETE   CYPRUS   Palmyra   Babylon

Damascus

A N   S E A   JUDAEA

yrene

Alexandria   Petra

ENAICA

ARABIA
PETRAEA

EGYPT   A R A B I A

A   D E S E R T A

I

The Ancients and Their Economy

In 1742 Francis Hutcheson, Professor of Philosophy in the University of Glasgow and teacher of Adam Smith, published in Latin his *Short Introduction to Moral Philosophy*, followed reluctantly five years later by an English translation, the author having discovered that "the preventing a translation was impossible". Book III, entitled "The Principles of Oeconomics and Politics", opens with three chapters on marriage and divorce, the duties of parents and children, and masters and servants, respectively, but is otherwise exclusively about politics. It is in Book II, entitled "Elements of the Law of Nature", that we find an account of property, succession, contracts, the value of goods and of coin, the laws of war. These were evidently not part of "oeconomics".

Hutcheson was neither careless nor perverse: he stood at the end of a tradition stretching back more than 2000 years. The word "economics", Greek in origin, is compounded from *oikos*, a household, and the semantically complex root, *nem-*, here in its sense of "regulate, administer, organize". The book that became the model for the tradition still represented by Hutcheson was the *Oikonomikos* written by the Athenian Xenophon before the middle of the fourth century B.C. Cast in the form of a Socratic dialogue, Xenophon's *Oikonomikos* is a guide for the gentleman landowner. It begins with a long introduction on the good life and the proper use of wealth, followed by a section on the virtues and leadership qualities necessary for the householder and on the training and management of his slaves, an even longer section on wifely virtues and the training of a wife, and the longest section of all, on agronomy (but agronomy in plain Greek, so to speak, demanding no technical knowledge of the reader). Fundamentally, this is a work of ethics, and Francis Hutcheson was surely familiar with it when he wrote his own chapters on marriage, parents and children, masters and servants, in the "economic" section of his *Introduction to Moral Philosophy*. In his preface, addressed to "the students in universities", he explains that if his book is carefully studied, it "may give the youth an easier access to the well known and admired works either of the ancients: Plato, Aristotle, Xenophon, Cicero; or of the moderns, Grotius, Cumberland, Puffendorf, Harrington and others." He then adds a charming apology for sparing himself the "disagreeable and unnecessary labour" of giving references "all along to the more eminent writers, . . . considering that this could be of no use except to those who have the cited books at hand, and that such could easily by their indexes find the corresponding places for themselves."

Not that there were always corresponding places. Hutcheson's conception of marriage and divorce, for example, was Christian (though liberal and deistic, without reference to a sacrament) and significantly different from both the Greek and the Roman. And he could not have found a precise ancient equivalent for the key word in his definition of "oeconomics", which "treat of the rights and obligations in a family".[1] Neither Greek nor Latin has a word with which to express the commonest modern sense of "family", as one might say, "I shall spend Christmas with my family". The Latin *familia* had a wide spectrum of meanings: all the persons, free or unfree, under the authority of the *paterfamilias*, the head of the household; or all the descendants from a common ancestor; or all one's property; or simply all one's servants (hence the *familia Caesaris* comprised all the personal slaves and freedmen in the imperial service, but not the emperor's wife or children). As with the Greek *oikos*, there was a heavy accent on the property side; the necessity never made itself felt to provide a specific name for the restricted concept evoked by our word "family". The *paterfamilias* was not the biological father but the authority over the household, an authority that the Roman law divided into three elements (I state this schematically), *potestas* or power over his children (including adoptees), his children's children and his slaves, *manus* or power over his wife and his sons' wives, and *dominium* or power over his possessions.[2]

This three-way classification is a precise account of a peasant household; the head manages and controls both the personnel and the property of the group, without distinction as to economic or personal or social behaviour, distinctions which could be drawn as an abstract intellectual exercise but not in actual practice. It is the same three-way classification on which Xenophon's *Oikonomikos* was constructed, though his aim was well above the peasant level, and it remained at the base of European society well into the eighteenth century (and even later in considerable areas).

There is no word in English for *patria potestas*, but there is in German, namely, *Hausgewalt*. German, too, lacked its own word for "family" in the narrow sense, until *Familie* became current in the eighteenth century.[3] The German *Wirtschaft* had a history much like that of "economics", and there was a corresponding literature neatly labelled *Hausvaterliteratur* by a modern student.[4] By the time we reach Wolf Helmhard von Hohenberg's *Georgica curiosa oder Adeliges Land- und Feldleben*, published in 1682, which employs the word *oeconomia* in the preface, the range of matter covered is much more varied and more technical than in Xenophon, but the fundamental conception of its subject, the *oikos* or *familia*, has not changed.

These were practical works, in their ethical or psychological teaching as in their agronomic instruction and their exhortations to maintain correct relations with the deity. In Xenophon, however, there is not one sentence that expresses an economic principle or offers any economic analysis, nothing on efficiency of production, "rational" choice, the marketing of crops.[5] The Roman agricultural manuals (and no doubt their lost Greek forerunners) do occasionally consider marketing and soil conditions and the like, but they too never rise above rudimentary common-sense observations (when they do not simply blunder or mislead). Varro's advice (*De re rustica* 1.16.3) to cultivate roses and violets on a farm near a city but not if the estate is too far from an urban market, is a fair sample of common sense.[6] "The layman's knowledge," Schumpeter correctly insisted, "that rich harvests are associated with low prices of foodstuffs" is "obviously prescientific and it is absurd to point to such statements in old writings as if they embodied discoveries." In economics as elsewhere, he continued, "most statements of fundamental facts acquire importance only by the superstructures they are made to bear and are commonplace in the absence of such superstructures."[7] *Hausvaterliteratur* was never made to bear a superstructure, and therefore it led nowhere insofar as the history of economic analysis or theory is concerned. There was no road from the "oeconomics" of Francis Hutcheson to the *Wealth of Nations* of Adam Smith, published twenty-four years later.[8]

Lexicographically the road began not with the literal sense of *oikonomia* but with its extension to any sort of organization or management. Thus, in the generation after Xenophon, a rival politician ridiculed Demosthenes as "useless in the *oikonomiai*, the affairs, of the city", a metaphor repeated two centuries later by the Greek historian Polybius.[9] When the word crept into Latin, we find Quintilian employing it for the organization or plan of a poem or rhetorical work.[10] And as late as 1736, Francois Quesnay could entitle a work, *Essai physique sur l'économie animale*—the same Quesnay whose *Tableau économique* of 1758 must rank with *The Wealth of Nations* as a foundation-stone of the modern discipline we call "economics".

Since revenues loom so large in the affairs of a state, it is not surprising that occasionally *oikonomia* also was used to mean the management of public revenues. The one Greek attempt at a general statement is the opening of the second book of the pseudo-Aristotelian *Oikonomikos*, and what is noteworthy about these half a dozen paragraphs is not only their crashing banality but also their isolation in the whole of surviving ancient writing. It was the French, apparently, who first made a practice of speaking of *l'économie politique*, and even they normally meant by it politics rather than economics until about 1750. By then a large body of writing had 'grown up on trade, money, national income and economic policy, and in the second half of the eighteenth century "political economy" at last acquired its familiar, specialized sense, the science of the wealth of nations. The shorter "economics" is a late nineteenth-century innovation that did not capture the field until the publication of the first volume of Alfred Marshall's *Principles of Economics* in 1890.

Marshall's title cannot be translated into Greek or Latin. Neither can the basic terms, such as labour, production, capital, investment, income, circulation, demand, entrepreneur, utility, at least not in the abstract form required for economic analysis.[11] In stressing this I am suggesting not that the ancients were like Molière's M. Jourdain, who spoke prose without knowing it, but that they in fact lacked the concept of an "economy", and, *a fortiori*, that they lacked the conceptual elements which together constitute what we call "the economy". Of course they farmed, traded, manufactured, mined, taxed, coined, deposited and loaned money, made profits or failed in their enterprises. And they discussed these activities in their talk and their writing. What they did not do, however, was to combine these particular activities conceptually into a unit, in Parsonian terms into "a differentiated sub-system of society".[12] Hence Aristotle, whose programme was to codify the branches of knowledge, wrote no *Economics*. Hence, too, the perennial complaints about the paucity and mediocrity of ancient "economic" writing rest on a fundamental misconception of what these writings were about.[13]

It then becomes essential to ask whether this is merely accidental, an intellectual failing, a problem in the history of ideas in the narrow sense, or whether it is the consequence of the structure of ancient society. Let me restate the question through two concrete instances. David Hume, whose reading in ancient authors was wide and careful, made the important (and too often neglected) observation: "I do not remember a passage in any ancient author, where the growth of a city is ascribed to the establishment of a manufacture. The commerce, which is said to flourish, is chiefly the exchange of those commodities, for which different soils and climates were suited."[14] More recently, an economic historian, Edgar Salin, contrasted modern cyclical crises, which he called "rational disturbances of a rational process" (I hold no brief for the language), with ancient crises, always attributed to natural catastrophes, divine anger or political disturbance.[15] Were these only distinctions (or failures) in analysis or were there fundamental differences in the reality under investigation?

Modern economists do not agree on a precise definition of their subject, but few, I believe, would quarrel, apart from nuances, with the following, which I take from Erich Roll: "If, then, we regard the economic system as an enormous conglomeration of interdependent markets, the central problem of economic enquiry becomes the explanation of the exchanging process, or, more particularly, the explanation of the formation of price."[16] (The word "market" is used abstractly, of course, and I cannot refrain from pointing out that in that sense it is untranslatable into Greek or Latin.) But what if a society was not organized for the satisfaction of its material wants by "an enormous conglomeration of interdependent markets"? It would then not be possible to discover or formulate laws ("statistical uniformities" if one prefers) of economic behaviour, without which a concept of "the economy" is unlikely to develop, economic analysis impossible.

"The moment seems to me to have come," wrote Count Pietro Verri in the preface to the 1772 edition of his *Meditazioni sull' economia politica*, "when political economy is developing into a science; there had been wanting only that method and that linking up of theorems which would give it the form of a science."[17] As a working hypothesis, I suggest that such a moment never came in antiquity because ancient society did not have an economic system which was an enormous conglomeration of interdependent markets; that the statements by Hume and Salin, which I selected to exemplify the point, were observations about *institutional* behaviour, not about an *intellectual* failing. There were no business cycles in antiquity; no cities whose growth can be ascribed, even by us, to the establishment of a manufacture; no "Treasure by Foreign Trade", to borrow the title of Thomas Mun's famous work stimulated by the depression of 1620–24, with its sub-title, "the Balance of our Foreign Trade is the Rule of our Treasure"— and that work belongs to the early prehistory of economic analysis.[18]

It will be objected that I am arbitrarily restricting "economics" to the analysis of a capitalist system, whereas non-capitalist or precapitalist societies also have economies, with rules and regularities and even a measure of predictability, whether they conceptualize them or not. I agree, save for the word "arbitrarily", and I obviously agree that we have the right to study such economies, to pose questions about their society that the ancients themselves never thought of. If I have taken so long over this introduction, with perhaps an excess of lexicography, that is because there is a fundamental question of method. The economic language and concepts we are all familiar with, even the laymen among us, the "principles", whether they are Alfred Marshall's or Paul Samuelson's, the models we employ, tend to draw us into a false account. For example, wage rates and interest rates in the Greek and Roman worlds were both fairly stable locally over long periods (allowing for sudden fluctuations in moments of intense political conflict or military conquest), so that to speak of a "labour market" or a "money market" is immediately to falsify the situation.[19] For the same reason, no modern investment model is applicable to the preferences of the men who dominated ancient society.

Among the interest rates which remained stable were those on maritime loans, the earliest type of insurance, going back at least to the late fifth century B.C. A considerable body of legal doctrine grew up round this form of insurance, but no trace of an actuarial concept, and that may be taken as a reasonable symbol of the absence of statistics, and hence of our difficulty in trying to quantify ancient economic data—the subject of frequent grousing by historians. Even the rare figure to which an ancient author treats us is suspect a priori: it may be no more than his guess or he may be giving it to us because it is exceptional, and we cannot always distinguish. It is frustrating to try to analyse landholding in classical Athens from precisely five figures for individual estates, scattered over a time span of about a century, at least one of which depends on difficult interpretation of the contours of the estate being described. Our lack of precise knowledge about Roman holdings is no less frustrating.[20]

Or when Thucydides (7.27.5) tells us that more than 20,000 slaves escaped from Attica in the final decade of the Peloponnesian War, just what do we in fact know? Did Thucydides have a network of agents stationed along the border between Attica and Boeotia for ten years counting the fugitives as they sneaked across? This is not a frivolous question, given the solemnity with which his statement is repeated in modern books and then used as the basis for calculations and conclusions. The context indicates that Thucydides thought the loss a severe blow to Athens. A modern historian would surely have gone on to indicate what proportion of the total slave population 20,000 represented. Thucydides did not, because he did not know the total, nor did anyone else in Athens. It follows that the 20,000 is no more than a guess; we can only hope that it was an educated guess. And I doubt if we can be even that hopeful about the figure of 120,000 armed slaves said to have marched on Rome in 72 B.C. under the leadership of Spartacus.[21]

But grousing is not good enough. Even in modern economic history, Fogel pointed out in a programmatic statement on econometric history, the "new economic history", it "is often true that the volume of data available is frequently below the minimum required for standard statistical procedures. In such instances the crucial determinant of success is the ability of the investigator to devise methods that are exceedingly efficient in the utilization of data—that is, to find a method that will permit one to achieve a solution with the limited data that are available."[22] For us there are very narrow limits: no ancient historian can begin to parallel

Fogel's study of the economic significance of railroads in the nineteenth century, starting from the counter-factual assumption that the railroad had not been invented and that the canal network had been increased instead. We shall see, however, that methods can sometimes be found by which to organize ancient data that appear beyond redemption at first sight.

We shall also see the dangers. Ancient historians are not immune from current number fetishism. They are beginning to claim quantitative proof where the evidence does not warrant it, or to misjudge the implications that may legitimately be drawn from their figures. Patterns, modes of behaviour, are at the heart of any historical inquiry such as the present one. "Apart from a presupposed pattern," said Whitehead, "quantity determines nothing."[23] Statistics help both to uncover and to elucidate the patterns, but there are also facets that are not susceptible to quantification.[24]

There is the further danger, when we have succeeded in producing a good set of figures, of then imputing that knowledge to the ancients themselves as an important component in their choices and decisions. "After all, a society does not live in a universe of statistics"[25]—not even today, and a thousand times not in antiquity. In the end, therefore, our problem is less one of devising new and complicated methods, which, given the available evidence, will of necessity remain simple, than of posing the right questions. And, I must add, of abandoning the anecdotal technique of dredging up an example or two as if that constituted proof.

As for the ancients, their statistical innocence, like their lack of economic analysis, resists a purely intellectual explanation. A society that produced the work of Apollonius of Perge on conic sections had more than enough mathematics for what the seventeenth-century English and Dutch called "political arithmetic" and we call "statistics", defined by Sir Charles Davenant in 1698, in his *Discourse on the Public Revenues*, as "the art of reasoning by figures, upon things relating to government".[26] The ancient world was not wholly lacking in figures of things relating to government. When Thucydides (2.13.3–8) tells us the number of available Athenian hoplites, cavalrymen and ships and the amount of cash in reserve at the outbreak of the war, that was not a guess. All ancient states kept rosters of their fighting forces, at least, and some states, chiefly the autocratic ones, took censuses for tax purposes and filed other information in the interest of the public (royal) revenue.[27] However, reasoning by figures is more than mere counting and recording, and there lies the great divide. Reasoning by figures implies a concept of relationships and trends, without which the categories that were counted were narrowly restricted, and what is equally important, few records were normally retained once they had served their immediate purpose. Hence no time series was available in antiquity, in either the public or the private sector, save exceptionally, and without a time series there can be no reasoning by figures, no statistics. Thucydides could not (or at least did not) provide the data necessary for a continuous assessment of the manpower position in the course of the Peloponnesian War.

I have not been saying anything particularly new. As long ago as 1831 Richard Jones protested that Ricardo's theory of rent rested on the assumption that what he (Jones) called "farmer's rent" was the universal form of rent, an assumption that historical inquiry proved to be false.[28] More recently the inapplicability to the ancient world of a market-centred analysis was powerfully argued by Max Weber and by his most important disciple among ancient historians, Johannes Hasebroek; in our own day by Karl Polanyi.[29] All to little avail.[30] The currently standard work in English on Greek economics has neither "household" nor *oikos* in its index.[31] Sir John Hicks offers a model for the "First Phase of the Mercantile Economy", in the city-state, which presupposes that "the trade (oil for corn) is *unlikely to get started* unless, to begin with, it is a handsome profit" (my italics).[32] A classical scholar tells us about the "investment of government capital in rural development" competing with "investment capital in trade" in Athens under the Pisistratid tyranny in the sixth century B.C.[33] Their assumptions, expressed or implied, amount to "a chemical doctrine of society" which claims "that all forms of society can be objectively analysed into a finite number of immutable elements".[34] If such assumptions prove invalid for antiquity, then all that follows must be false, about economic behaviour and the guiding values alike. We have, I suggest, to seek different concepts and different models, appropriate to the ancient economy, not (or not necessarily) to ours.

But first it is time that I specified what I mean by "ancient". In the nineteenth century I should not have had to bother. The division of European history into the ancient, medieval and modern periods, a conception that had its roots in the Renaissance, was a universally accepted convention. In our century there have been challenges and objections of various kinds—epistemological, psychological, political. Yet in the end, when all the difficulties and exceptions are duly noted, when we allow that the "concept of historical period depends more on stipulation than on inferences from commonly accepted evidence",[35] when we agree to abandon the value judgment implicit in such a phrase as "the Dark Ages", when we recognize that China and India also had histories that are not to be ignored, it remains true, first, that European civilization has a unique history, which it is legitimate to study as a distinct subject;[36] second, that even casual acquaintance with the sweep of European history gives an unmistakable sense of qualitative differences among the traditional periods (whatever further differences there may be within the periods);[37] third, that history and prehistory should remain distinct subjects of inquiry, that Neolithic settlements, like the contemporary non-literate societies studied by the anthropologists, belong to yet another "period" so to speak.

But is it also legitimate, with the vast new knowledge now available, to exclude from "ancient history" the important, seminal civilizations of the ancient Near East, the Sumerians, Baylonians and Assyrians, the Hittites, Canaanites, Hebrews and Phoenicians, the Egyptians, the Persians? It is not a valid argument for exclusion that these civilizations existed on the continents we now call Asia and Africa rather than in Europe; nor that mostly they spoke languages outside the Indo-European family (to which in fact Hittite and Persian do belong). On the other hand, it is no argument for inclusion to stress the borrowings and the economic or cultural connections between the Graeco-Roman world and the Near Eastern: the appearance of Wedgwood blue porcelain does not require the inclusion of China as an integral part of an analysis of the industrial revolution in England. What matters is the way in which the two civilizations (or complexes of cultures) diverge fundamentally at every point, in their social structures, in their power structures (both internally and externally), in the relationship between the power structure and religion, in the presence or absence of the scribe as a pivotal figure. It is almost enough to point out that it is impossible to translate the word "freedom", *eleutheria* in Greek, *libertas* in Latin, or "free man", into any ancient Near Eastern language, including Hebrew, or into any Far Eastern language either, for that matter.[38]

The Near Eastern economies were dominated by large palace- or temple-complexes, who owned the greater part of the arable, virtually monopolized anything that can be called "industrial production" as well as foreign trade (which includes inter-city trade, not merely trade with foreign parts), and organized the economic, military, political and religious life of the society through a single complicated, bureaucratic, record-keeping operation for which the word "rationing", taken very broadly, is as good a one-word description as I can think of. None of this is relevant to the Graeco-Roman world until the conquests of Alexander the Great and later of the Romans incorporated large Near Eastern territories. At that point we shall have to look more closely at this Near Eastern kind of society. But otherwise, were I to define "ancient" to embrace both worlds, there is not a single topic I could discuss without resorting to disconnected sections, employing different concepts and models. The exclusion of the Near East is therefore not arbitrary, though retention of the label "ancient" is frankly less easy to defend other than on grounds of tradition and convenience.

I do not wish to over-simplify. There were private holdings of land in the Near East, privately worked; there were "independent" craftsmen and pedlars in the towns. Our evidence does not permit quantification, but I do not believe it is possible to elevate these people to the prevailing pattern of economy, whereas the Graeco-Roman world was essentially and precisely one of private ownership, whether of a few acres or of the enormous domains of Roman senators and emperors, a world of private trade, private manufacture. Both worlds had their secondary, atypical, marginal people, such as the nomads who were a chronic threat to the settled river-valley communities in Mesopotamia and Egypt, perhaps the Phoenician cities on the coast of Syria, certainly the Spartans in Greece. Furthermore, Phrygians, Medes and Persians were not Babylonians or Egyptians, while the government of the Roman Empire became as autocratic and bureaucratic, in some ways, as the Ptolemies, and before them the Pharaohs, of Egypt. But not in all ways. We must concentrate on the dominant types, the characteristic modes of behaviour.[39]

The Graeco-Roman world is of course an abstraction, and an elusive one when we try to anchor it in time and space. In very round numbers we shall be dealing with the period between 1000 B.C. and A.D. 500.* At the beginning that "world" was restricted to a little corner of the Balkans and a few toeholds on the Turkish coast of the Aegean Sea. Gradually, spasmodically, it expanded in all directions, until at one moment, at the death of the emperor Trajan in A.D. 117, the Roman Empire extended nearly 3000 miles from the Atlantic Ocean to the edge of the Caucasus; and from Britain and the Rhine in the north to a southern line running more or less along the border of the Sahara Desert and then to the Persian Gulf, a north–south axis of some 1750 miles without counting in Britain. At that moment, the area was perhaps 1,750,000 square miles, approximately half the land area of the United States at present.

That is an impressive figure, but to appreciate the scale of

* Neither date is a meaningful one in the sense that anything significant occurred in either 1000 B.C. or A.D. 500. The date 1000 B.C. is a symbol for the beginning of the "Dark Age" in Greece, which I believe to be reflected in the Homeric poems.

human activity we must look a little more closely. Gibbon made the acute observation that the Roman army in the heyday of the empire was no larger than that of Louis XIV, "whose kingdom was confined within a single province of the Roman empire".[40] The army is not necessarily an index of the population as a whole: Gibbon himself added in a footnote that it must "be remembered that France still feels that extraordinary effort". However, we have learned something: the Roman empire was incapable of a comparable effort, whatever the price. Our best guess of the maximum population ever attained in the Graeco-Roman world is 50–60,000,000 at the beginning of the Christian era, roughly the same as in the United Kingdom or Italy today, no more than treble that of the state of California.[41] These millions were un-evenly distributed, not only among the regions but also between town and country, and, within the urban sector, between five or six swollen administrative capitals on the one hand, such as Rome, Alexandria or Carthage, and on the other hand a number of communities, mostly in the eastern half, in the 100,000-class and then hundreds of little towns we dignify with the proud label of "cities". It is salutary to remember that in an earlier epoch the famous and powerful Sparta could never count more than 9000 adult male citizens, and not even that for most of its history.

One aspect of the distribution of the population requires con-sideration. It is a commonplace that for much of its history the Graeco-Roman world was tied together by the Mediterranean Sea, *mare nostrum*, "our sea", the Romans called it. The roll of nearly all the great centres—Athens, Syracuse, Cyrene, Rome, Alexan-dria, Antioch, Constantinople—can be called without going more than a few miles inland. For a long time everything beyond this thin belt was periphery, land to be drawn upon for hides, food, metals and slaves, to be raided for booty, to be garrisoned for defence, but to be inhabited by barbarians, not by Greeks or Romans. "We inhabit a small portion of the earth," wrote Plato (*Phaedo* 109B), "from Phasis [on the east coast of the Black Sea] to the Pillars of Heracles [Straits of Gibraltar], living around the sea like ants and frogs around a pond."

The Mediterranean area constitutes a single "climatic region",[42] marked by winter rains and long summer droughts, by light soils and dry farming for the most part, in contrast to the irrigation farming on which so much of the ancient Near Eastern economy was based. It is a region of relatively easy habitation and much outdoor living, producing on its best soils, the coastal plains and the large inland plateaus, a good supply of the staple cereal grasses, vegetables and fruits, in particular grapes and olives, with suitable pasture for small animals, sheep, pigs and goats, but not on the whole for cattle. The ubiquitous olive—the chief source of edible fat, of the best soap and of fuel for illumination—is an essential clue to the Mediterranean life-style. The olive-tree flourishes even in summer drought but, though not labour-intensive, it demands attention and it requires time, since the tree does not bear for the first ten or twelve years. It is thus a symbol of sedentary existence —its longevity was celebrated—and the Mediterranean on the whole is no place for nomadic peoples.

On the other hand, neither the olive nor dry farming generally requires the complex social organization that made possible the great river-valley civilizations along the Nile, the Tigris and Euphrates, the Indus and Yellow rivers. Irrigation farming is more productive, more consistent and more conducive to a dense population. It is no accident that the main centre within the Roman empire of irrigation farming, Egypt, had a population in the first century of 7,500,000 exclusive of Alexandria[43]—one of the very few ancient population figures we have that is likely to be accurate. In compensation, the river-valleys turned into virtual deserts the moment the central organization broke down, whereas the ancient dry-farming regions recovered rapidly from natural disasters and human devastation.

Of course there were inhabited districts in Greece, central and northern Italy, central Turkey which were at a sufficient distance from the sea not to have easy access to it for their products. Nevertheless, what I have said about the Mediterranean axis holds for about the first 800 years of our 1500-year period, and then a significant change set in, the spread of the Graeco-Roman world inland, especially to the north, on a scale to be reckoned with. Eventually France, Belgium, Britain and central Europe to the Danube basin were fully incorporated, with consequences that have perhaps received insufficient attention. Two simple facts enter into the reckoning: first, these northern provinces were outside the Mediterranean climatic region and also tended to have heavier soils; second, they were barred by the prohibitive cost of land transport from fully sharing in the advantages of Mediterranean traffic, save for those districts in close proximity to navigable rivers (unknown in Asia Minor, Greece, most of Italy, and Africa apart from the Nile).[44] Not only did the great arteries, such as the Rhône, Saône, Rhine, Danube and Po, carry an active traffic but, in Gaul in particular, the many secondary rivers as well.

Thus far, in speaking of a Mediterranean axis and a Mediterranean climatic region, I have been playing down the extent of variation within the area, and I must now turn to that, still only in a preliminary way. I am thinking not of the self-evident variations in fertility, in suitability for specific crops, in the presence or absence of important mineral resources, but of the variations in the social structure, in land tenure, in the labour system. The world the Romans brought together into a single imperial system had behind it not one long history but a considerable number of different histories, which the Romans neither could nor wished to wipe out. The exceptional position of Rome itself and of Italy with its exemption from the land tax is an obvious example. The continuation in Egypt and other eastern provinces of a peasant system that left no place for the slave plantations of Italy and Sicily is another. I do not think I need enumerate further; the position was summed up by André Déléage in his fundamental study of the radically new tax system introduced by Diocletian throughout the empire. This system, Déléage wrote, was "extremely complex" because it took "different forms in the different sections of the empire",[45] not for reasons of royal caprice but because, in order to be effective, to produce the required imperial revenues, the tax system had to acknowledge the profound, historically created differences in the underlying land regime.

Is it legitimate, then, to speak of the "ancient economy"? Must it not be broken down by further eliminations, as I have already eliminated the older society of the Near East? Walbank, following in the steps of Rostovtzeff, has recently called the Empire of the first century "a single economic unit", one that was "knit together by the intensive exchange of all types of primary commodities and manufactured articles, including the four fundamental articles of trade—grain, wine, oil and slaves".[46] The industries of Gaul, he specifies, "rapidly became serious competitors on the world market" and the "metalware of Egypt found a ready sale everywhere; examples have been dug up even in South Russia and India".[47] Similarly Rostovtzeff says that "the exchange of manufactured goods, articles not of luxury but of everyday use, was exceedingly active".[48]

This is all too vague: such generalizations cry out for a more sophisticated effort to approach quantification and pattern-construction. Wheeler tells the cautionary tale of the discovery on the Swedish island of Gotland of 39 sherds of *terra sigillata* pottery scattered over an area of some 400 square metres, which turned out in the end all to be broken bits of a single bowl.[49] Around the year 400 the wealthy Bishop Synesius of Cyrene (in modern Libya) wrote to his brother from Alexandria (*Epistles* 52) asking him to purchase three light summer mantles from an Athenian, who, Synesius had heard, had arrived in Cyrene. That is the man, he added, from whom you bought me some shoes last year, and please hurry before all the best ware has been sold. Here are two examples of "ready sale" in a "world market".[50] I cite them neither to caricature nor to imply that ancient trade was all on that level, but to concretize my demand for more specification, more qualification, where possible quantification, of such otherwise misleading vague phrases as "intensive exchange", "exceedingly active", "examples have been dug up". The imperial city of Rome lived on grain imported from Sicily, Spain, North Africa and Egypt, but in Antioch, during the famine of A.D. 362–363, it required the forcible intervention of the emperor Julian to have grain brought in from two inland districts of northern Syria, one fifty, the other a hundred miles away.[51]

To be meaningful, "world market", "a single economic unit" must embrace something considerably more than the exchange of some goods over long distances; otherwise China, Indonesia, the Malay Peninsula and India were also part of the same unit and world market. One must show the existence of interlocking behaviour and responses over wide areas—Erich Roll's "enormous conglomeration of interdependent markets"—in the dominant sectors of the economy, in food and metal prices, for example, and one cannot, or at least no one has.[52] "Neither local nor long-distance trade," a distinguished economic geographer has pointed out, "disturbed the subsistence base of the householding units in peasant societies. The role of modern central-place hierarchies is, on the other hand, predicated upon the extreme division of labour and the absence of household self-sufficiency in necessities."[53] Neither predicate existed to a sufficient degree in antiquity.

It will be obvious by now that I reject both the conception and the approach I have briefly criticized. The few isolated patterns regularly adduced, the ending of the brief monopoly held by the north Italian town of Arezzo in the production of *terra sigillata*, the rough correlation between large-scale wars and the price of slaves, cannot bear the great edifice erected upon them. My justification for speaking of "the ancient economy" lies in another direction, in the fact that in its final centuries the ancient world was a single political unit, and in the common cultural-psychological framework, the relevance of which to an account of the economy I hope to demonstrate in subsequent chapters.

II

Orders and Status

ANYONE WHO reads much in ancient authors will eventually be struck by the fact that, in a culture lacking statistics in general, there was a curious abundance of precise figures, readily and publicly proclaimed, of the size of individual fortunes or at least of individual financial transactions. When, in the *Odyssey* (14.98–104), the swineherd Eumaeus remarks to the "stranger" about his absent master, "not twenty men together have so much wealth; I will give you the inventory, twelve herds of cattle on the mainland, as many of sheep, so many droves of swine", and so on, there is no trace of satire, nothing of Shaw's Captain Bluntschli, the Swiss hotelkeeper who announced at the close of *Arms and the Man*, "I have nine thousand six hundred pairs of sheets and blankets, with two thousand four hundred eiderdown quilts. I have ten thousand knives and forks, and the same quantity of dessert spoons . . . and I have three native languages. Show me any man in Bulgaria that can offer as much!" Eumaeus was demonstrating the greatness of Odysseus in the most matter-of-fact way, just as the emperor Augustus recorded in the account of his reign which he himself prepared for posthumous publication: I paid out about 860,000,000 sesterces for the purchase of land for veterans; I handed out in cash altogether 2,400,000,000 sesterces to the treasury, to the plebs of the city of Rome and to demobilized soldiers; and lots more.[1]

The judgment of antiquity about wealth was fundamentally unequivocal and uncomplicated. Wealth was necessary and it was good; it was an absolute requisite for the good life; and on the whole that was all there was to it. From Odysseus, who told King Alcinous of the Phaeacians that he would wait a year if necessary for the many gifts he was promised, and not just overnight, before departing, because "more advantageous would it be to come to my dear fatherland with a fuller hand, and so should I be more reverenced and loved among men" (*Odyssey* 11.358–60), the line was continuous to the end of antiquity. I shall quote only Trimalchio, the freedman-"hero" of the *Satyricon*, addressing his dinner-guests: "If you don't like the wine I'll have it changed. It's up to you to do it justice. I don't buy it, thank heaven. In fact, whatever wine really tickles your palate this evening, it comes from an estate of mine which as yet I haven't seen. It's said to adjoin my estates at Terracina and Tarentum. What I'd like to do now is add Sicily to my little bits of land, so that when I go to Africa I could sail there without leaving my own property."[2]

The *Satyricon*, written by a courtier of Nero's of consular rank, is not an easy work to assess in its values, judgments or implications. It is a work which mocks and sneers, but it is not *Alice in Wonderland*; Trimalchio may not be a wholly typical ancient figure, but he is not wholly untypical either.[3] In the passage I have just quoted, except perhaps for the use of the diminutive *agellae* (little bits of land), with its spurious modesty, the mockery is in the *reductio ad absurdum*, in the extension of accepted values to the point of unreasonableness. In two respects Trimalchio was expressing perfectly good doctrine, which he merely exaggerated: he was openly delighted with his wealth and boastful about it, and he was equally pleased with his self-sufficiency, with his possession of estates capable of producing everything he needed, no matter how expanded the needs and extended the desires.

There were exceptions. Socrates went so far as to suggest, in his own way of life, that wealth was neither essential nor even necessarily helpful in achieving the good life. Plato went further, at least in the *Republic* where he denied his philosopher-rulers all property (along with other normally accepted goods). The chief disciple of Diogenes the Cynic was a rich man, Crates of Thebes, who voluntarily gave up his possessions, much like the heroes of the saints' lives in the later Roman Empire.

Anthologies have been produced of statements idealizing the simple life, philosophical or bucolic, and even poverty.[4] But they must be treated with discrimination. "Poverty," said Apuleius in the middle of the second century (*Apology* 18.2–6), "has always been the handmaiden of philosophy.... Review the greatest rogues whose memory has been preserved, you will find no poor men among them.... Poverty, in sum, has been from the beginning of time the founder of states, the inventor of arts." Out of context that seems straightforward enough. The context, however, is not irrelevant. Apuleius, son of a high official of Madaurus, a Roman colony in North Africa, had spent many years abroad, chiefly in philosophical and rhetorical study. On his return to North Africa, he married a wealthy woman older than himself, a widow for fourteen years, and was brought to trial by her son on the charge of seduction through magic. The bill of particulars included the claim that Apuleius was a poor fortune-hunter; he replied, in his defence from which I quoted, with the inconsistency permitted in a pleader. First, he argued, what is wrong with poverty? Second, he continued, I am in fact a fairly rich man, having inherited (with my brother) nearly two million sesterces from my father, most of which remains despite the costs of my travels and my liberality.

In another sphere, there is the famous remark the historian Thucydides (2.37.1) attributes to Pericles: "Neither is poverty a bar, but a man may benefit his city whatever the obscurity of his condition." Again very straightforward, but it was precisely the exceptional character of Athens that Pericles was praising. Not many Greek states of the classical period, and none at all in the ancient world at any other period, allowed poor men of obscure condition to play a positive constructive role in political life, and even in Athens it is almost impossible to find a man of modest means, let alone a really poor man, in a position of leadership.

Nevertheless, I do not wish to argue away the exceptions. There are always exceptions, and it is perhaps more significant that the anthologies I mentioned are not very large. Our concern must be with the prevailing ideology. One can quote Plato to "disprove" almost any general statement one tries to make about Greek society, but that is a stultifying and fundamentally wrong historical method. Fourth-century B.C. Greeks did not, after all, abolish, or even question, monogamy and the family despite the arguments adduced against them in the *Republic*. Nor is it a legitimate objection that the writers from whom our knowledge of the ideology comes, for Greece as for Rome, were in the vast majority men from, or attached to, the upper classes. Ideology never divides neatly along class lines; on the contrary, its function, if it is to be of any use, is precisely to cross those lines, and about wealth and poverty there was a remarkable unanimity in antiquity. Trimalchio was a more authentic spokesman than Plato.

Ancient moralists, at least from the time of the Sophists (and in a rudimentary way even earlier, in such poets as Solon and Theognis), examined all the received values of their society — including wealth. They examined, and they debated and they disagreed, not about the economy but about the private ethical aspects of wealth, a narrow topic. Is wealth boundless? Is wealth a good if it is not used properly? Are there morally good and morally evil ways of acquiring wealth? Even, among a minority of moralists, is it possible to live a life of virtue without wealth? Fundamentally, however, "Blessed are the poor" was not within the Graeco-Roman world of ideas, and its appearance in the Gospels — whatever one's exegesis of the texts — points to another world and another set of values. That other world eventually achieved a paradoxical ideology, in which a fiercely acquisitive temper was accompanied by strains of asceticism and holy poverty, by feelings of unease and even of guilt.

The history of the word *philanthropia* ("love of man") illustrates the distinction.[5] Originally it was employed to define a divine quality or a beneficent act by a god, and that sense survived to the end of antiquity, in Christian as in pagan usage. Soon, however, *philanthropia* also came to be attributed to highly placed human beings, in the sense of a humane feeling or simply an act of kindness or courtesy. When individuals or communities appealed to a monarch or high functionary to redress a grievance or grant a favour, they appealed to his *philanthropia*. If successful, they received a *philanthropon*, which might be an immunity from a tax or other obligation, and therefore have a monetary value, but which was more often an amnesty, the right of asylum, an intervention against some administrative wrong. The ruler and his agents were the protectors of the people against oppression and wrongful injury, and one appealed to their *philanthropia* along with good will and justice, essentially synonymous terms.[6] A characteristic third-century anecdote reports that when a defeated gladiator appealed for his life to Caracalla, who was present in the amphitheatre, the latter denied having the power and suggested an appeal to the victor, who dared not make the concession lest he appear "more philanthropic" than the emperor (Dio 78.19.4). There the development of the word stopped in antiquity; it remained for later ages to express humanity in purely monetary terms, to degrade it to the level of gifts to the poor and needy, to charity.

To be sure, the ancient world was not wholly lacking in charitable acts, in the narrow modern sense. Normally, however, generosity was directed to the community, not to the needy, whether as individuals or as groups.[7] (I exclude generosity to poor relations, clients and favourite slaves as a different situation.) The benefactions of the younger Pliny, probably unsurpassed in Italy or the western empire, were typical in this respect.[8] One can cite exceptions, but one can also almost count them, and that is the decisive fact. The very poor aroused little sympathy and no pity throughout antiquity. "Give to one who gives, but do not give to one who does not give," advised the poet Hesiod in the seventh century B.C. (*Works and Days* 355), and Hesiod, of all ancient writers, was no mere mouthpiece for upper-class values. What was lacking was a sense of sin. A Greek or Roman could offend his gods easily enough, and at times, though not often, we meet with notions that come close to the idea of sin. Basically, however, their wrong acts were external, so to speak, and therefore amends were made by ritual purification, or they were intellectualized, as in the

Socratic doctrine that no man does evil knowingly. The accent is on the word "action", not on a condition or state of sinfulness that could be healed only by divine grace. Hence there need be no ambiguity about wealth as such, or about poverty as an evil.[9]

Not even the state showed much concern for the poor. The famous exception is the intensely political one of the city of Rome (and also of Constantinople in the final period), where, from the time of Gaius Gracchus, feeding the populace became a political necessity, which not even the emperors could escape (and when the emperors could no longer cope, the popes stepped in). If ever an exception proved the rule, this is the one. Quite apart from the nuance—far from insignificant—that until the third century A.D. resident citizens were eligible as beneficiaries without a means test, it is proper to ask, who provided free corn and pork as a regular matter in any other city of the empire? No one, and such an occasional attempt at numaneness as Julian's, when Antioch was suffering from a severe famine, was a complete and bitter failure. Trajan established an interesting and unique scheme of family allowances in Italy, known as the *alimenta*, but he was able to get it started in only a minority of the cities, and, though it survived for more than a century, even indirect evidence of a further extension is remarkably thin. Besides, there is reason to believe that Trajan's main concern was to increase the birth rate in Italy (but not in any other region of the empire).[10] Again an exception that proves the rule.

If one wishes to grasp the basic attitude to the poor, one must look not at the occasional philanthropy but at the law of debt (as it applied to them, not among status-equals in the upper classes). That law was uniformly harsh and unyielding. Even where the archaic system of debt-bondage disappeared, the defaulting debtor continued to make amends, in one way or another, through compulsory labour, his own and sometimes his children's.[11]

Underpinning the positive Graeco-Roman judgment of wealth was the conviction that among the necessary conditions of freedom were personal independence and leisure. "The condition of the free man," wrote Aristotle (*Rhetoric* 1367a32), "is that he not live under the constraint of another," and it is clear from the context that his notion of living under restraint was not restricted to slaves but was extended to wage labour and to others who were *economically* dependent. There is a clue in Greek linguistic usage. The Greek words *ploutos* and *penia*, customarily rendered "wealth" and "poverty", respectively, had in fact a different nuance, what Veblen called "the distinction between exploit and drudgery".[12] A *plousios* was a man who was rich enough to live properly on his income (as we should phrase it), a *penēs* was not. The latter need not be propertyless or even, in the full sense, poor: he could own a farm or slaves, and he could have a few hundred drachmas accumulated in a strong-box, but he was compelled to devote himself to gaining a livelihood. *Penia*, in short, meant the harsh compulsion to toil,[13] whereas the pauper, the man who was altogether without resources, was normally called a *ptochos*, a beggar, not a *penēs*.[14] In Aristophanes' last surviving play, the *Plutus*, Penia is a goddess (an invention of the playwright's) and she strongly resists (lines 552–4) the suggestion that she and *ptocheia* are sisters: "The life of the *ptochos* . . . consists in having nothing, that of the *penēs* in living thriftily and applying oneself to one's work, in not having a surplus but also in not lacking necessities."

The *Plutus* is anyway a most complicated work and cannot be adduced as a text glorifying *penia*, which retained in the popular mind a pejorative undertone, for all its difference from beggary, precisely like Apuleius's *paupertas*.[15] Its relevance for us is as a footnote to Aristotle, and, if I may put it that way, also to a famous passage in Cicero, which I must quote nearly in full (*De officiis* 1.150–1):

"Now in regard to trades and employments, which are to be considered liberal and which mean, this is the more or less accepted view. First, those employments are condemned which incur ill-will, as those of collectors of harbour taxes and money-lenders. Illiberal, too, and mean are the employments of all who work for wages, whom we pay for their labour and not for their art; for in their case their very wages are the warrant of their slavery. We must also consider mean those who buy from merchants in order to re-sell immediately, for they would make no profit without much outright lying. . . . And all craftsmen are engaged in mean trades, for no workshop can have any quality appropriate to a free man. Least worthy of all are those trades which cater to sensual pleasures: 'fishmongers, butchers, cooks, poulterers and fishermen,' as Terence says; to whom you may add, if you please, perfumers, dancers and all performers in low-grade music-halls.

"But the occupations in which either a higher degree of intelligence is required or from which society derives no small benefit — such as medicine or architecture or teaching — they are respectable for those whose status they befit. Commerce, if it is on a small scale, is to be considered mean; but if it is large-scale and extensive, importing much from all over and distributing to many without misrepresentation, is not to be greatly censured.* Indeed, it even seems to deserve the highest respect if those who are engaged in it, satiated, or rather, I should say, content with their profits, make their way from the harbour to a landed estate, as they have often made it from the sea to a harbour. But of all things from which one may acquire, none is better than agriculture, none more fruitful, none sweeter, none more fitting for a free man."

Why, one will promptly ask, should Cicero be accepted as more representative than other moralists whom I have previously labelled exceptional, Socrates, Plato, the Cynics? His opening "this is the more or less accepted view" (*haec fere accepimus*) is the kind of *ex parte* statement that has no standing as evidence. It is perhaps more cogent that the *De officiis*, in which the passage appears, was until quite recently one of the most widely read ethical treatises ever written in the west. Tully's *Offices* "give the Mind a noble set", wrote Bishop Burnet when commending it to the clergy in his *Discourse of the Pastoral Care*, published in 1692 and

---

* Note that foreign trade is evaluated positively because it provides goods for consumers, not, in Thomas Mun's language, because it increases national treasure.

reaching a fourteenth edition in 1821, approved by the Society for Promoting Christian Knowledge for anyone contemplating Holy Orders.[16] The distinction between writers who are more and less representative of a particular social environment is a familiar one in the history of ideas, between John Stuart Mill or Emerson and Nietzsche, for example, as between Cicero and Plato. "Unrepresentative" moralists certainly offer penetrating insights into the realities of their society, but they have to be read differently, they cannot be read straight, so to speak, as mere reporters.

However, I shall not argue on those lines. Instead, I shall treat the Cicero passage as the foundation for a hypothesis. Does it or does it not accurately reflect the prevalent pattern of behaviour in Cicero's time? And beyond? The issue is one of choice. Given that no man, not even Robinson Crusoe, is absolutely free, how free was a Greek or Roman to choose among a range of possible "employments", whether of his energies or his goods? More precisely, perhaps, how much weight was attached to what we should call economic factors in the choice, maximization of income, for example, or market calculations? Still more precisely, how free was a rich Greek or Roman, since obviously fishmongers, craftsmen and performers in low music-halls were rigidly restricted and could think of leisure and independence only as Utopian?

A recent inquiry into the junior officers of the Roman imperial army opens with the following two sentences: "There was, it may be agreed, in the society of the Empire as in all societies a desire on the part of the individual and the family to advance socially. It was the task of the emperor not to frustrate this desire but to provide for its satisfaction in a way that would be of maximum benefit to society."[17] That this is a valid generalization for all societies or for all sectors within a society is demonstrably incorrect, and the role assigned to the Roman emperor would be extraordinarily difficult to document or defend. However, those weaknesses apart, we are here presented with one familiar viewpoint, not argued, not demonstrated, simply asserted, "it may be agreed". It reflects a modern "individualist" view of social behaviour which a distinguished Indologist has called the greatest obstacle to an understanding of the social structure of India: "it is our misunderstanding of hierarchy. Modern man is virtually incapable of fully recognizing it. For a start, he simply fails to notice it. If it does force itself on his attention he tends to eliminate it as an epiphenomenon."[18]

Where did the Graeco-Roman world stand, in its economic behaviour, between the two extremes of "individualism" and "hierarchy"? That is a central question; it merits careful consideration, employing clearly defined categories. There are contexts in which loose reference to classes, for example, is harmless: I myself refer to the "upper classes" in this way, when I trust the meaning is intelligible. Now, however, I must try to establish the social situation with greater precision.

It will be noticed that Cicero's classification cannot be pinpointed exactly. Most of the specific employments he enumerates are occupations, but not all: wage labour is not an occupation, nor is agriculture when it embraces everyone from a poor tenant to the absentee owner of hundreds, even thousands, of acres. Although Cicero himself was a large landowner, his "occupation" was not agriculture but the law and politics, both of which he understandably neglected to mention. He is an excellent exemplar of the truth that in antiquity land ownership on a sufficient scale marks "the absence of any occupation",[19] not only in the particular circumstances of Rome at the end of the Republic but equally in classical Sparta or Athens. Plutarch tells us that Pericles inherited a landed estate from his father and "organized its management in the way he thought would be simplest and most strict. He sold all the year's produce in bulk and then bought all the necessities in the market. . . . Every expenditure and every receipt proceeded by count and measure. His agent in securing all this exactitude was a servant, Evangelus, who was either gifted by nature or trained by Pericles to be unsurpassed in household management." Pericles' sons and daughters-in-law, Plutarch continues, were displeased with his methods, "there being no abundance, as in a great house and under generous circumstances" (*Pericles* 16.3–5). The disagreement in this instance was not over how to acquire wealth but over how to spend it. Neither Pericles nor his disgruntled sons revealed any more interest in farming as a profession than did Xenophon when he wrote the *Oikonomikos*.

For the *plousioi* of antiquity—and they alone are at present under consideration—categories of social division other than occupation have priority in any analysis, and I shall examine three in turn: order or estate (as used in France before the Revolution, German *Stand*), class and status.[20] "Order" is of course the Latin *ordo*, but, predictably, the Romans did not use it in a sociologically precise way any more than we do with comparable English terms, and I shall not follow their usage too closely. An order or estate is a juridically defined group within a population, possessing formalized privileges and disabilities in one or more fields of activity, governmental, military, legal, economic, religious, marital, and *standing in a hierarchical relation to other orders.* Ideally membership is hereditary, as in the simplest and neatest ancient example, the division of the Romans in their earliest stage into two orders, patricians and plebeians. But no society that is not wholly stationary can rest on that simple level, especially not if, as was the case in Rome, there was no way to replace a patrician house that lacked male heirs.

Once Rome ceased to be a primitive village of peasants and herdsmen on the Tiber and began to extend its territory and power, the existing system of two orders, though firmly sanctioned by law, religion and tradition, had to be adapted to the new circumstances if the community was not to be violently destroyed. The Romans' own version of the early centuries of the Republic, known to us from the histories by Livy and Dionysius of Halicarnassus writing at the time of Augustus, has as its central theme the struggle between the patricians and plebeians. Among the plebeian "victories" in these accounts were the removal in 445 B.C. of the prohibition of marriage between the orders and, by a law of 366 B.C., the concession to plebeians of eligibility for one of the two consulships, the highest offices in the state. No special knowledge of Roman history is required to appreciate who among the plebeians were the beneficiaries of such victories. The story "is unintelligible unless there were rich plebeians".[21] Another victory was the abolition of *nexum*, a form of bondage for debt; this time the beneficiaries would have been the poor plebeians, against both patricians and rich plebeians.

From 366 on the names of no more than twenty-one patrician houses are attested. The patriciate continued to exist for centuries thereafter, but its practical significance was soon reduced pretty much to certain priestly privileges and to ineligibility for the office of tribune, while "plebeian" came to mean about what it means in English today. The original patrician-plebeian dichotomy had lost its relevance. The highest order was now the senatorial *ordo*, members of the senate, plebeian in the increasing majority as the years went on, an order in the strict sense but not hereditary in law, however near to being hereditary it was in fact. A further adaptation came in the late second century B.C. when the equestrian order came to be defined *de facto* to include all non-senators with a minimum property of 400,000 sesterces.* The old name *equites*, knights, was no longer taken literally, though the ancient ritual of assigning the "public horse" to a select number (1800 or 2400) went on, with honorific overtones. Even for the other *equites*, now the great majority within the order, there was genuine social-psychological meaning in an archaic title "with its associations of high rank and property-census, antique tradition, and decorative imagery".[22]

This criss-crossing of categories reveals that by the late second century B.C., when Rome had become an empire that included not only the whole of Italy below the Po River but also Sicily, Sardinia and Corsica, as much of Spain as they were able to control, North Africa, Macedonia and Greece, orders alone were inadequate as an integrating institution, but that at the same time the tradition of orders was too strong to be abandoned. The hierarchy was in fact headed no longer by the senatorial order as a whole but by an inner group, the "nobility" (their own word), which had no juridical standing but which was above all con-

---

* The roughness of the classification is to be noted: the richest equestrians had more wealth than the poorest senators.

fined, *de facto*, to families who could claim a consul, past or present, among their members.[23]

The nobility was not an order but what I shall shortly define as a status. When the Republic was replaced by a monarchy under Augustus, the emperor revitalized the system of orders to a considerable extent, but for my purposes it is unnecessary to pursue the story further in Roman history,[24] except to make one more point. Everything I have said so far about orders pertained exclusively to the Romans themselves. But who were the Romans of the second century B.C. or of the age of Augustus? They were neither a nationality nor a race but the members of a formally defined group, the Roman citizen-body, and that, too, must be counted among the orders, though with reference to outsiders rather than internally and for that reason not so classified by the Romans themselves.* Our word "citizen" has the same philological connection with "city" as the Latin *civis* and the Greek *politēs*, but a much weaker connotation, since in the formative centuries of both civilizations the "city" was a community bound together by religion, tradition, intimacy and political autonomy in ways that no modern city pretends to. Hence citizenship entailed a nexus of privileges and obligations in many spheres of activity, juridically defined and jealously protected; it was membership in an order in the strictest sense of that term, especially once "outsiders" in noticeable numbers began to reside inside.[25] Roman citizenship was, after all, something Rome's so-called Italian "allies" went to war for in 91 B.C. Augustus (*Res gestae* 8.3–4) recorded 4,233,000 Roman citizens in a census of 8 B.C., 4,937,000 in A.D. 14, most of them living in Italy, in the period when we guess the total population of the empire to have been fifty or sixty million.

The history of the orders in Greece is less complex yet comparable in important respects.[26] The differences, in my opinion, can be explained, first by the absence in Greece of large-scale expansion, the major complicating factor in Rome; second, by the emergence in Greece of democracy, never achieved in Rome. It

---

* The Romans sometimes referred to *status civitatis* (cf. *status libertatis*), but in the classification I am employing, "order", not "status", is correct.

was precisely in the democratic states that the shift from orders to status-groups was most complete in the classical period, say after 500 B.C.[27] Earlier, orders were sufficiently in evidence; there is the example of Solon's reform of the Athenian constitution, traditionally in 594 B.C., whereby he divided the citizen-body into four categories, each defined by a fixed minimum property holding.[28] But for the study of the Greek economy, the distinction of the most far-reaching significance, one that continued right through the classical period in both democratic and oligarchic states, was between the citizen and the non-citizen, because it was a universal rule—I know of no exception—that the ownership of land was an exclusive prerogative of citizens. The privilege was occasionally extended to individual non-citizens, but rarely and only under powerful stimulus.

Consider for a moment the consequences in such a city as Athens, where the ratio of resident non-citizen males to male citizens ranged at different times from possibly 1:6 to perhaps 1:2½. Many of the non-citizens were actively engaged in trade, manufacture and moneylending and some moved in the highest social circles, Cephalus of Syracuse, for example, in whose house Plato later (and of course fictitiously) sited the dialogue we know as the *Republic*. Cephalus could own neither farmland nor a vineyard nor the house he lived in; he could not even lend money on land as security since he had no right of foreclosure. In turn, Athenian citizens who required cash could not easily borrow from non-citizens, the main moneylenders. This wall between the land and liquid capital was an impediment in the economy, but, the product of a juridically defined and enforced social hierarchy, it was too firmly based to be torn down.[29]

What I have called the Solonic "orders" are commonly referred to as the Solonic "classes". In principle, of course, the members of any classification system are "classes" by definition. However, there is a distinction we must express somehow in language, between groups which are and groups which are not juridically defined, and some students have suggested "order" for the first, "class" for the second. There could be no disagreement, except on the accuracy of the facts alleged in a particular instance, whether a man was or was not a member of one of Solon's orders or of the patrician or senatorial order in Rome; the test is an objective one, whereas, at least in modern society where it can be examined, there is persistent uncertainty, even in a self-assessment, whether a man belongs to the upper or lower middle class.[30]

There is little agreement among historians and sociologists about the definition of "class" or the canons by which to assign anyone to a class. Not even the apparently clearcut, unequivocal Marxist concept of class turns out to be without difficulties. Men are classed according to their relation to the means of production, first between those who do and those who do not own the means of production; second, among the former, between those who work themselves and those who live off the labour of others. Whatever the applicability of that classification in present-day society,[31] for the ancient historian there is an obvious difficulty: the slave and the free wage labourer would then be members of the same class, on a mechanical interpretation, as would the richest senator and the non-working owner of a small pottery. That does not seem a very sensible way to analyse ancient society.[32]

The pull on the historian of the capitalist, market-oriented economy reveals itself most strongly at this point. An influential book on the Roman *equites* was published in 1952 (by H. Hill) under the title, *The Roman Middle Class*, and the middle class, we all know, are businessmen. Nothing has bedevilled the history of the later Roman Republic more than this false image of the *equites*, called businessmen, capitalists, the new moneyed class, *ad lib.*, resting on the large, deeply entrenched assumption that there must have been a powerful capitalist class between the land-owning aristocracy and the poor. We have already seen that the *equites* were an order in the strict sense, and it has been proved that the overwhelming majority of them were landowners. There was, it is true, a small but important section among them, the publicans, who engaged in public contracts, tax-farming and large-scale moneylending, chiefly to communities in the provinces who were in difficulties over the taxes these same publicans were collecting

4

for the Roman state. I do not underestimate these men, but they were neither a class—they were required to offer land as security for their contracts, it is important to note—nor were they representative of the equestrian order as a whole, nor were they engaged in large-scale manufacture and commerce, nor was there a class struggle between them and the senators. A vast fictitious edifice, erected on a single false assumption about classes, still passes for Roman history in too many books.[33]

Half a century ago Georg Lukács, a most orthodox Marxist, made the correct observation that in pre-capitalist societies, "status-consciousness . . . masks class consciousness". By that he meant, in his own words, that "the structuring of society into castes and estates means that economic elements are *inextricably* joined to political and religious factors"; that "economic and legal categories are objectively and *substantively so interwoven as to be inseparable*".[34] In short, from neither a Marxist nor a non-Marxist standpoint is class a sufficiently demarcated category for our purposes—apart from the safe but vague "upper (or lower) classes" to which I have already referred—and we are still left with the necessity of finding a term that will encompass the Spartan "Inferiors" (citizens, technically, who had lost their holdings of land), the nobility of the late Roman Republic, the "friends of the king" who made up the ruling circle around the early Hellenistic kings,[35] the men Cicero had in mind when he allowed the professions of medicine, architecture and teaching to "those whose status they befit",[36] and Trimalchio.

Trimalchio was an ex-slave, a freedman, and the Romans recognized an *ordo libertinorum*, but they appreciated the virtual meaninglessness of such an order and rarely referred to it. In his wealth, Trimalchio ranked with the senators, in his "class", too, in the Marxist sense, and even in his life-style so long as we consider only his esoteric luxury and his acceptance of certain "senatorial" values, the ownership of large estates as a "non-occupation" and the pride in his economic self-sufficiency. But not when we look beyond, to the activities from which he was legally excluded as a freedman, to the social circles from which he was equally excluded, and which he made not the slightest effort to break into. Trimalchio, unlike Molière's *bourgeois gentilhomme*, was no parvenu, it has been cogently said, for he never arrived.[37]

It is for such distinctions that I suggest the word "status", an admirably vague word with a considerable psychological element. Trimalchio has been likened to the Pompeiian who called himself *princeps libertinorum*, first among the freedmen,[38] and that is status. Rich Greeks and Romans were, in the nature of things, members of criss-crossing categories. Some were complementary, for example, citizenship and land ownership, but some generated tensions and conflicts in the value system and the behaviour pattern, as between freedmen and free men, for instance. Although an order or estate had a position of superiority or inferiority to other orders, it was normally not egalitarian internally[39]—as was acknowledged, or at least implied, in Pericles' pride in the privilege of the poor Athenian to benefit his city—and the tensions that ensued could turn into open rebellion, as when impoverished Roman nobles joined the conspiracy of Catiline in 63 B.C.

I shall not pile on examples, which are very numerous; I shall pause only to indicate the development in the final centuries of antiquity. Roman expansion introduced the further complication of separate local and national (Roman) status, in particular of local and Roman citizenship—a free man could possess one or both or neither—and then the Roman emperors gradually depressed Roman citizenship until Caracalla, probably in A.D. 212, rendered it effectively meaningless by extending it to virtually all the free men of the empire. Orders proliferated recklessly, with abundant use of the superlative in the titles, *clarissimus, perfectissimus*, and so on.[40] Though the appearance is of a *reductio ad absurdum*, the reality was that men struggled for imperial favour so as to climb from order to order, not only for the honour but also for the pecuniary emoluments.

And now, finally, what has all this to do with the question of Cicero's moral strictures and the economic realities of ancient society? The conventional answer appears with monotonous regularity, as in a recent book on the freedmen of Cicero's day.

Cicero's "rigid views", we read, represented "aristocratic prejudice", "snobbery and nostalgia for an agricultural past". In
"practice things were different. Cicero certainly profited, even if
indirectly, from his oratory; senators like Brutus often dabbled in
usury; the irreproachable *eques*, Atticus, was involved in publishing, banking, and agricultural production."[41] Another scholar
proves Cicero irrelevant by making a complicated case for the
possibility, perhaps probability (but no more), that two of the
leading manufacturers of Arretine pottery in this same period were
members of landowning senatorial families.[42] Yet another assures
us that, all in all, "little in this respect separated the senator from
the wealthy non-senator".[43]

If only social and economic history were so simple. Cicero states
what he claims to be a prevailing social judgment (similar sentiments abound in both Greek and Roman literature), and he is
brushed aside by the enumeration of a few men who did not obey
his precepts. In such an argument, neither precision nor accuracy
seems required. Words like "prejudice", "snobbery", "double-
think" have no place in the discussion; agricultural production is
what landowning is about, and can hardly be used against Cicero;
advocacy, as I have already said, was omitted by Cicero from his
catalogue. No attempt is made at a quantitative analysis. Nor are
distinctions drawn, though there are some quite obvious ones
readily at hand.

Let us be clear about the issues. Neither in Cicero's Rome nor in
any other complex society did all men behave according to the
accepted canons. One is driven to repeat such a platitude because
of the prevalence of argument by exception. Nor will it be maintained that the archaic values of Homeric Greece or legendary
early Rome were still intact and binding in later periods. But the
alternative is not necessarily between archaic values and no values
at all. Before Cicero is finally dismissed, it must be decided whether
or not the new freedom of enrichment was total, even for the
nobility, or whether, by law or convention, men were still being
pressed towards certain sources of wealth according to status.[44]
Cicero's age offers the best possible test case: it was an age of

political breakdown, of the bitterest power struggles in which few holds were barred, of profound changes in traditional moral behaviour, of great tension between values and practices. Then, if ever in antiquity, one might expect to find signs of a "modern" style of economic activity, and therefore to find such formulations as Cicero's in the *De officiis* to be empty bombast.

I begin with moneylending and usury. The Romans, unlike the Greeks, tried from early times to control interest rates by law, on the whole not unsuccessfully.[45] But the age of Cicero was abnormally complicated: the demands of politics, as they were then being played, and of conspicuous consumption, an element in politics, involved the nobility, as well as others, in moneylending on a stupendous scale. Electoral bribery, an expensive life-style, extravagant public games and other forms of public largesse had become necessary ingredients of political careers. For men whose wealth was in land, the pressures were exacerbated by a shortage of liquid assets, of cash. In consequence, much political manœuvering included a complicated network of loans and guarantees. To borrow created a political obligation—until one was assigned a provincial governorship and recouped. Hence extortion in the provinces often became a personal necessity, and all the time there was much tension, at this high level of Roman society, about money matters. Only a few, such as Pompey and Crassus, were so rich as to be fairly immune from anxiety. The risks were also considerable: bankruptcy could lead to disaster if one's creditors decided to desert one politically; then it could mean expulsion from the senate and foreclosure of one's estates.[46]

Cicero himself borrowed 3,500,000 sesterces at 6% from professional moneylenders in order to purchase a luxurious house on the Palatine from Crassus. As he explained in a letter, he was considered a good risk because he was a consistent protector of the rights of creditors.[47] At a later date, Cicero borrowed 800,000 sesterces from Caesar, which caused him much embarrassment when he began to edge into Pompey's camp;[48] still later, in 47 or 46, when Caesar was in full control, Cicero lent the dictator's secretary Faberius a large (unspecified) sum, and recovery of that loan proved a difficult, squalid business.[49] Whether or not either of those two loans was interest-bearing is uncertain, but there is no doubt that both Crassus and Caesar, among others, made large interest-free loans to politically useful men.[50] Repellant though the comparison may seem, they were demonstrating in practice what Aristotle meant when he wrote (*Nicomachean Ethics* 1133a 4–5) that "it is a duty not only to repay a service done but also to take the initiative oneself in doing a service".

One more instance needs to be recorded. At some time between 58 and 56 B.C., Brutus, that paragon of nobility, still a young man, lent a considerable sum to the city of Salamis in Cyprus at 48% interest. When the time came for Brutus to collect, Cicero was saddened, and as governor of Cilicia he tried to have the affair settled at the legal 12% rate.[51] That was not the only Roman debt Cicero was busy trying to collect during his governorship, nor even the only debt to Brutus. What remains then of "those employments are to be condemned which incur ill-will, as those of . . . moneylenders (*faeneratores*)"? Did not Cicero the practical man make a mockery of Cicero the moralist?

I believe not, once proper distinctions are drawn. Nowhere did Cicero dismiss the mean employments as unnecessary. Where, outside Never-Never-Land, could they have been? Moneylenders were as indispensable in his world (and for him personally) as shopkeepers, craftsmen, perfumers and doctors. The only question he was concerned with was the moral (and social) status of the practitioners. There was no contradiction between his borrowing from professional *faeneratores* in order to buy a house appropriate to his status and his denigration of these same *faeneratores* as persons.* Brutus, Crassus and Caesar were another matter. They lent large sums of money but they were not moneylenders; they were men of war and politics, the two activities most befitting the nobility. Such men, it was recognized, could properly put some of

---

* "No youth of proper character," wrote Plutarch (*Pericles* 2.1–2), "from seeing the Zeus at Olympia or the Hera at Argos, longs to be Phidias or Polyclitus. . . . For it does not of necessity follow that, if the work delights you with its grace, the one who has wrought it is worthy of your esteem."

their excess cash to work through loans, an amateur activity that did not distract them from their full-time, noble careers. In Cicero's day there was the added virtue that this sort of money-making was largely political, conducted in the provinces, at the expense of the defeated and the subjected. Cicero would not have dreamed of calling these amateurs *faeneratores*.[52]

The opportunity for "political moneymaking" can hardly be over-estimated. Money poured in from booty, indemnities, provincial taxes, loans and miscellaneous exactions in quantities without precedent in Graeco-Roman history, and at an accelerating rate. The public treasury benefited, but probably more remained in private hands, among the nobles in the first instance; then, in appropriately decreasing proportions, among the *equites*, the soldiers and even the plebs of the city of Rome.[53] Nor should the civil wars be forgotten: some of the great fortunes were founded through Sulla's proscriptions and confiscations,[54] and again after the victory of Augustus over Antony. Nevertheless, the whole phenomenon is misunderstood when it is classified under the headings of "corruption" and "malpractice", as historians still persist in doing.[55] Cicero was an honest governor of Cilicia in 51 and 50 B.C., so that at the end of his term he had earned only the legitimate profits of office. They amounted to 2,200,000 sesterces,[56] more than treble the figure of 600,000 he himself once mentioned (*Stoic Paradoxes* 49) to illustrate an annual income that could permit a life of luxury. We are faced with something structural in the society.

What set the last age of the Roman Republic apart was the scale and wholeheartedness of the effort. In the Greek city-states, even in the Hellenistic period, the rule was that the commander in the field "could dispose of the proceeds from the sale of booty in various ways, . . . but whatever was brought back became the property of the state".[57] To be sure, we do not know the proportions, an obviously important matter, but the attested cases of generals who acquired considerable wealth are of men performing mercenary service for tyrants or foreign kings. The Roman rules were similar, but a change in behaviour, if not in the law, became visible with the first conquests outside Italy, in the wars against Carthage in the third century B.C. The enrichment of army commanders out of booty was the counterpart of the engrossment by the senatorial aristocracy of confiscated and conquered land in Italy.[58]

Then, when the relative peace and quiet of the Roman Empire (and the emperors' interest) put an end to such possibilities, private enrichment from war and administration was achieved through another technique, royal favour on the Hellenistic model. That, so to speak, was the imperial version of politics as a road to enrichment. We are told that Mela, the brother of Seneca, "refrained from seeking public office because of a perverse ambition to attain the influence of a consul while remaining a Roman *eques*; he also believed that a shorter road to the acquisition of wealth lay through procuratorships for the administration of the emperor's affairs" (Tacitus, *Annals* 16.17). Seneca himself, a senator and for a time Nero's tutor and closest adviser, was credited with having amassed a fortune worth 300,000,000 sesterces,[59] some of it no doubt his share of the confiscated estates of Britannicus, Nero's brother-in-law who died shortly before his fourteenth birthday in A.D. 55, probably by poisoning.

Complicating this ravenous hunger for acquisition in the upper strata was the fact that their basic wealth was land, and that they therefore faced chronic shortages of cash—which in this world meant gold and silver coin and nothing else—whenever they needed larger sums for either the conventional expenditure of men of high status, such as fine houses or dowries for their female relations, or the equally conventional expenditures required by political ambition. Such expenditures possessed a momentum of their own, which helped determine the extent of the rapacity at the expense of both internal enemies in a civil war and conquered or subject peoples at any and all times. To include the military and political activity that produced this kind of income among "employments" may seem logical to a modern mind; it would have been false according to ancient canons, and Cicero was perfectly correct not to mention it, as he was correct and consistent to distinguish professional moneylenders from the moneylending activity of his fellow-senators.

He was equally correct, and not disingenuous, to omit from the occupations requiring "a higher degree of intelligence" the very one which raised him to a leading position in the state, the practice of public law. In Rome, barristers and jurisconsults occupied a special place in the hierarchy; their work was closely tied in with politics and was considered equally honorific. A law of 204 B.C. prohibited barristers from taking fees or from going to court to recover money from their clients on any pretext. Such a law was not easily enforced, and violations are on record. Not on Cicero's level, however, for the simple reason that the great Republican barristers and jurisconsults had no need for fees. "If Cicero did a client proud the client's purse, friends and influence would be available to Cicero later at call,"[60] precisely as if he had lent a fellow-politician 2,000,000 sesterces interest-free. This was not the case in Rome with the other professions (in our sense). The jurist Julian, writing in the second century after Christ, laid down the following rule (*Digest* 38.1.27): "If a freedman carries on the trade of a pantomimist, he must offer his services gratis not only to his patron but also for the diversion of the latter's friends. In the same way, a freedman who practises medicine must, at his patron's request, treat the latter's friend without charge." The status of doctors in fact varied greatly in different periods and places of the ancient world. Among the Greeks they were generally esteemed, also under the Roman Empire, but among the Romans themselves the profession drew its practitioners largely from slaves, freedmen and foreigners,[61] so that Julian's thinking of doctors alongside the very low-grade occupation of pantomimist was no mere gratuitous insult.

Thus far, in sum, Cicero the moralist has proved to be not a bad guide to prevailing values. The argument becomes more difficult when we turn to commerce and manufacture, in some ways the nub of the problem. A negative argument is always difficult to substantiate. It must be conceded that the ancient sources are distorted by incompleteness and partiality; that there was evasion of

the Ciceronian code through silent partnerships and through slave-
and freedman-agents.[62] These are legitimate points, though they
often descend to illegitimate conjecture: Why should the *pragma-
teutai* of the Piraeus have erected a statue to the wife of Herodes
Atticus (the wealthiest and most powerful man in Athens in the
second century A.D.)?, asks one scholar, and he replies, without
any warrant: Because they were the commercial agents of
Herodes.[63] The decisive point remains that, against the relatively
few known instances of silent partnerships and similar devices, not
a single prominent equestrian can be identified "who was
primarily a merchant"[64] or any *equites* "who were themselves
active in the grain trade or engaged personally in sea-borne
commerce"[65]—even *equites*, let alone senators.

Landowners were of course concerned with the sale of their produce (unless their lands were leased to tenants), concerned through
their bailiffs and stewards, like Pericles' man Evangelus, and in
Italy at least, if their land included good clay-pits, brickmaking
and tilemaking acquired the status of agriculture. Hence "brickmaking is practically the only industry at Rome in which the
aristocrat does not hesitate to display his connections with the
profits of a factory".[66] Again a distinction has to be drawn. When
Cicero ended his long passage with "But of all things from which
one may acquire, none is better than agriculture", the last thing
he had in mind was subsistence farming. We still speak of a
"gentleman farmer", never of a "gentleman merchant" or a
"gentleman manufacturer". But whereas today that is a fossilized
survival in our language, because agriculture, too, is a capitalist
enterprise, for most of human history the distinction was fundamental. Anyone who confuses the gentlemanliness of agriculture
with a disinterest in profits and wealth closes the door to an
understanding of much of the past. No one ever recommended
squeezing a penny more fervently than that self-appointed
preacher of the old virtues, of the *mos maiorum*, the elder Cato.

As a control, let us turn from Rome to the commercial centres of
the provinces. Rostovtzeff, writing about Lugdunum (modern
Lyons), a Gallic village which, after a Roman colony was founded

there in 43 B.C., rapidly became the biggest and richest city in Gaul, thanks to its location at the confluence of the Rhône and Saône rivers and to its conversion into a main administrative centre, says: "To realize the brilliant development of commerce and industry in Gaul" in the second century, "it is sufficient to read the inscriptions in the twelfth and thirteenth volumes of the *Corpus*" of Latin inscriptions "and to study the admirable collection of sculptures and bas-reliefs. . . . The inscriptions of Lyons, for instance, whether engraved on stone monuments or on various articles of common use (*'instrumenta domestica'*), and particularly those which mention the different trade associations, reveal the great importance of the part played by the city in the economic life of Gaul and of the Roman Empire as a whole. Lyons was not only the great clearing-house for the commerce in corn, wine, oil, and lumber; she was also one of the largest centres in the Empire for the manufacture and distribution of most of the articles consumed by Gaul, Germany and Britain."[67]

This may be excessively exuberant, but there can be no dispute about the volume and importance of the trade passing through such centres. That is not at issue, but the status of the men who dominated, and profited from, the trade and the related financial activity. A. H. M. Jones noticed that although there were indeed men of substance among the Lyons merchants, they were freedmen and foreigners (not only from other Gallic towns but from as far afield as Syria), not a single one of whom identifies himself even as a citizen of Lyons, let alone as a member of the local aristocracy, not to mention the imperial aristocracy.[68] A similar analysis has been made for Arles[69] and for the recently excavated trading centre on the Magdalensberg in the province of Noricum,[70] both great "clearing-houses" in Rostovtzeff's terminology. Of course there were exceptions, not only exceptional individuals but also exceptional cities, such as the Roman harbour-town of Ostia, the caravan-city of Palmyra, perhaps Arezzo briefly while it was the centre for *terra sigillata*, but I trust I need not comment on the argument from exception again. Insofar as the epigraphical evidence has been properly analysed—and on this subject the necessary inquiry has hardly been started—it confirms what both the literary sources and the legal texts say about the low status of the professional traders and manufacturers throughout Roman history.

Even in ancient communities less luxurious and less complex than Ciceronian and imperial Rome or even classical Athens—and most ancient communities were less luxurious, less complex, as well as more traditional—someone had to import food, metals, slaves and luxuries, construct houses, temples and roads, and manufacture a wide range of goods. If it was the case, as I believe the evidence shows with sufficient certainty, that a very large part of that activity was in the hands either of men of low status or of men like the wealthy metics of Athens, who were more respectable socially but outsiders politically, there has to be an explanation.

Why did Athens, which passed a variety of laws, with stringent penalties, to ensure its imported corn supply, vital for its very existence, fail to legislate about the personnel of the corn trade, much of which was in the hands of non-Athenians? Why did Roman senators leave a clear field for the *equites* in the lucrative and politically important activity of tax-collection in the provinces?[71] The answer is that they did so because the citizen-élite were not prepared, *in sufficient numbers*, to carry on those branches of the economy without which neither they nor their communities could live at the level to which they were accustomed. The élite possessed the resources and the political power, they could also command a large personnel. They lacked the will; that is to say, they were inhibited, as a group (whatever the responses of a minority), by over-riding values. It is then decisive to notice that, in the familiar denunciation of freedmen and metics, from Plato to Juvenal, the invariable theme is moral, not economic.[72] They were condemned for their vices and their evil ways, never as competitors who were depriving honest men of a livelihood.

Stated differently, a model of economic choices, an investment model, in antiquity would give considerable weight to this factor of status. I do not say it was the only factor or that it weighed equally with all members of any order or status-group, nor do I know how to translate what I have said into a mathematical equation. Much depended at any given time both on the ability to obtain sufficient wealth from the reputable sources and on the pressures to spend and consume. I chose Ciceronian Rome for special analysis precisely because that was the period when the status-based model appeared to be nearest to a break-down. It did not break, however, it bent, it adapted, by extending the choices in some directions, not in all; in directions, furthermore, which can be seen to have followed logically from the very values that were being threatened and defended. And if the model survived even that extraordinary period, then it was surely secure in other periods and regions. Trimalchio remains an authentic spokesman.

III

Masters and Slaves

PARADOXICAL THOUGH it may seem, nothing creates more complication in the ancient status picture than the institution of slavery. It all looks so simple: a slave is property, subject to the rules and procedures of property, with respect to sale, lease, theft, natural increase and so on. The swineherd Eumaeus, the favourite slave of Odysseus, was property; so was Pasion, the manager of the largest banking enterprise in fourth-century B.C. Athens, who soon enough was freed and eventually was honoured with Athenian citizenship; so was any slave working in the notorious Spanish silver mines; so was Helicon, slave of the emperor Caligula, singled out by Philo (*Embassy to Gaius* 166–72) as chiefly responsible for the difficulties of the Jewish community of Alexandria; so was Epictetus, the Stoic philosopher born about A.D. 55, originally the slave of one of Nero's freedman-secretaries. That gives pause, but, after all, houses and estates and all sorts of objects of property also vary greatly in their quality. Slaves fled and were beaten and branded, but so were animals; both slaves and animals caused damage to other persons and property, for which their owners were responsible through what the Roman law called noxal actions. Then we come to two qualities in which the slave was unique as property: first, slave women could and did produce children sired by free men; second, slaves were human in the eyes of the gods, at least to the extent that their murder required some form of purification and that they were themselves involved in ritual acts, such as baptism.

This ineradicable double aspect of the slave, that he was both a person and property, thus created ambiguities, beautifully exemplified in Buckland's book, *The Roman Law of Slavery*, published in 1908. Buckland was an austere writer, he restricted himself to the Empire and to legal doctrine in the narrow sense, yet he needed 735 pages because, as he said in his preface, "There is scarcely a problem which can present itself, in any branch of the law, the solution of which may not be affected by the fact that one of the parties of the transaction is a slave." Ambiguity was compounded by the not uncommon practice of freeing slaves, who, though they still continued to suffer certain disabilities as freedmen, had nevertheless crossed the great divide, and whose children, if born afterwards, were fully free from birth, the poet Horace for example. In Rome, though not normally in Greece, the freedmen of citizen-owners automatically became citizens by the formal act of manumission, the only situation in which that prize could be granted by a strictly private act of a private individual.

However, these ambiguities, profound though I believe them to be, do not constitute the whole of the paradox with which I began. I shall exemplify further with two specific institutions. The first is the helot system of Sparta. The helots were a numerous group, far more numerous than the Spartans whose estates they worked in Laconia and Messenia, and for whom they acted as servants and performed various other tasks. The Greeks regularly referred to the helots as "slaves", but they are easily and significantly differentiated from the chattel slaves of, say, Athens. They were not free men, but they were also not the property of individual Spartans; they were not bought or sold, they could not be freed (except by the state), and, most revealing of all, they were self-perpetuating. Wherever we find chattel slaves in antiquity, we find the stock recruited not only by birth but also by continual import from outside. But never in the case of the helots, who must therefore have had their own families, *de facto* if not *de iure*, and their own possessions, transmitted from generation to generation, no doubt their own cults, and, in general, all the normal human institutions except their freedom. One consequence was that they also revolted, unlike genuine slaves in the Greek world in pre-Roman times. Another was that, in times of heavy military commitment, they were impressed into the Spartan army (as proper, heavy-armed soldiers, not merely as orderlies and clerks).[1]

My second example, the institution of *peculium*, is better known from, and more fully developed, in Rome than in Greece. What the Romans called *peculium* was property (in whatever form) assigned for use, management, and, within limits, disposal to someone who in law lacked the right of property, either a slave or someone in *patria potestas*. In strict law, a *peculium* was a purely voluntary grant by the master or *pater*, which involved him in legal responsibility to third parties up to the amount of the *peculium*, and which he was free to withdraw at any time. In practice, however, the possessor normally had a free hand in the management, and, if a slave, he could expect to buy his freedom with the profits, to continue the business as a freedman thereafter if he wished, and to transmit it to his heirs. In practice, furthermore, a substantial part of the urban commercial, financial and industrial activity in Rome, in Italy, and wherever else in the empire Romans were active, was being carried on in this way by slaves and freedmen from the third century B.C. on. Unlike slave bailiffs and managers, those who had a *peculium* were working independently, not only for their owners but also for themselves. And if the business were on any scale above the minimal, their *peculium* was likely to include other slaves along with cash, shops, equipment and stock-in-trade.[2]

Now it is apparent that, though household servants, slaves with a *peculium* and slaves working in chains on a large farm all fell within a single juridical category, the legal status masked the economic and social differentiations among them.[3] And legal status itself becomes very opaque when we consider such categories as the helots. The Greeks, lacking a developed jurisprudence, never made a serious effort to define the helot status juridically: "between the free men and the slaves" (Pollux, *Onomasticon* 3.83) is the best they achieved. And it is a fair speculation that the Romans would not have been successful had they tried. Roman lawyers concerned themselves with the internal Roman world, and the social complexities of the increasingly hybrid world of the empire baffled them; hence their inability to pigeonhole the so-called *coloni* of the later Empire[4] and their resort to such classificatory monstrosities as the *liber homo bona fide serviens* and the *servus quasi colonus*. We are the heirs of the Roman law, filtered through the Middle Ages, and we are mesmerized by the notion that at the lower end of the social scale, in the work force, there are three and only three possible categories, slaves, serfs and free wage-earners. So the helots become serfs[5] and the slaves with a *peculium* are discussed in the first instance as slaves, when, economically and in terms of the structure and functioning of the society, they were mostly self-employed craftsmen, pawn-brokers, moneylenders and shopkeepers. They did the same kind of civilian work as their free counterparts, in the same ways and under the same conditions, despite the formal difference in legal status. The members of neither group worked under the restraint of another, in the sense condemned as slavish and unfree by Aristotle and Cicero, and there is the paradox inherent in ancient slavery.

Historically speaking, the institution of wage-labour is a sophisticated latecomer. The very idea of wage-labour requires two difficult conceptual steps. First it requires the abstraction of a man's labour from both his person and the product of his work. When one purchases an object from an independent craftsman, whether he is free or a slave with a *peculium*, one has not bought his labour but the object, which he had produced in his own time and under his own conditions of work. But when one hires labour, one purchases an abstraction, labour-power, which the purchaser then uses at a time and under conditions which he, the purchaser, not the "owner" of the labour-power, determines (and for which he normally pays after he has consumed it). Second, the wage-labour system requires the establishment of a method of measuring the labour one has purchased, for purposes of payment, commonly by introducing a second abstraction, namely, labour-time.[6]

We should not underestimate the magnitude, speaking socially
5

rather than intellectually, of these two conceptual steps; even the Roman jurists found them difficult.[7] The need to mobilize labour-power for tasks that are beyond the capacity of the individual or family is an old one, reaching far back into prehistory. When any society we can trace attained a stage of sufficient accumulation of resources and power in some hands (whether king, temple, ruling tribe or aristocracy), so that a labour force was demanded greater than could be provided by the household or kinship group, for agriculture or mining or public works or arms manufacture, that labour force was obtained not by hiring it but by compelling it, by force of arms or by force of law and custom. This involuntary labour force, furthermore, was normally not composed of slaves but of one or another "half-way" type, such as the debt-bondsman, the helot, the early Roman client, the late Roman *colonus*. The occasional slave is found, especially the female captive, as is the occasional free hired man, but neither was for a long time a significant factor in production, whether on the land or in towns.

A proper balance of these low statuses is difficult to achieve. In a famous Homeric passage, Odysseus visits Hades, meets the shade of Achilles and asks after his well-being. The reply is a bitter one. Rather than be king over all the dead, said Achilles, "I would rather be bound down, working as a *thes* for another, by the side of a landless man" (*Odyssey* 11.489–91). Not a slave, but a landless *thes*, was the lowest human status Achilles could think of. And in the *Iliad* (21.441–52), the god Poseidon reminds Apollo of the time when both of them worked a full year as *thetes* for Laomedon king of Troy, "for an agreed upon wage". At the end of the year they were driven off unpaid, with no means of obtaining redress.[8] *Thetes* were free men, the swineherd Eumaeus a slave, but the latter had a more secure place in the world thanks to his attach-ment to an *oikos*, a princely household, an attachment more meaningful, more valuable, than the status of being juridically free, of not being owned by someone. Another nuance can be seen in the struggle, in early sixth-century Athens and fifth- and fourth-century B.C. Rome, to bring about the abolition of debt-bondage. In both communities a substantial number of citizens had fallen into actual bondage through debt—Aristotle even says (*Constitution of Athens* 2.2), about Athens, that "the poor, with their wives and children, were 'enslaved' to the rich"—but their successful struggle was never looked upon, either by themselves or by our ancient authorities on the subject, as a slave revolt. They were citizens reclaiming their rightful place in their own community—for themselves alone, not for the few genuine chattel slaves who had been brought from outside into Athens and Rome at that time.[9]

Were these citizen-bondsmen, before their liberation, free men or not? I find this a meaningless question and worse, a misleading question, reflecting the false triad I mentioned earlier, whereby we try to force all labour into one of three categories, slave, serf or free. Conceptually there are two polar extremes of legal "freedom". At one pole is the slave as property and nothing else; at the other pole, the perfectly free man, all of whose acts are freely and voluntarily performed. Neither has ever existed. There have been individual slaves who had the bad luck to be treated by their owners as nothing but a possession, but I know of no society in which the slave population as a whole were looked upon in that simple way. At the other end, every man except Robinson Crusoe has his freedom limited in one way or another in consequence of living in society. Absolute freedom is an idle dream (and it would be psychologically intolerable anyway).

Between these two hypothetical extremes there is a whole range or spectrum of positions, some of which I have already exemplified, often co-existing within the same society. A person possesses or lacks rights, privileges, claims and duties in many respects: he may be free to retain the surplus of his labour after payment of dues, rents and taxes, but not be free to choose the nature and place of his work or his domicile; he may be free to select his occupation but not his place of work; he may have certain civil rights but no political rights; he may have political rights but no property rights so long as he is, in Roman terms, *in potestate*; he may or may not have the right (or obligation) of military service, at his own or public expense; and so on. The combination of these rights, or lack of them, determines a man's place in the spectrum, which is, of course, not to be understood as a mathematical continuum, but as a more metaphorical, discontinuous spectrum, with gaps here, heavier concentrations there. And even in a colour spectrum, which can be translated into a mathematical continuum, the difference among the primary colours remains perfectly visible.[10]

This may all seem unnecessarily abstract and sophistical. I think not. In the previous chapter I tried to show how at the upper end of the social scale, the existence of a spectrum of statuses and orders (though I did not use the word "spectrum") explains much about economic behaviour. Now I am suggesting that the same analytical tool helps resolve otherwise intractable questions about the behaviour at the lower end. I have already indicated that helots revolted, while chattel slaves did not in Greece, precisely because the helots possessed (not lacked) certain rights and privileges, and demanded more. Invariably, what are conventionally called "class struggles" in antiquity prove to be conflicts between groups at different points in the spectrum disputing the distribution of specific rights and privileges. When genuine slaves did finally revolt, three times on a massive scale in Italy and Sicily in the period 140–70 B.C., their concern was with themselves and their status, not with slavery as an institution, not, simply stated, to abolish slavery.[11] The spectrum-idea also enables us to locate the slave with a *peculium* in relationship both to the slave-farmhand and to the free independent craftsman and shopkeeper. And it helps immunize us from the injection of our moral values into such more narrowly economic questions as the comparative efficiency of slave labour and other forms of labour.

The majority of the free men, even of the free citizens, in antiquity worked for their livelihood. Even Cicero allowed that. But the total labour force also included another substantial sector, men who were to a greater or lesser extent not free, a category for which our language provides no appropriate one-word label once it is accepted that chattel slavery is only a sub-category. In the broad category, which I shall call "dependent (or involuntary) labour", I include everyone who worked for another not because of membership in the latter's family, as in a peasant household, and not because he had entered a voluntary, contractual agreement (whether for wages, honoraria or fees), but because he was bound to do so by some pre-condition, birth into a class of dependents or debt or capture or any other situation which, by law or custom, automatically removed some measure of his freedom of choice and action, usually for a long term or for life.

Historians have traditionally concentrated on the sub-category of chattel slaves (as shall I), and for intelligible reasons. In the great "classical" periods, in Athens and other Greek cities from the sixth century B.C. on and in Rome and Italy from early in the third century B.C. to the third century A.D., slavery effectively replaced other forms of dependent labour, and those are the ancient centres and periods that grip the attention for many reasons. However, neither the rise nor the decline of slavery in antiquity can be understood in isolation. Little as we are able to grasp the situation concretely, we can be confident that in the archaic periods in both Greek and Roman history, slavery was unimportant, clientage, debt-bondage and the like the prevalent forms of dependent labour. Furthermore, Sparta was by no means unique in this respect in the classical era: something very like helotage existed in Crete and Thessaly, in Greek Sicily for a time, and on a large scale and for many centuries among the Greek colonies in the Danube basin and along the shores of the Dardanelles and the Black Sea,[12] altogether a very substantial portion of Hellas in quantitative terms.

Debt-bondage, too, even after it had been abolished in Athens and Rome, remained more widespread than we allow, formally in many areas,[13] informally where we might least have expected it, in Italy itself. The Roman law pronounced categorically that contractual farm-tenants were free to leave at the completion of their tenure, normally five years (*Code* 4.65.11). And so they were—provided they were not in arrears. As long ago as 1885 Fustel de Coulanges suggested that the tenants with whom L.

Domitius Ahenobarbus privately equipped a fleet in 50 or 49 B.C. (together with his slaves and freedmen) do not seem to have been all that free,[14] and he noticed further that the tenants in arrears about whom the younger Pliny complained in a frequently cited letter were still labouring on his estates after the expiry of their tenure, and that they therefore should be linked with the undefined *nexus* of Columella and the *obaerati* of Varro, who were unmistakably bondsmen.[15] Fustel's argument has attracted little attention because historians have been too obsessed with the evils of slavery to appreciate the evils of short-term tenancy under the harsh Roman law of debt. The argument is no less valid for this neglect.[16]

One stimulus for chattel slavery came from the growth of urban production, for which the traditional forms of dependent labour were unsuitable. On the land, slavery made significant inroads wherever helotage and comparable labour-statuses failed to survive, for whatever reason, on a sufficient scale to meet the needs of landowners (hence not in Sparta, for example). That is to say, in the absence of a free labour market, a slave labour force was imported—for slaves are always in the first instance outsiders—only when the existing internal force became insufficient, as after the Solonic reforms in Athens. This correlation was also central to the development when Alexander and his successors, and later the Romans, conquered large portions of the old Near East. There they found an independent peasantry coexisting with a large dependent labour force on the land, in ratios we cannot even guess at, and they took the obvious course, as conquerors who came to exploit and profit, of retaining the tenure system they found, making only such modifications in detail as were required, for example by the establishment of Greek cities, whose land was traditionally free from royal or temple controls.[17] Why should they have done otherwise? Why, to be precise, should they have tried either to convert already dependent peasants, with a tradition of centuries of acceptance of their status, into a different kind of subjection, or to drive them off and import a substitute labour supply? This rhetorical question requires no answer. The consequence was that in Asia Minor, Syria and Egypt, slavery never became an important factor on the land. And Rome's acquisitions in western Europe and North Africa, with their different pre-Roman social structures, underwent yet another development.[18]

If we put aside for the present the questions of the rise and the decline of slavery and concentrate on the great "classical" periods in Greece and Italy, then we are faced with the first genuine slave societies in history, surrounded by (or embedded in) societies that continued to rely on other forms of dependent labour. None of this can be translated into neat quantitative terms. We do not know the numbers of slaves in Greece or Italy at any given time, not even the number in any particular community or in any particular individual's possession, save for exceptions. Estimates by modern scholars for classical Athens range wildly, all the way from 20,000 to 400,000, both impossible figures but indicative of the sad state of our information.[19] They also reveal an obsessively tendentious, subjective and basically false approach to the problem. Certainly we should try to discover the numbers as closely as the evidence allows, but argument from simple arithmetical ratios may turn into number mysticism rather than systematic quantification. The impossibly low estimate of 20,000 slaves in Athens in the time of Demosthenes gives a ratio of slaves to citizen households of not much below one to one.[20] What would that prove even if it were correct? In the American slave states in 1860, the slave population was slightly less than one third of the total, and perhaps three fourths of the whites owned no slaves at all, according to official census figures.[21] No one will deny that the American slave states were slave societies: given the presence of enough slaves, above an undefinable minimum, the test is not numbers but social and economic location. No matter how many slave women a historian may manage to tot up in the harems of the Caliphate of Baghdad, they count for nothing against the fact that agricultural and industrial production was largely carried on by free men.

Admittedly, a "sufficient minimum" is not a precise concept, but it is good enough in the light of the large-scale and continuous enslavement of the victims of war and "piracy" recorded through-out ancient history; Caesar alone is said to have been responsible for one million during his campaigns in Gaul between 58 and 51 B.C., a not wildly incredible figure.[22] Xenophon, writing in the middle of the fourth century B.C., reports the popular belief that half a century earlier the general Nicias owned a thousand slaves whom he leased out to concessionaires in the Athenian silver mines, that another man had six hundred and that a third had three hundred (*Poroi* 4.14–15). That is often dismissed as fantasy,[23] and I know of no way to "prove" Xenophon right. I do not have to; it is enough that Xenophon assumed his readers would not find these figures unreasonable and that he based a very elaborate proposal on them; that Thucydides (7.27.5) thought it a reason-able guess that 20,000 slaves had fled in the final decade of the Peloponnesian War, the majority of them skilled workmen; that the best modern estimate suggests a slave force in the mines in Xenophon's time running to five figures.[24] It is enough that the metic Cephalus employed nearly 120 slaves in the manufacture of shields, an undisputed figure,[25] or, to turn to Rome, that the prefect of the city, Lucius Pedanius Secundus, assassinated by one of his slaves in the reign of Nero, had four hundred slaves in his town house alone (Tacitus, *Annals* 14.43). Not surprisingly, the numerous gravestones of the common people of the city of Rome in that period reveal a preponderance of freedmen (ex-slaves) over freeborn.[26]

By "location" I mean two interlocking things, location in em-ployment (where the slaves worked) and location in the social structure (which strata possessed and relied on slave labour), and that is what we must now consider. The starting-point is that both slaves and free men are found in every kind of civilian employ-ment, though mining comes very near to being a monopoly of slaves and domestic service of slaves and ex-slaves (freedmen), and it is perhaps noteworthy that Cicero omitted both activities from his catalogue. Mining has always been an exceptional occupation, reserved (as it still is in South Africa for example) for the depressed sectors of the population, slaves where they are available, free men whose freedom is fragile and easily encroached upon where slavery no longer exists.[27] Throughout antiquity free miners were a negligible element, so much so that Xenophon thought it reasonable to propose that the Athenian state should enter the business of purchasing slaves to be leased to the concession-holders in the silver mines, and support the entire citizen-body from the income it would derive. As for domestic service, I note only that this category included, in the richer households, not merely cooks, butlers and maids but also nannies, "pedagogues", spinners and weavers, bookkeepers, administrators; in the household of the Roman emperors, the lower echelons of the imperial civil service.

The refinement the analysis then requires is again pointed to by Cicero: he calls a whole range of employments mean and illiberal, but he restricts the slave metaphor to those who work for wages, to hired labour. Free men were found in all occupations, but usually as self-employed workers, either as smallholders or tenants on the land, or as independent craftsmen, traders and moneylenders in the towns. That is the first fundamental distinction to be made in locating slavery in ancient society. The evidence, small though it may be in quantity, is overwhelming in its impact. Free hired labour was casual and seasonal,* its place determined by the limits beyond which it would have been absurd to purchase and maintain a slave force, most obviously to meet the exceptional short-term needs of harvesting in agriculture. Similarly in the cities there were men who were compelled to struggle for subsistence on wages, picking up odd jobs as porters, at the docks or in the building trades, the men the Greeks called *ptochoi*, beggars, in contrast to the hard-working "poor".[28] Harvesting and portering were essential activities, to be sure, but the men who performed them were either these marginal figures or they were independent peasants and craftsmen happy to be able to add something to their regular, low earnings.

Whenever we know of a private establishment, urban or rural, regularly employing the services of numbers of workmen whose

---

* There was of course the one major exception, irrelevant in the present context, of rowers in the navy and, where they existed, professional soldiers.

status is identified, these were slaves. Enterprises hiring free men on even a semi-permanent basis are simply not found in the sources. The Athenian orator Demosthenes could therefore use the words, "the slaves" and "the workshop" (*ergasterion*), as perfect synonyms when he was trying in a court of law to recover his inheritance from his guardians.[29] Half a century later, an unnamed Athenian landowner, lusting after a slave boy, was tricked, so he says (Hypereides 5), by the owner, a perfumer, into buying the *ergasterion* itself, which consisted of three slaves (the boy, his father and his brother), some stock-in-trade and a large number of debts. In the Italy of Augustus, the flourishing potteries of Arezzo employed only slaves, the largest number known in a single establishment being some sixty. When the centre of manufacture of "Arretine ware" shifted to Gaul, the local potters, nearly all of them Celts in origin, were independent craftsmen in small individual enterprises, apparently without numerous slaves or wage-workers.[30] In the later Roman Empire, finally, when the distinction between slaves and other forms of involuntary labour had been diminished to almost the vanishing point, in the imperial factories and the mint, the largest industrial enterprises of the time now that the state produced directly, among other things, the uniforms and arms required by its armies, the workers were all servile in the broad sense, and often still slaves in the narrow sense, a work force, furthermore, that was recruited by breeding.[31]

Apart from this late development under a complete autocracy, public works reveal certain nuances differentiating them from private enterprises. Insofar as they required specialized skills, extremely so with marble temples, three distorting factors must be allowed for: first, the element of piety, attracting free labour as private employment might not; second, the opportunity, recognized by some states, to provide supplementary income for its citizen-craftsmen; third, the absolute shortage of the requisite specialists outside a few atypical centres such as Athens and Rome. For this work, therefore, slaves appear to have been little used. However, the same distorting features made it almost impossible to have the work carried out by large-scale contractors. The work was commonly broken down into small jobs, each given out on a separate contract rather than on a wage-basis.[32] The distinction which the Roman lawyers eventually acknowledged between the two contracts of hire, *locatio conductio operis* and *locatio conductio operarum*, expressed a fundamental status-distinction, the difference between independence and dependence; between the free man who, though he worked for his livelihood, worked for clients (private or public), and the man who worked for wages.[33]

The beauty of fine temples should not distract us from the fact that most public works—roads, walls, streets, aqueducts, sewers—required more muscle than skill. But at that point our sources, with their disinterest in such matters, desert us, and archaeology cannot help. That is the kind of work that could be equally imposed on soldiers and on captives. Yet I think one pair of contemporary Roman texts provides the clue. The story is told (Suetonius, *Vespasian* 18) that someone came to the emperor Vespasian with a new device for transporting heavy columns to the Capitol at small cost. The emperor rewarded the inventor for this ingenuity and then refused to use the device, "exclaiming, How will it be possible for me to feed the populace?" That is charming, but the large, continuing imperial outlay for the Roman populace went for bread and circuses, not for jobs.[34] Vespasian's reference is to the kind of casual labour I have already noticed; transporting columns to the Capitol could hardly have provided permanent employment for large numbers of people, whereas maintenance of the water supply did, and for that there was a permanent staff of seven hundred slaves (including the "architects").[35]

We know that from a book written by Sextus Julius Frontinus, who was appointed *curator aquarum* by the emperor Nerva in A.D. 97. Frontinus was a senator of some distinction, having been urban praetor, suffect consul and governor of Britain long before he took over the Roman water supply. The contrast between his status and that of the slave "architects" who were the technical managers of the system points up something fundamental. Political administration was one thing, management something else again, and management throughout the classical period, Greek as well as

Roman, urban as well as rural, was the preserve of slaves and freedmen, at least in all larger establishments, those in which the owner himself did not normally take an active part. That men of the highest status would not and indeed could not devote themselves to managing their own estates and other business affairs is self-evident: their life-style made that impossible, doubly so for the larger landowners, city-dwellers who visited their estates from time to time. That emerges wherever we look, whether at Xenophon's *Oikonomikos* or Cato's manual or the letters of Pliny.

Even public administration was problematical below the highest echelons. There is a revealing text from the latter half of the second century, the *Apology* of Lucian, a Syrian-Greek who had become a distinguished rhetorician and belle-lettrist, but who, towards the end of his life, took a post in the imperial service. He had once written an essay bitterly attacking the "slavishness" of literary men who accepted places, for a salary, in the homes of wealthy patrons. Was he not in effect doing the same, he now asks? It is true, he replies, that I and they both receive a wage and work "under the power of another", but whereas "their slavery is manifest and they differ little from purchased or bred slaves"—I find the echoes of Aristotle and Cicero irresistible, even if not deliberate —my position is incomparable because I serve the public interest.[36] A *jeu d'esprit* no doubt, but none the less indicative: today an apology for accepting a minor governmental post would not take that line.

In the urban economy, slave-managers were closely linked with slaves with a *peculium,* and therefore, particularly in Roman society, with freedmen, since these were the slaves who were more commonly manumitted, not the agricultural slaves. We must then ask why so important a role in the economy—or to speak in more precise ancient terms, in the acquisition of wealth—was left to slaves and freedmen. One suggestion is to find the explanation in the "relatively greater efficiency and better training of the unfree and newly freed".[37] Perhaps, but there is an element of circularity in the reasoning. If the freeborn were unavailable for training, which means that they were unwilling to enter the employ of others, then the stress ought to be placed there in order to avoid the implication of a genuine choice between two kinds of managerial personnel.[38]

Now it is a peculiarity inherent in the status of freedman that it is evanescent, restricted by law to a single generation. A freedman's sons remained slaves if born before his manumission (unless they were also manumitted), but were fully free if born later. It was on his sons, therefore, that a freedman placed his hopes for those social and political consequences of wealth that the law denied him personally, public office in particular. A close analysis, made nearly half a century ago,[39] of epitaphs from Italy during the Empire revealed that a high proportion of members of the municipal senates were the sons of freedmen, highest in a city like Ostia, where the figure is estimated to have reached 33% or more, lowest in the more rural district of Cisalpine Gaul, say 12%. The figures have been challenged as too high because of the author's loose tests for determining who was or was not a freedman's son. The criticism of the statistics is correct, but ill-directed. No one is claiming that vast numbers of freedmen's sons became local aristocrats, or that municipal senates were becoming dominated by such men, or that they constituted a new "class" in Roman society. Even a reduction of the percentages by half would not invalidate the conclusion that a significant number of freedmen had succeeded through their sons in attaining high social and political status. The emperor Claudius was not making a meaningless gesture when in A.D. 41 he ordered the Alexandrians to exclude "those born of slaves" from the ephebate, the upper-class Greek youth corps of the city.[40] Nor was Marcus Aurelius, who in about the year 175 instructed Athens to remove from the elite Council of the Areopagus anyone who was not freeborn in the third generation, while expressly permitted the sons of freedmen membership in the Council of Five Hundred.[41] In Rome tself, according to Tacitus (*Annals* 13.27), it was argued in Nero's time that most equestrians and many senators were the descendants of slaves; a tendentious hyperbole, no doubt, but not a view to be simply dismissed.

Success was achieved by the normal method of an extensive outpouring of funds on the community and its citizens, and the easy explanation is that these fortunes were gained in trade, manufacture and moneylending. Yet one must pause a bit at the fact that among these most successful freedmen there was a heavy concentration of men risen from the ranks of the imperial and municipal civil service. Furthermore, the question remains open as to what proportion, either of the richer freedmen themselves, like Trimalchio, or of their now upper-class sons steered their wealth into the safe harbour of the land. It is probably impossible to find a convincing answer, but there are occasional hints, such as the fact that of the larger farms (and vineyards) in the neighbourhood of Pompeii, employing tens of slaves (evidenced, among other things, by the chains found in excavation), perhaps half were the property of freedmen.[42] But whatever the answer, that is, whatever the proportion whose families continued in urban economic activity, the important conclusion is that the ephemeral stratum who managed the affairs of the aristocratic landed magnates could never become Rostovtzeff's bourgeoisie;[43] they did not play the creative role of the estate-managers, surveyors and lawyers of Europe on the eve of the Industrial Revolution, who stitched "the landed gentleman . . . into the new economic fabric of society".[44] No Trimalchio could become the Stolz of Goncharov's *Oblomov*.[45]

The Greek pattern, it must be admitted, is less clear, not with respect to slave-managers, who are sufficiently attested, but with respect to freedmen and their descendants. Our difficulty is both technical and substantive. Greek freedmen became metics, not citizens; their nomenclature did not reveal freedman status as did the Roman; the Greeks never adopted the Roman practice of summarizing their careers on their tombstones (at least not until the Roman Empire). Hence we simply cannot say what proportion of the metics who loomed so large in the urban economy were freedmen or their descendants, as distinct from free immigrants. Granted that gap in our knowledge and granted other variations and shifts in nuance, I believe the generalization is fully war-

ranted that, in terms of their "location", slaves were fundamental
to the ancient economy in what I have been calling, for lack of a
more precise label, the "classical period", Greek and Roman.
They were fundamental both in their employment (where they
worked) and in the social structure (the reliance placed on them
and their labour by the highest strata, the ruling classes).

In short, classical Greece and Italy were slave societies in the
same broad sense as was the American South. There were significant differences, among them the fact—at least one has the firm
impression that it is a fact—that the slave-owning section of the
population in antiquity was proportionally greater than the
estimated twenty-five per cent in the southern states. "Who has no
slaves and no money-box" is how a Roman poet describes the
penniless man, when we might say "not a bean".[46] About
400 B.C., an Athenian appealed to the Council against his removal
from the list of those entitled to public assistance, physically
incapacitated citizens possessing a property worth less than two
hundred drachmas, equal to about two hundred days' wages. In
his plea (*Lysias* 24.6) he argued that he was not yet able to purchase a slave who could maintain him (the actual words used are
"replace him"), but that he hoped eventually to be in a position
to do so. Nearly eight hundred years later, the world famous
rhetorician and teacher Libanius appealed to the council of
Antioch for an increase in the stipend of his lecturers, so poor and
miserably underpaid that they could not afford more than two or
three slaves each.[47] At that time, even privates in ordinary
regiments sometimes owned personal slave-batmen.[48]

As in other slave societies, slaves and free men could be found
working side by side. Fragments have survived of the public
accounts for the final stage in the construction, at the end of the
fifth century B.C., of the temple on the Acropolis of Athens known
as the Erechtheum.[49] They are broken down into daily records
because in this instance the Athenian state itself acted as the contractor. Of the 86 workmen whose status is known, 24 were
citizens, 42 metics and 20 slaves. In a number of instances, a
slaveowner worked alongside one or more of his own slaves; the

metic Simias, a mason, with five slaves. They all seem to have been paid at the same rate, five or six obols a day, including the architects, whose only advantage was that they could expect continuous employment on the project.[50] Simias, of course, pocketed both his own pay and that of his slaves, but that does not affect the issue.

Wage rates in antiquity generally remained remarkably stable and undifferentiated. *We* may believe that the free men were thus being kept down by the slaves, both in the competition for employment and in the rates of pay. But *they* never argued that; as I said before, the complaints about slaves and slavery that have come down are moral, not economic. The one major exception drives the point home: the growth of the large slave-worked estates in Italy during the late Republic brought serious protests— Tiberius Gracchus made a public issue of the masses of slaves in the countryside[51]—but they were on behalf of the dispossessed small landowners, the peasantry, not on behalf of free labour, agricultural or urban.[52] The dispossessed wanted their land back, not employment on the large estates. Strictly speaking, they had no interest in the slaves, no objection to slave labour on the traditional holdings of the upper classes.

At the beginning of the Industrial Revolution in England, Arthur Young wrote, "Every one but an idiot knows that the lower classes must be kept poor, or they will never be industrious."[53] The Graeco-Roman poor, the citizen poor, were kept free instead during the classical period, and available for military and naval service.[54] There were times when they exercised their freedom in order to rebel, either for fuller political rights or for the perennial revolutionary programme of antiquity, cancel debts and redistribute the land, the slogan of a peasantry, not of a working class. Veterans constantly demanded land grants upon demobilization; the latest inquiry suggests that in the unusually active allotment period of the civil wars in the last century of the Roman Republic, a quarter of a million veteran families were given land in Italy alone by Sulla, Caesar, the triumvirs and Augustus.[55] Often they were willing to accept allotments so small that there was no margin even with tax exemption, indeed a near certainty of eventual failure: allotments of three to five acres are attested for the second century B.C.; Caesar's bill of 59 B.C. provided ten *jugera* (slightly over six acres) for a veteran (or poor man) with a family of three or more children.[56] Or they clung to the cities and demanded more and more bread and circuses.

What is totally absent is anything we can recognize as a labour programme, anything to do with wages, conditions of employment, the competition of slaves. In the innumerable little benevolent societies, commonly organized by trade or occupation, that mushroomed in the cities and towns of antiquity, especially in the Hellenistic world and the Roman Empire, the communal activity was restricted to religious, social and benevolent affairs; in no sense were they guilds trying to foster or protect the economic interests of their members, nor did they reveal a trace of the hierarchical pattern of apprentice, journeyman and master that characterized the medieval and early modern guilds.[57] Slaves and free men (chiefly free independent craftsmen) could be fellow-members of a society, precisely because of the absence of any feeling of competition.

Neither in Greek nor in Latin was there a word with which to express the general notion of "labour" or the concept of labour "as a general social function".[58] The nature and conditions of labour in antiquity precluded the emergence of such general ideas, as of the idea of a working class. "Men never rest from toil and sorrow by day, and from perishing by night," said Hesiod (*Works and Days* 176-8). That is a descriptive statement, a statement of fact, not of ideology; so is the conclusion, that it is therefore better to toil than to perish, and better still to turn to the labour of slaves if one can. But the world was not one of toil and sorrow for everybody, and there lay a difficulty. The expulsion from Eden had the saving feature that it embraced all mankind, and hence, though it linked work with sin and punishment, it did not degrade labour as such. A fate which is everyone's may be tragic, it cannot be shameful. Sin can be washed away, not natural moral inferiority. Aristotle's theory of natural slavery in the first book of

6

the *Politics* was an extreme position, but those who did not accept it merely turned the doctrine round: men who engaged in the mean employments or in the slavish conditions of employment were made inferior by their work. Either way there was no consolation.

All this, it will be objected, is based on the views of the upper classes and their spokesmen among the intellectuals, not on the views of those who worked but were voiceless. But they were not wholly so. They expressed themselves in their cults, for example, and it is to be noted that though Hephaestus (the Roman Vulcan), the craftsman among the gods, was in a sense a patron of the crafts, and especially of the metallurgists, he was an inferior deity in heaven and he received little formal worship and few temples on earth.[59] The most "popular" classical cults were the ecstatic ones, particularly that of Dionysus/Bacchus, the god of intoxication (in more senses than one). Through Dionysus one did not celebrate toil, one obtained release from it. Those who worked also expressed their views in their demands for land, already noticed, and in their failure to ally themselves with the slaves on those relatively rare occasions when the latter revolted.[60]

Skill was honoured and admired, to be sure, but pride in craftsmanship is a psychological phenomenon that is not to be confused with a positive evaluation of work as such. Even Plato was a great admirer of workmanship and made innumerable positive analogies to the skilled craftsman, while ranking that skill very low in his hierarchy of values. Slaves revealed a similar pride, not in their words, which we do not possess, but in the work itself. No one can distinguish, in the ruins of the Erechtheum, which mouldings were carved by Simias, which by his five slaves. The *terra sigillata* ware of Arezzo, made by slaves, was much finer than the products of the free potters of Lezoux.

The psychology of the slave is complex and, for antiquity at least, probably impenetrable. A proper analysis would have to consider the deracination of the slave from both homeland and kin; the implication of the ubiquitous "boy" as a form of address for male slaves of any age; the impact on sexual mores, exemplified by the sexual relations between the young Trimalchio with both his master and his mistress, repeated by the old Trimalchio with *his* slaves;[61] the predominance of rural slaves in the great revolts, with the urban slaves at times not merely remaining neutral but fighting on the side of their masters;[62] the active participation of slaves in siege-defence;[63] and much else that would take us outside the limits of this discussion.

The qualitative performance of slave labour is the essential point from which to proceed to a consideration of its efficiency and profitability, and hence of the choices available to the employers of labour in antiquity. This is a subject bedevilled by dogma and pseudo-issues, most of them growing out of moral judgments. There is a long line of writers, of the most varied political coloration, who assert that slave labour is inefficient, at least in agriculture, and ultimately unprofitable.[64] This suggestion would have astonished Greek and Roman slaveowners, who not only went on for many centuries fondly believing that they were making substantial profits out of their slaves but also spending those profits lavishly. It would equally have astonished the planters of Brazil and Mississippi, whose return on investment was fairly comparable with the profits in the non-slave regions of the New World.[65]

It is then asserted, as a second "line of defence", that slavery impeded technological progress and growth in productivity, that even the servile "colonate" of the later Roman Empire, the forerunner of medieval serfdom, was more efficient because *coloni* (not to mention free tenants) "were more interested than the slaves in the results of their labour".[66] Dogma again: one has to come down to the fourteenth century in England and France before wheat production, for example, regularly matched the fourfold yield which appears to have been considered as the target for the slave-worked estates in ancient Italy;[67] and one can point to some technological progress precisely where slavery showed its most brutal and oppressive face, in the Spanish mines and on the Roman *latifundia*.[68]

We lack the data from which to calculate the profitability of ancient slavery, anyway a very difficult exercise, as current study of the American South has revealed; and we have no way to assess its relative profitability in antiquity as compared to other types of labour.*The ancients could not have made the first calculation either, but they did know that they regularly emerged with satisfactory incomes. The second, the relative calculation, they could not even imagine. Against what realistic alternative were they to measure? Southern planters and manufacturers could look to their northern counterparts. To whom could Greeks or Romans look? Having looked, furthermore, the South decided to go to war in order to retain slavery, and that simple historical fact ought to put an end to the kind of argument that still casts such a spell in ancient history. Economic growth, technical progress, increasing efficiency are not "natural" virtues; they have not always been possibilities or even desiderata, at least not for those who controlled the means by which to try to achieve them.

Moral judgments and practical judgments are frequently at odds. "There is no inherent need for immoral social arrangements to be economically inefficient, and even a greater presumption that they *do* yield tangible, material rewards for the dominant class."[69] The literature of the Roman Empire is filled with doubts and qualms about slavery; fear of slaves, of being murdered by them, of possible revolts, is a recurrent (and old) theme. But this literature can be matched, passage by passage, from the American South, and in neither society was the practical conclusion drawn that slavery should be replaced by other forms of labour, should be abolished, in short.[70]

Yet in the end there was a "decline" of slavery in antiquity, and that requires explanation. Let us be clear what is at issue. Ancient slavery was neither abolished, as in the United States in 1865, nor did it disappear nor was it replaced by a system of free wage-labour. Again we are plagued by the lack of statistics. Slaves were still ubiquitous in late antiquity. In the latter half of the fourth century, Roman officers holding the line against the Goths in

* How would one include in the calculation the immunity of slaves from military service?

Thrace were so busily engaged in slave-dealing with the enemy that the imperial defences were neglected.[71] A generation later, the emperors, in the midst of a war with the Goth ruler Alaric, were struggling to prevent the enslavement in Illyricum (Yugoslavia) of peasants fleeing from the barbarians, of captives who had been ransomed from them, and even of a barbarian tribe known as the Scirians who had been forcibly settled on the land within the empire.[72] Bishop Palladius found nothing incredible in reporting (*Lausiac History* 61) that, at just that moment, Melania the Younger, a noble Roman lady who had decided to shed her worldly goods for a saintly Christian life, manumitted a fraction of her slaves, to the number of eight thousand.

Nevertheless, the impression is firmly founded that by the fourth and fifth centuries of our era, chattel slavery had lost its key place even in the old classical heartland, in the productive urban activity to free labour (independent for the most part), in the countryside to tied peasants known as *coloni*.[73] What happened, and why? If, as I have already argued, neither efficiency and productivity nor economies of scale were operative factors, what motivated the upper classes, in particular the owners of large estates, to change over from slave gangs to tied peasants? A simple cost-accounting explanation is sometimes offered. It runs like this. Rome had to pay the price of her successful expansion; as more and more of the world was incorporated into the empire, more and more tribes and nations were protected from enslavement; Rome's eastern conquests threw hundreds of thousands of men, women and children onto the slave market while the conquest was proceeding, but not after the final settlement, first in the Balkans, then in Asia Minor and Syria; likewise with Caesar in Gaul, and so on.

There is an obvious element of truth in such a picture. Both the end of mass captures and the greater distances the slave traders had to travel to the sources of supply ought to have increased the price of slaves, on a straight arithmetical computation, though we lack the price statistics with which to do the sums. But there are also flaws in the argument as a *sufficient* explanation. The first is chronological. Systematic Roman conquest was finished by A.D. 14, and the supposed depressing effects on the slave supply were not visible for too long a time thereafter. Secondly, there is the failure to appreciate the full extent of "internal enslavement", in blatant defiance of legality, through the sale or exposure of children and through well-organized kidnapping.[74] Another flaw is the curious assumption that Germans, who remained outside the empire, were somehow unsatisfactory as slaves unlike all the other "barbarian" peoples who had been suitable for many preceding centuries, to the Greeks as to the Romans. The assumption is not only unsupported in the ancient sources, it is belied, for example by the slaving activities in the course of the wars with the Goths.

The fourth flaw is the assumption that a reduction in the supply of captive or imported slaves cannot be met by breeding. That a slave population can never reproduce itself is a fiction, but it dies hard, despite the simple proof from the American South, where the virtually complete cessation of the slave trade at the beginning of the nineteenth century was countered by systematic breeding, an activity which also contributed substantially to profits from the investment in slaves. Many slaves were bred in antiquity, too, more than we appreciate because this has been a badly neglected subject of research.[75] The practical Columella, in the middle of the first century, was not motivated by sentiment when he exempted a mother of three children from work on his estates, and freed her if she produced further offspring (1.8.19).

Nevertheless, it appears to be the case that, despite the hypothetical possibilities, the employers of labour in the later Empire were not making the efforts needed to maintain a full complement of slave labour. If the explanation for their behaviour is not to be found in the drying up of the slave supply or in decisions about efficiency, productivity and the like, then it must lie in a structural transformation within the society as a whole. The key lies not with the slaves but with the free poor, and I believe the elements can be pinpointed. The starting-point is the trend, visible from the beginning of the monarchic government in Rome, from Augustus on, in other words, to return to a more "archaic" structure, in which orders again became functionally significant, in which a broader spectrum of statuses gradually replaced the classical bunching into free man and slaves. There was, in effect, a reversal of the process that had transformed the archaic world into the classical. The replacement of the city-state form of government, with its intense political activity, by a bureaucratic, authoritarian monarchy made a major contribution; as the great majority of the citizen population lost their role in the selection of officials and their place in the army, which was now professionalized and increasingly composed of recruits from certain "backward" provinces, they lost ground in other respects, too.

This change is symbolized by the emergence of the two categories within the population known as *honestiores* and *humiliores*, roughly rendered as "upper classes" and "lower classes", formalized no later than the early second century and subject by law to different treatment in the criminal courts. The *humiliores*, for example, were liable to a series of cruel punishments which can fairly be called "slavish". Burning alive, wrote the jurist Callistratus (*Digest* 48.19.28.11), is usually a punishment for slaves who threatened the safety of their masters, but it is also applied to plebeians and persons of low rank (*humiles personae*).* That would never have been said while the citizens among them voted and fought in the legions.[76] It is no objection to say that the reality of equality before the law has always fallen short of the ideal. We are here faced with a change in the ideology itself, reflecting (and contributing to) a cumulative depression in the status of the lower classes among the free citizens.

One well known text will suffice to illustrate. In the first years of the reign of Commodus, barely outside Gibbon's Golden Age, the tenants on an imperial domain in the district of Carthage appealed to the emperor against excessive demands being made upon them by the tenants-in-chief (*conductores*), abetted by the imperial procurator who had not only "for many years" ignored

* Another jurist, Aemilius Macer, phrased it the other way round: "In regard to slaves, the rule is that they should be punished after the manner of *humiliores*" (*Digest* 48.19.10 pr.).

their petitions for redress but had sent in soldiers to fetter, beat and torture the protesters, some of whom were even Roman citizens. The emperor solemnly instructed his African officials to restore the peasants to their lawful condition.[77] The document tells us only that much, and we may reasonably doubt that the imperial order made much impact, even momentarily in Carthage, let alone on the vast imperial domains throughout the empire. In four eloquent pages, Rostovtzeff long ago pointed out that the elaborately detailed regulations for the African domains provided the sole defence of the tenants against the *conductores* and procurators on the one hand, and on the other hand delivered the peasants into the hands of the very same officials.[78] Appeal to the emperor was always possible in principle, but we could guess that the chances for a group of peasant *humiliores* would have been slight even if we did not have proof that so much more powerful a stratum as the members of the provincial city aristocracies were also "further from their imperial protector than was safe".[79]

In such a context, it was an inevitable corollary that moralists would call attention to the humanity of slaves. It is sometimes argued that Stoics and Christians in this way helped bring about the decline of slavery in antiquity, despite the uncomfortable fact that they never called for its abolition.[80] The logic of the argument is not easy to perceive. There is in fact relatively little discussion of slavery in the surviving writings of Roman Stoics of the imperial age—anthologies of relevant passages are in this respect misleading. The stress is on the master's moral obligation to behave, for his own sake, with self-restraint and moderation, at least as much as on the humanity of the slave. The latter is also required to behave appropriately, and, in the end, either to accept his status or to pay the penalty for violence, dishonesty, rebellion. No doubt individuals were influenced by such views, but the impact on the institution of slavery was consequentially insignificant.[81]

As for Christianity, after the conversion of Constantine and the rapid incorporation of the church into the imperial power structure, there is not a trace of legislation designed to turn away from slavery, not even by gradual steps. On the contrary, it was that most Christian of emperors, Justinian, whose codification of the Roman law in the sixth century not only included the most complete collection of laws about slavery ever assembled but also provided Christian Europe with a ready-made legal foundation for the slavery they introduced into the New World a thousand years later.[82]

It was in the reign of Commodus, too, that the first peasant revolt occurred in Gaul of a type that was to persist in the western provinces well into the fifth century. The rebels, who came to be called Bacaudae for reasons unknown to us, seem to have had no social programme other than an exchange of roles between themselves and the landlords. At times they created enough of a threat to require suppression on a military rather than a mere police scale, and the damage they did in the areas in which they operated must have been considerable, though we have few details because late Roman writers ignored them as a deliberate policy.[83] Two points emerge nevertheless. The language employed in the occasional reference implies that slaves and tenants cooperated, an exception to the rule that slave revolts and peasant struggles never came together, but not a genuine exception because the Bacaudae are testimony to the very status transformation at the lower end of the scale I have been discussing. They are also testimony—this is the second point—to the breakdown of such social equilibrium as the early Empire had achieved. More precisely, the cost burden borne by the agricultural producers had before the end of the second century passed the point of tolerance for many of them. In the following centuries, this question became steadily more acute, with a decisive impact on the history and the transformation of the imperial system.

The commonplace that the land was the chief source of wealth in antiquity must be understood in the Roman Empire, from its beginning, to include the wealth of the state. That is to say, not only was the emperor himself by far the largest landowner but the bulk of the taxes fell on the land. Although it is meaningless to assert, as do many historians, that in the early Empire taxation "was not very oppressive",[84] it is correct that the burden was bearable in the sense that grumbling led to appeals for a tax reduction, not to mass desertion from the land nor to revolt. It is not irrelevant that such appeals are attested as early as the reign of Tiberius.* Then, imperial expenses increased steadily, if slowly and spasmodically. Vespasian is said (Suetonius, *Vespasian* 16.2) to have increased, even doubled, the land-tax in some provinces, but on the whole the needs were for some two centuries met by new indirect taxes, by various schemes designed to bring marginal and deserted land into production, by confiscations and by requisitioning devices, for example, for road construction and the imperial post. That these amounted to substantial additional burdens cannot be doubted, to which there was then added the burden of steadily increasing taxation on the land from the third century. One estimate, perhaps exaggerated, is that by Justinian's reign the state took between one fourth and one third of the gross yield of the land of the empire.[85] To that must be added the substantial amount that never reached the treasury but was diverted by a horde of tax-collectors and officials, partly as legal perquisites (known as *sportulae*), partly as illegal exactions.

The increasing requirements can be attributed in the first instance to that iron law of absolutist bureaucracy that it grows both in numbers and in the expensiveness of its life-style. From the imperial court down, there were, decade by decade, more men to support from public funds, at a steadily growing standard of luxury. Then an external, contingent factor entered the scene. In the reign of Commodus' father, Marcus Aurelius, who died in A.D. 180, the Germanic tribes on the northern European edge of the empire became seriously aggressive again for the first time in more than two centuries. And they never stopped for very long thereafter, until they destroyed the western Empire. The Persians in the east also made their contribution, as did lesser military forces, such as native tribes on the edge of the desert in North Africa.

Military requirements and military expenditure thus became

* Tacitus (*Annals* 2.42) uses the term "worn out" (*fessae*) for the provincials of Syria and Judaea in just this context.

the permanent, dominant concern of the emperors, and the limit to their military activity was set by the maximum amount they could squeeze in taxation and compulsory labour or compulsory deliveries; and by the political chaos that ultimately set in within the Empire, notably in the half-century between 235 and 284 when there were no fewer than twenty Roman emperors formally sanctioned by the senate, another twenty or more who claimed the title with the backing of an army, and countless others who aspired to the claim. The burden was unevenly distributed geographically, first by the accident of devastation, whether by foreign invaders or by the Roman armies themselves, especially during the civil wars;[86] second because there was no local correlation between agricultural production and army requirements, so that, for example, the disproportionately large armies kept in Britain took a disproportionately larger bite out of local production.[87]

The social distribution of the burden was far more uneven. Land taxation lay most heavily, directly or indirectly, on those who actually worked the land, peasants and tenants. The owners of slave-worked estates could of course not pass the tax on, but the imperial aristocracy, at least, were adept at tax evasion (and Italian land was virtually exempt from taxation until the beginning of the fourth century), as the emperor Julian acknowledged when he refused the traditional remission of tax arrears on the express ground that "this profited only the wealthy" while the poor had to pay on the dot.[88] It is in the nature of things that the peasant, independent or tenant, has a fragile hold on his land: he has little margin when times are hard. The combined effect of the various developments I have been examining—increasing taxation, depredations and devastations, depression in status as symbolized by the establishment in law of the category of *humiliores*—were to drive him either into outlawry or into the arms of the nearest powerful landlord (or landlord's agent). And the latter, as we saw in the case of the tenants on the imperial domain at Carthage, meant protection and oppression at the same time.

"Who could be more oppressive than landlords" and their agents, asked Julian's contemporary, St. John Chrysostom, a pupil of Libanius. He specified at some length (*Homily on St. Mathew* 61.3): oppressive services employing "their bodies like asses and mules", beatings and tortures, extortionate interest and lots more. Half a century later, Salvian, writing in Gaul, summed up all the threads: the peasant's choice, he said, was to flee, either to the Bacaudae or to the invading barbarians or to the nearest landed magnate, exchanging his little plot for "protection".[89] Historians are understandably uncomfortable with the testimony of preachers and moralists, but in this instance the latter confirm what all the other signs suggest and none contradicts. For Salvian, there is archaeological support in Gaul.[90] More generally, there is the evidence of the law codes that from Diocletian at the end of the third century, tenants were tied, not free. The emperor's interest was in taxation, not in the status of tenants, but the effect was nonetheless to convert into law what had gradually been happening in practice.[91] And with the disappearance of the free tenant went the disappearance from the legal texts of the classical Roman tenancy contract, the *locatio conductio rei*.[92]

It can be pointed out, of course, that if Salvian is to be accepted as a witness, then there were still free peasant proprietors in Gaul in the fifth century. No doubt there were—the capacity of some peasants to survive in virtually every society despite massive pressure against them is a remarkable historical fact[93]—as there were still slaves on the land not only in the fifth century, but also in the sixth and the seventh. There is no possible way of our counting these hardy peasant owners, absolutely or relatively. But our concern is with the labour on the large estates, imperial, senatorial and other, where there was an undeniable (and undenied) shift in the dominant pattern from slaves to tenants, whose precarious status as wholly free men was gradually eroded, decisively perhaps in the third century. We apply the generic term *coloni* to them, but the sources, both Greek and Latin, use a profusion of terms, often with great imprecision. The attractive suggestion has been made that the terminological pattern reflects the social realities of the later Empire; regional variations, for example, or different statuses with different origins that may or may not have converged.[94] The suggestion has been allowed to go untested so far, but it has an *a priori* plausibility because the Roman conquest embraced regions of widely differing social structures, leading, as I said earlier, to different systems of land organization within the empire.

In the east, the effect of the later imperial development would have been chiefly to intensify and solidify the pre-existing dependent status of the peasantry. In Italy and elsewhere in the west, where for some centuries we found genuine slave societies, the effect was the more drastic one of the shift from slavery to the colonate. The decline of slavery, in other words, was a reversal of the process by which slavery took hold. Once upon a time the employers of labour in these regions imported slaves to meet their requirements. Now their own lower classes were available, as they had not been before, from compulsion, not from choice, and so there was no need for a sustained effort to keep up the slave supply, nor to introduce wage-labour.

The cities of the empire also responded to the structural changes. Fiscal burdens eroded the curial order (the municipal senates); in the regions under heaviest barbarian attack, the wealthy tended to withdraw to their estates as a protective measure, and to increase the production of manufactured goods on them; the state paid the armies and the civil service largely in kind, supplying the armies with requisitioned food and with manufactures from its own slave-workshops. The consequent disappearance of larger private manufacturing units in the cities had a radical effect on the labour situation in the urban crafts. The *plebs urbana* of the later Empire are a remarkably neglected subject in modern histories, except when they rioted.[95] Yet no one doubts that they were present in large numbers or that they still counted among the free men, unlike *coloni* and slaves: as late as A.D. 432 an imperial constitution (*Theodosian Code* 9.45.5) still referred to the *ordo plebeiorum*. They included not only the unskilled, the "beggars", but also the artisans of the cities, highly specialized, hard working and mostly very poor. It was the urban slaves who were now the parasitical element. We must judge from impressions, but it is striking that in all the sources of the late Empire, when productive slaves appear they are working in the rural sector, as farmers or craftsmen, whereas the still numerous urban slaves (outside the imperial factories) appear with equal regularity as domestics and administrators, as a luxury for conspicuous consumption not only of the wealthy but also of such modest men as the lecturers in Libanius's school at Antioch.

IV

Landlords and Peasants

IN THE close link between status and the possession of
land, the law played its part. It was the Greeks who most fully
preserved for citizens a monopoly of the right to own land, and
who in the more oligarchic communities restricted full political
rights to the landowners among their members, most completely
in Sparta. But the law, as I have said before, was often less important than custom, tradition, social and political pressures.
Roman expansion in Italy, for example, entailed a more open
citizenship policy, so that Latins obtained the privilege of owning
Roman land from an early date, all free Italians by the early first
century B.C. *De facto* there was a fundamental change in the
land-citizenship link (unknown to the Greek city-states) which is
concealed by a narrowly juristic account.

In a city-state, furthermore, the land was in principle free from
regular taxation. A tithe or other form of direct tax on the land,
said the Greeks, was the mark of a tyranny, and so firmly rooted
was this view that they never allowed an emergency war tax, such
as the Athenian *eisphora*, to drift into permanence (nor did the
Romans of the Republic), unlike the pattern with which other
societies have been very familiar. Empires, on the other hand,
drew their main revenues from the land, in rents and taxes,

though the Greek cities managed to wring from their Hellenistic rulers some freedom for the land attached to a city, and Italy retained its traditional exemption until the beginning of the fourth century A.D. (Land owned by Roman citizens in the provinces, in contrast, was subject to taxation at least by Cicero's day.) I stress the point, paradoxically, not because of its implication for the upper classes but for what it meant to the peasantry, to the free, citizen-peasant. Wealthy Greeks bore the substantial share of the costs of the state despite the tax exemption on their estates; if wealthy Republican Romans did not, at least not after the third century B.C., that was only because Roman imperial expansion enabled them to shift the burden onto their subject peoples, the provincials. The situation was then reversed under the empires: the tax on the land was passed in large part to the poor, and in time also to the middle classes, while the upper stratum carried less and less of the public financial burden.[1]

This is a correlate of the distinction commonly formulated in political terms, between the liberty of the classical citizen in the city-state and the lack of freedom, relative or total, under the empires (and under the earlier, archaic regimes). I suggest that tax exemption was an important underpinning for that novel and rarely repeated phenomenon of classical antiquity, the incorporation of the peasant as a full member of the political community.[2] Ideologically this was expressed in the celebration of agriculture, of which the best known and most artistic expression is surely Virgil's *Georgics*. All strata of the citizen-body shared the ideology in general. Then they diverged in the particular. As Heitland wrote, "The glorification of unyielding toil as the true secret of success was (and is) a congenial topic to preachers of the gospel of 'back to the land'." But "the ever-repeated praises of country life are unreal. Even when sincere, they are the voice of town-bred men, weary of the fuss and follies of urban life, to which nevertheless they would presently come back refreshed but bored with their rural holiday."[3] For them, I have already remarked, land ownership signified the absence of an occupation; for the others, it meant unyielding toil. All shared a hunger for land, expressed at one level in the piling of one estate onto another as the opportunity arose, at the other level in a dogged willingness to try again after failure and dispossession.

None of this can be translated into quantitative terms. There were always substantial areas in which the proportion of the citizen body who were landowners or tenant farmers approached one hundred per cent (quite apart from the unique case of Sparta), even when they had urban centres and are called "towns" or "cities".[4] And there were a few swollen cities, notably in the early Roman Empire, such as Rome itself, Alexandria, Carthage, Antioch, with a population running well into six figures, many of whom had no connection with land or agriculture. But what of the vast areas between the extremes, spread over fifteen hundred years of history? We are told that a proposal was made in Athens in 403 B.C. to limit the political rights of any citizen who did not own some land, and that, had the measure been enacted, which it was not, 5000 citizens would have been the victims. That is something, if the report is accurate (there are those who doubt it). But how much? We do not know the total number of citizens in 403; "some land" could well mean no more than an urban garden plot on which a stonemason grew beans and perhaps some grapes.[5] Or we are told (Josephus, *Jewish War* 2.385), probably on the basis of a census, that the population of Egypt in the first century of our era was 7,500,000 apart from Alexandria. That is more helpful in one respect because outside the city of Alexandria, where the population could not have been greater than half a million, if that, almost everyone was totally involved with agriculture, including the soldiers and the innumerable petty officials. On the other hand, Egypt was the densest and most poverty-stricken province in the empire, so that no generalization follows.

We must therefore rest content with the vague but sure proposition that most people in the ancient world lived off the land, in one fashion or another, and that they themselves recognized the land to be the fountainhead of all good, material and moral. When we then turn to the question of the scale of holdings, we find ourselves little better off. To begin with, the total number of

7

individual figures in our possession over the whole time period and the whole region is ludicrously small: at a guess, since no one has assembled them all, I should doubt if they run to two thousand.[6] Second, the available figures are not readily commensurable: there is a tendency among ancient writers to report either a monetary value, normally self-assessed and dubious for more than one reason, or a single year's gross income, rather than acreage; and to report on a particular estate rather than on a man's total holding. There have been attempts by modern historians to translate one type of figure into another for purposes of computation, on the basis of a 6% or 8% "normal return on investment in land". I then find myself in the embarrassing position, given my insistence on the search for quantifiable regularities and patterns, of having to demur. A small number of texts do in fact produce such a rate in specific circumstances, but some turn out to be worthless,[7] there are too few figures altogether, and there are too many variables of soil and crop and land regime. Nor was it a frequent practice, familiar in England since the late Middle Ages, to express land values as so many years' purchase. Third, ancient writers frequently give a figure or describe a farm only because it is unusual or extreme, such as Varro's list of examples (*De re rustica* 3.2) of the high profitability derived from bees, flowers, hens, doves and peacocks on villas near the city of Rome. What little we have is therefore not a random sample.

Nevertheless, I believe we can discover something meaningful about the range of landholdings and the trends. Let us begin with the extreme and untypical case of Egypt, untypical because its irrigation farming produced relatively stable, high yields (perhaps tenfold for grain), because there was little waste land (as little as five per cent in the Fayum), because the native peasantry was never a free population like the classical Graeco-Roman. In a typical Fayum village of the Ptolemaic period, such as Kerkeosiris with a population of perhaps 1500 farming some 3000 acres, many peasants lived at a bare subsistence minimum with holdings as small as one or two acres, some on one-year leases and all subject to dues and taxes.[8] At the upper limit, two incomplete figures will suffice to suggest both scale and trend. The first is the estate in the Fayum of one Apollonius, for a time the highest official in the country early in the third century B.C., which ran to some 6500 acres.[9] (Apollonius had at least one other large estate, at Memphis, and everything reverted to the crown when he fell out of favour.) The second figure relates to the Apion family, natives of Egypt who in the sixth century A.D. twice achieved the top post in the Byzantine Empire, that of praetorian prefect. This family was one of a number of extraordinarily wealthy landowners in Egypt. How wealthy is not known, but it has been calculated that one of their estates alone amounted to some 75,000 acres, from which they contributed possibly 7,500,000 litres to the annual grain levy for Constantinople.[10]

So extreme a range was uncommon in the ancient world, but the gap between smallest and largest landowner was generally wide enough, and, I believe, steadily widening. We have already seen that Roman citizens were being settled in colonies in Italy in the second century B.C., on holdings as low as three acres, with six acres more or less the norm for men with larger families in Caesar's day. When a small Greek community was founded in the Adriatic island of Curzola in the third or second century B.C., the first settlers were each allotted an unspecified amount of arable and about three quarters of an acre of vineyard.[11] That peasant holdings on this small scale were common cannot be doubted, though the documentation is inadequate. At least they were tax-free holdings in the classical world, unlike Egypt, and to that extent more viable. They were also unlikely to show any significant changes over the centuries, until the general debasement of the free peasantry set in under the Roman emperors.

For movement, one must look to the upper classes. Already in fifth- and fourth-century Athens there were landowners possessing from three to six estates in different parts of Attica. The most valuable known to us were two farms, one in Eleusis, the other in Thria, included among the property of the family line founded by a certain Buselos, which can be traced through the fifth and fourth centuries B.C. and included a considerable number of men of some prominence in the military and political affairs of Athens. The Eleusinian farm was said to be worth 12,000 drachmas, the other 15,000. These are likely to be undervaluations, but even so, 12,000 drachmas was forty times the maximum possession allowed a man who sought public assistance, six times the minimum property requirement for the full franchise in the oligarchic constitution imposed on Athens in 322 B.C.[12]

The Buselos family were among the more wealthy in fourth-century B.C. Athens, but their fortune would have ranked as very modest in the Athens of the Roman Empire. The case I want to present is admittedly an extreme one, but extremes are what mark out the range. Athenian life in the second century A.D. was dominated by one man, Herodes Atticus, patron of the arts and letters (and himself a writer and scholar of importance), public benefactor on an imperial scale, not only in Athens but elsewhere in Greece and Asia Minor, holder of many important posts, friend and kinsman of emperors.[13] His family, originally from Marathon, was among the city's élite at least as far back as the late second century B.C., and continued to rise in status and power, being granted Roman citizenship under Nero. Then, probably in A.D. 92 or 93, Hipparchus, the grandfather of Herodes, got into trouble and his estates were confiscated by Domitian, who sold them off, we are told, for 100 million sesterces (2,500,000 drachmas), one hundred times the minimum property qualification for a senator, some fifty times the annual income of his contemporary, the by no means poverty-stricken Pliny the Younger. But Hipparchus had prudently hidden away a very large sum in cash, so that a few years later, his son, the father of Herodes Atticus, was able to recoup the family fortune in the more liberal reign of Nerva; on his death, he left a trust providing an annual income of 100 drachmas for every Athenian citizen, which implies a total fortune very much in excess of 100 million sesterces.

The Athenians never received the money, but that is another story. What matters to us is that this was basically landed wealth (the only other source of family income attested is moneylending on a great scale[14]) and that Herodes Atticus owned villas at

Cephisia near the city of Athens and at Marathon, house property in the city, landed estates in both districts, in northern Attica, on the island of Euboea, at Corinth and elsewhere in the Peloponnese, in Egypt, and from the dowry of his very aristocratic Roman wife, property on the Appian Way and in Apulia in Italy.[15] In and around Marathon, furthermore, the holding appears to have been one great consolidated tract.[16]

The wealth of this family was remarkable even by Roman standards: that emerges from the tone in which Suetonius (*Vespasian* 13) reports the hundred-million profit accruing to Domitian from the confiscated estates of Herodes' grandfather. Normally, the scale of things in Roman society reduced the Greek to paltriness. Some idea of the upward curve of accumulation among the Roman élite can already be gained from the Gracchan reform. In 133 B.C. Tiberius Gracchus forced through a law restricting individual holdings of *ager publicus*, that is, of land in Italy confiscated by the Roman state in the course of its conquering wars and then leased, usually for nominal rents. The limit set was 500 *jugera*, and an additional 250 for each of two sons, a maximum of about 625 acres per family. (Holdings of "private land" were left untouched.) That many senators and others had succeeded in acquiring substantially more *ager publicus* than 625 acres is demonstrated both by the violence of their reaction to the law, and by the jump in the census figures for the ensuing decade in consequence of the Gracchan confiscation and redistribution of holdings above the limit.[17] A century later, the wealth arrayed against Julius Caesar enabled Pompey to enrol 800 of his personal slaves and herdsmen in his armies, and Ahenobarbus to promise each of his men twenty-five acres from his estates in Etruria (and larger grants to officers and veterans).[18] Ahenobarbus' offer was extended to either 4000 or 15,000 soldiers, depending on differing interpretations of the phrase, "his men", and of course the test of his sincerity and of his ability to find so much land never came. Nevertheless, even as propaganda it is a pointer.

I cannot resist two more examples. When Melania the Younger decided to abandon her worldly life in the year 404, the estates she and her husband possessed in various parts of Italy, Sicily, Spain, North Africa and Britain were bringing in an annual income of 1150 pounds of gold (1600 Roman pounds). One domain near Rome included 62 hamlets, each said to have 400 slaves engaged in agriculture, a total of 24,000.[19] I would not want to insist on the details: hagiographies are not noted for being moderate or scrupulous. But I would insist on the verisimilitude (except for the size of the slave force), since there is too much contemporary evidence along the same lines, both documentary and archaeological, to be dismissed.[20] The data about the Apion family in Egypt are firm. More modestly, a legal document dated 445 or 446, the accuracy of which also cannot be disputed, reveals that a former Grand Chamberlain of the emperor Honorius, whose origin, far from being noble like Melania's, was among the slave boys who were castrated and employed in the imperial household, was receiving some thirty pounds of gold a year from six properties in Sicily alone.[21] And of course not even Melania could stand comparison with the emperors themselves, whose accumulation of land through confiscation, gift, bequest and reclamation added up to a total which, did we know it, would strain the imagination. From the fourth century on, the church began to rival them, in the holdings of popes, bishoprics and monasteries.[22]

Now, despite my own strictures about the argument by example, I think one may conclude, from the accumulation of individual instances, that the trend in antiquity was for a steady increase in the size of landholdings; not a simple straight line upward, as much an accumulation of scattered, sometimes very widely scattered, estates as a process of consolidation; but a continuing trend nevertheless. This generalization applies to the class of wealthy landowners, not to any given individual or family. One can find failures enough, because of war or political disaster. But it is a reinforcing fact that out of each such crisis there emerged men who were richer, whose landed possessions were greater, than those before. The Hannibalic War devastated much of southern Italy, but it also gave a great boost to the occupation of more and more of the *ager publicus* by a small ruling élite in Rome. The half-century of equally devastating civil war, from Sulla to Augustus, had comparable results (quite apart from the vast profits made abroad). There is a nice example at the very beginning: an expensive villa on the Bay of Naples belonging to Marius was bought by a lady named Cornelia, presumably Sulla's daughter, for 300,000 sesterces and resold by her to Lucullus for ten million.[23] This may be a moral fable, but like all good fables, it illustrates a fundamental truth.[24]

We may also conclude that large estates produced large incomes, that the familiar recurrence of what historians call "agrarian crisis" in antiquity was a crisis among the peasantry or in military recruiting or in something else, not a drastic fall in the profits of *latifundia*. We cannot produce a balance-sheet, but we can point to the life-style of the rich, to the large outlays they made, whether for personal, conspicuous consumption or for public support in elections or for any other reason. These never ceased, and they rarely ceased to become larger and larger.[25] Clearly the exploitation of agricultural labour was intense, of tied peasants and dependent labour in the eastern and some other conquered territories, primarily of slaves and of the marginal free men who took small tenancies in the classical heartland. Then came the double blow to the peasantry, the steady reduction in the meaning of citizenship for the lower classes and the burden of taxation and other dues on the land. In time they were forced into the ranks of fully exploitable subjects, as we saw in the context of the decline of ancient slavery. That brought about a change in the social structure of the agricultural labour force and in the tenurial system, while preserving the intensity of exploitation and the profitability.*

It is perhaps futile to seek a realistic idea of the middle range of landed properties, though, to my knowledge, no one has even tried. One firm testimony of extensive middle-range holdings in Italy under the early Empire is worth noticing as an indicator. The evidence is in a bronze tablet from Velleia, near Piacenza,

---

* Nothing is more revealing about our source material than the fact that we know virtually nothing about the marketing procedures employed by landowners.

spanning the period between 98 and 113 and linked to Trajan's *alimenta* programme, which, in effect, siphoned imperial funds to local children through larger properties that guaranteed the solvency of the scheme.[26] In this group, there were forty-six properties in the main scheme, four of them evaluated at over one million sesterces each, the average approximating 300,000. At the arbitrary, but surely modest, figure of six per cent per annum, the average income would be about 18,000 sesterces in value, or fifteen times the gross pay of a legionary (from which his food and other expenses were deducted), the difference, say, between $45,000 and $3,000 a year. And it was probably the case that some of the Velleian proprietors had other holdings, in the same district or elsewhere. Nearly half of them appear to have been absentee owners, which is surely suggestive.

I make no claim, naturally, that this single text proves anything of itself. Nor, by itself, would the figure given by Ausonius, professor of rhetoric and eventually consul, for the estate he inherited near Bordeaux in the mid-fourth century, some 125 acres of arable, half as much in vineyards, meadowland and over 400 acres of woodland.[27] However, estates of just that order appear to be common in the archaeology of Gaul, and when this evidence is taken in conjunction with what I showed in the previous chapter about the Pompeian vineyards and the sons of freedmen who attained municipal aristocratic status, or with the landed base of this (curial) class in the cities throughout the Empire, the hypothesis seems reasonable that in the early Empire, and still in many areas in the later Empire, there was a considerable spectrum of landholdings from the peasant to the highest stratum, and particularly that comfortable possessions were numerous in the hands of families who left little mark on the historical record.[28] I am willing to hazard the proposition that this was also the case in most parts of the ancient world at most times, allowing for divergent standards of comfort.

It is even more difficult to obtain a picture of the range among peasants, but a comparison with other societies suggests the existence of a peasant spectrum, too. There is a strange reluctance among historians, and even among sociologists, to define the term "peasant", and a tendency in the English-speaking world to dismiss the peasant as an inferior type to be found in other countries only. I say "strange" because, on a historical view, the peasant is the most common and most widely distributed social type of all, the man "whose ultimate security and subsistence lie in his having certain rights in land and in the labour of family members on the land, but who is involved, through rights and obligations, in a wider economic system which includes the participation of non-peasants".[29] All the elements are essential, in order to distinguish the peasant on the one hand from the primitive agriculturalist or pastoralist, who is not involved in a "wider economic system"; on the other hand from the modern family farm, in which the family is an "entrepreneurial unit" rather than a productive unit.[30] And that definition encompasses the vast majority of the population of the ancient world, both the free small landowners and the tied peasants, the *coloni*. Strictly speaking, it does not fit the free tenants, who had no rights in land beyond the term of their normally short contracts, but, as we shall see, there was a relevance in practice, limiting the choice of the large landowners whose tenants they were.

The optimum size of a peasant farm is an obviously meaningless notion: there are too many variables. But let us take as a basis of discussion the Caesarian settlement, ten *jugera* (six-plus acres) for a veteran with three children. The Roman unit, the *jugum*, was the area of land one man could (hypothetically) plough in a day. Ten *jugera* of good arable would produce enough food to sustain a small family (but not an ox in addition) even with the alternate fallow system, especially when free from rents and taxes.* The size of the family itself then became a major crux, first because there were few crops to spare; second, because ten *jugera* cannot keep a family employed full time; third, because, under the Greek and

* I assume the optimum, that veterans' allotments consisted entirely of good arable, which was not necessarily always the case in practice. Furthermore, I know of only two texts which explicitly refer to a yoke of oxen and an amount of seed accompanying the allotment, and these are both from the fourth century A.D.[31]

Roman rules of inheritance, an estate was in principle divided equally among legitimate sons (and sometimes daughters), with no trace of primogeniture; fourth, because a peasant cannot dismiss his excess labour. What Hesiod said, in his characteristic fashion, in the seventh century B.C. remained valid for the whole of ancient history: "There should be an only son to feed his father's house, for so wealth will increase in the home; but if you leave a second son you should die old" (*Works and Days* 376–8). High rates of infant mortality helped; when nature failed, one turned to infanticide and infant exposure (often merely a device to get round the law prohibiting the sale of free children into slavery[32]), a reflection of which survives in the frequency of foundlings in myths and legends and in comedy, both Greek and Roman.

It is difficult to overestimate the implications of five- and six-acre holdings. In Germany in the 1950s, by comparison, farms under twenty-five acres were to be found almost exclusively in the possession of the elderly, of war widows or of worker-peasants.[33] The small ancient peasant holdings meant chronic underemployment of labour in terms of production, though not underemployment of energy, which is not the same thing. Modern studies show that the smaller the holding, the greater the number of man-hours expended per acre. What else can a peasant householder do? Since he cannot fire members of his family, if he cannot send them away to take tenancies on larger estates he must keep them busy at home somehow; in jargon, his aim is to "maximize the input of labour rather than maximize profit or some other indication of efficiency".[34]

This built-in inefficiency also meant inaccessibility to technological or other improvement, and stress on the requirements of subsistence, at the cost of other possible approaches to the utilization of resources. We may well wonder with the elder Pliny (*Natural History* 18.187), for example, how far a ten-*jugerum* holder could resist breaching the traditional alternating fallow system, regardless of the deleterious consequences to the fertility of his land. And we may be certain of a diversification of crops at the expense of specialization and its benefits. Subsistence farming is by definition not market farming, not the production of cash crops. The typical "peasant market" was a place where peasants (and no doubt village craftsmen) met from a radius of five or six miles in order to fill gaps in necessities by exchange with each other; there were only a few things a peasant could not produce himself— a metal ploughshare, for example—when everything went well. The paucity of coin finds in genuinely rural areas is no accident.[35]

There were circumstances which may have encouraged peasants, especially those nearer the upper limit of family holdings, to turn to cash crops. I am thinking of the presence nearby (ten to twelve miles, no more) of larger towns, of international shrines attracting visitors who needed catering (such as Olympia or Delphi), or of more or less permanent army camps. I suspect, however, that good land so located would have attracted the wealthier landlords, like the villa owners mentioned by Varro (*De re rustica* 1.16.3), with their speciality products, and that it was in those strata, rather than among the peasants, that the suppliers of city-army-shrine needs were normally to be found.[36] In the opening soliloquy of Aristophanes' *Acharnians*, the protagonist bewails the city life to which he has temporarily been driven by a marauding Spartan army in the early years of the Peloponnesian War. From his seat in the Assembly high on the Pnyx, he looks out on his farm at Acharnae and yearns for his village where "no one cries, 'Buy charcoal, vinegar, oil', where the word 'buy' is unknown". A poet's hyperbole, no doubt, but not, I think, a comic playwright's joke.

Not surprisingly, the ancient peasant was always at the margin of safety. Cato gave his chained slaves more bread than the average peasant in Graeco-Roman Egypt could count on as a regular staple.[37] The one normal source of subsidiary income for peasants was seasonal labour on larger neighbouring estates, especially during the harvest: the Roman agricultural writers assume, and indeed, require, the presence of such a reserve labour force in all their calculations. Beyond that, in a pre-industrial society, the opportunities for part-time employment were few and unreliable.

The Athenian navy in the fifth and fourth centuries B.C. was the great exception, and the key to Athenian freedom from agrarian troubles during the whole of that period. The Roman armies in that period before they became involved in long service outside Italy were perhaps another exception, but a less significant one.

There is a deep paradox here. The freer the ancient peasant, in the political sense, the more precarious his position. The client of the archaic period or the *colonus* of the later Empire may have been variously oppressed, but he was also protected by his patron from dispossession, from the harsh laws of debt, and on the whole from military service (which so often led to unavoidable neglect of the farm and ultimate dispossession[38]). The genuinely free peasant had no protection against a run of bad harvests, against compulsory army service, against the endless depredations in civil and foreign wars. Hence the variegated history of peasant responses, from the demands for land that lay behind the great Greek expansion beginning as early as the eighth century B.C., to "squatting" on vacant or derelict public or temple property,[39] flight from the land into the cities or the bush, open revolt; in the end, to an acceptance of the dependent status that became the rule in the course of the Roman Empire—a history that is, alas, yet to be written.

The fact that large landowners were essentially immune from crisis conditions was the consequence of the size of their holdings and their reserves, and, in some periods though not all, of the inflow of wealth from their political prerogatives, rather than of a qualitatively different approach to the problems and possibilities of farming. The family and universal succession played the same part in their lives. They had a "peasant-like" passion for self-sufficiency on their estates, however extravagant they may have been in their urban outlays. They were equally bound by a limited and fairly static technology, with the two-year fallow cycle as its base, and by the high costs of land transport. These points need to be made explicitly because they are repeatedly challenged by modern scholars, not so much on the evidence as on psychological grounds, on a disbelief that Greeks and Romans should have been so incapable of "simple" improvements. There were improvements of one kind or another in the course of antiquity, especially in the Roman classical period, in drainage and irrigation, in tools and mill-stones, in seed selection, but they were marginal, for, as our leading contemporary authority on Roman farming summed up the story, "the patterns of land use and the methods of tillage remained unchanged. As in ancient industry, new requirements were met by the transfer of old techniques."[40] But there is nothing mysterious about this "stagnation", no serious reason for disbelief: large incomes, absenteeism and its accompanying psychology of the life of leisure, of land ownership as a non-occupation, and, when it was practised, letting or sub-letting in fragmented tenancies all combined to block any search for radical improvements.[41]

As for the objective of self-sufficiency, that was neither an "archaizing" value judgment (of a Plato, for example) nor just a joke of Trimalchio's. At this level, we are of course considering estates that were farmed for their cash incomes, not for subsistence. Hence the stress on taking steps to avoid cash outlays for the purchase of vine-props, animal fodder, wine or anything else required for cultivation of the soil and maintenance of the labour force has to be explained within a framework of profit-making. There was nothing archaic or profligate about men who stock-piled in anticipation, or hope, of higher prices; who took the trouble to recommend sale of worn-out cattle and slaves, old wagons, discarded tools, blemished sheep and diseased slaves. Cato closed his exhortation with a maxim (*De agricultura* 2.7), "A *paterfamilias* should be a seller, not a buyer." That was less a moral judgment than an economic one (in our language), though I doubt if Cato would have drawn the distinction very finely. A long passage in a nineteenth-century Russian novel is not evidence, in a strict sense, for ancient thinking, but I wonder if the psychology was sufficiently different in this respect not to permit me to quote a portion:

"Oblomov's parents were extremely sparing with any article which was not produced at home but had to be bought. They gladly killed an excellent turkey or a dozen chickens to entertain a guest, but they never put an extra raisin in a dish, and turned pale when their guest ventured to pour himself out another glass of wine. Such depravity, however, was a rare occurrence at Oblomovka. . . . Generally speaking, they did not like spending money at Oblomovka, and however necessary a purchase might be, money for it was issued with the greatest regret and that, too, only if the sum was insignificant. . . . To pay 200, 300, or 500 roubles all at once for something, however necessary it might be, seemed almost suicidal to them. Hearing that a young local land-owner had been to Moscow and bought a dozen shirts for 300 roubles, a pair of boots for twenty-five roubles, and a waistcoat for his wedding for forty roubles, Oblomov's father crossed himself and said, with a look of horror on his face, that 'such a scamp must be locked up'."[42]

The moral tone is evident, and full allowance must be made for the difference between a leading Roman senator, residing and politically active in the capital city, and petty Russian nobility burrowed in their estates. What interests me, however, is another aspect, brought out by the novelist, writing at a moment of transition between two ways of life in Russia, when he concluded this passage as follows: "They were, generally speaking, impervious to economic truths about the desirability of a quick turnover of capital, increased production, and exchange of goods." Cato was not impervious to such "economic truths"; he never heard of them. There was no one in his world to suggest them or argue for them. Lacking the techniques by which to calculate, and then to choose among, the various options, for example the relative economic merits of growing or buying the barley for slaves and the stakes for vines; lacking the techniques by which to calculate the relative profitability, under given conditions, of one crop and another, or of agriculture and pasturage;[43] relishing independence from the market as buyers, from reliance on others for their own necessities, the landowners of antiquity operated by tradition, habit and rule-of-thumb, and one such rule was that "a *paterfamilias* should be a seller, not a buyer".[44]

There is a famous example of the approach in Cato's manual

(1.7) when he enumerates, in descending order of importance, the products of an ideal 100-*jugerum* farm: wine, garden fruit and vegetables, willows, olives, pasture, grain, forest foliage for fodder, and acorns. The passage is famous for the wrong reason: it is regularly cited as a general statement of the realities of Italian agriculture in the second century B.C., whereas it ought to be quoted as proof of the absurdity of what passes for economic analysis in the ancient sources. I need hardly enumerate the weaknesses: no consideration of the location of the farm with respect to available markets or to export possibilities; nothing about the nature of the soil beyond the single phrase, "if the wine is good and the yield is great"; no cost accounting of even a rudimentary nature.*

Not everyone was a Cato. There were other notions of the optimum employment of the land and its products, but these were socially and politically oriented, not economically. There was Pericles' method of disposing the whole of the produce in bulk in order to unburden himself for full-time political activity. There was Pericles' early political rival, Cimon, who, we are told by Aristotle (*Constitution of Athens* 27.3–4), "supported many of his fellow-demesmen, every one of whom was free to come daily and receive from him enough for his sustenance. Besides, none of his estates was enclosed, so that anyone who wished could take from its fruits." This was a rudimentary predecessor of the highly developed client system of the last centuries of the Roman Republic, when men like Pompey and Ahenobarbus appreciated the advantages of supporting large reserves of manpower for their votes and, ultimately, for their fighting abilities.

I have so far avoided speaking of economies of scale not because there were none, but because, in my view, they were slight, though I must concede that the foundation for any conclusion is a shaky one. Under ancient conditions, consolidation of holdings into large continuous tracts did not automatically imply economies of scale,

* I am not suggesting that Cato was wholly witless. In 1.3 he does say that a good water-supply and access to the sea, a river or a road are factors to consider in buying a farm. The fact remains, however, that his crop ranking ignores everything of the kind, not to mention soil variations from district to district.

particularly not where slaves were the main labour force. There is reason to believe, from hints in the writings of the agronomists and land-surveyors, that they believed 200 *jugera* to be the optimum holding a single bailiff could manage. Yet far larger holdings were to be found in the empire. In North Africa, according to the sober Frontinus writing at the end of the first century A.D., there were private domains larger than the territories of cities, with a work force large enough to inhabit hamlets (*vici*) ringing the villa like ramparts (*in modum munitionum*).[45] And the newly developed territories in the west were clearly open to Roman occupation in extensive tracts. For example, the recently excavated estate at Montmaurin, not far from Toulouse, had possibly 2500 acres of farmed land, run from a single building-complex, itself covering 45 acres, in which the *vilicus* and his labour force were housed, apparently the owner, too, and in which the animals were kept, the equipment and the produce were stored and all the ancillary activities were carried on. Built in the middle of the first century A.D., this "villa" prospered until the end of the second century, when it was devastated by a flood and never reconstituted as a single operating unit.[46]

In the long civilized portions of the empire, in contrast, the trend towards accumulation of land seems not to have been accompanied by a matching effort to consolidate into larger units of exploitation. Although some notable instances of consolidated estates are known, such as the *massa Calvisiana* in southern Sicily, an early third-century establishment that extended for some ten miles on the eastern side of the Gela River, there was apparently no reluctance to divide *massae* and *fundi* when the occasion arose.[47] That suggests little attention to economies of scale, and I believe that the dispersed holdings of Herodes Atticus represented the more common pattern. Earlier, two wealthy clients of the young Cicero owned numerous farms each treated as a separate unit of exploitation: Aulus Caecina's holding even included two adjacent but separate farms, and at least one let out to a tenant; Sextus Roscius of Ameria, in the extreme south of Umbria, owned thirteen units all in the Tiber Valley.[48]

Nor may we ignore the failure of writers of the period to refer to economies of scale. Trimalchio's frivolous reason for wishing to "add Sicily to my little bits of land" may not bear much weight, but one of Pliny's letters (3.19) is less easily dismissed. An estate adjoining one of his in Umbria was up for sale at a bargain price, thanks to mismanagement by the owner and his tenants. Pliny was thinking of buying it. The primary advantage, he writes, would be one of amenity (*pulchritudo*). There are also practical advantages: the two properties could be visited in one journey, both could be put under a single procurator (agent) and perhaps even under one *actor* (bailiff), only one country-house would have to be kept up to the standard appropriate for an occasional sojourn by a senator. On the debit side, he adds, are the risks in putting two holdings under the same "hazards of fortune" (*incerta fortunae*), the weather for example.

What is your advice? was the question Pliny put to his correspondent, even though he gave none of the information one might expect, neither the dimensions of the property nor the current rental nor the details about the produce. The anticipated advantages were largely psychological; apart from the bailiffs, there is not a whisper of possible economies of scale that could or would follow the consolidation of two adjoining estates, let alone any consideration of reorganizing the production, for example towards either greater diversity or greater specialization, or of a more efficient use of the labour force.

Direction and control of labour was a recurrent theme in all ancient writing concerned with estate management (even under a tenancy regime), obviously so in view of the fact that the typical large landowner was an absentee owner. However, the concern was for the honesty of the force, honesty in the full employment of labour-time and in the handling of money and goods, rather than for qualitative improvement in the efficiency of the force by better methods of tillage or by the introduction of labour-saving devices. It represents the viewpoint of the policeman, not of the entrepreneur. Modern study reveals that "absentee landlordism is a guarantee that customary methods of farming are strictly observed

8

though they may be antiquated".[49] Customary methods allowed for technical *refinements*[50]—this must be said repeatedly—but normally stopped there. Hence economies of scale were not a realistic possibility for the very men whose holdings were hypothetically large enough and growing larger.

Tenancy, the much discussed alternative to the slave *latifundia*,[51] was in this respect worse, because of the limiting effects of short terms and family life cycles. Who were tenants, after all? Single tenancies of large units are known, with exceptions, only on public land, in particular on the African domains of the Roman emperors, which were subdivided into small plots, so that the tenants-in-chief were imperial agents and administrators in fact, if not in strict law, rather than large-scale farmers. To generalize from the North African domains, as has become standard practice, is thus to falsify the situation in Italy and Sicily, in Greece and the Hellenistic east, perhaps in Spain and Gaul, too (as it is false, at the other end of the scale, to generalize from the Egyptian fellahin, Ptolemaic or Roman). The adjoining estate that Pliny was thinking of buying had been worked (badly) by tenants, in the plural, and this was surely the classical norm on private land. This was largely a matter of availability: one could not journey to Rome or any other larger city and simply pick up men able, financially and professionally, to take on large tenancies. The normal tenant was a man with few resources and without his own land, a failed peasant, a "superfluous" peasant's son, or a dispossessed peasant like Horace's Ofellus (*Satires* 2.2)—and he, of necessity, thought in peasant terms of a family-sized holding, hence Horace's word *patres* (*Epistles* 1.14.3) for his own tenants.[52]

On larger tenancies, the short-term lease remained a brake on improvements or economies of scale. A particularly dramatic example is provided by the twenty farms on Delos and two nearby islands owned by the temple of Apollo. These were relatively large units, let to richer members of Delian society and worked by slaves; the best of them earned the high rental of 1650 drachmas a year in the best period. But the term was ten years, and, though the lease was renewable by the tenant, the detailed evidence, stretching over a long period, between 313 and 170 B.C., shows that the tenants did only what was required of them, that is, they returned the property with the identical number of olive-trees, fig-trees and livestock that they received, no more and no less.[53] Ten-year leases are a disincentive to improvements, even with farms of this scale and surely with smaller, more typical family-size holdings. Land reclamation projects normally resolved one difficulty by resorting to leases in perpetuity, notably on the imperial estates, but the addiction to small family parcels soon put a brake on them too.

We are thus brought back to the fundamental question of choice that has been raised repeatedly in this discussion. I do not doubt that Columella, for example, despite his limitations, could have performed the simple arithmetical computation required to reveal the economies possible from an enlarged scale of exploitation. The question, in other words, was not an intellectual one. In modern jargon, the "threshold point in the spectrum of farm acreage" is determined by a combination of social and economic factors, in the absence of which the arithmetic becomes meaningless.[54] The powerful pull of the peasant-household, the attitudes to labour and management, the weak urban market, the satisfactory profits of the existing land regime, perhaps the difficulties inherent in organizing and managing a very large slave force—a subject which it is even more impossible to examine concretely, from the ancient evidence, than the profitability of slave labour—all served as disincentives to change. For all Pliny's complaining about troubles with tenants, whose difficulties are understandable enough, *he* "is never short of cash in these years".[55] Nor his kinsmen: he ends his letter about the Umbrian estate in this way: "You will ask whether I can easily raise the three million sesterces. Most of what I have is in land, but I have money out on loan and it will not be difficult to borrow. Besides, I can always have money from my mother-in-law, whose money-chest I can use as freely as my own."

Once again we turn to Trimalchio for the bald truth. The great banquet is suddenly interrupted by the arrival of a secretary, who reads off the journal for July 26th: on the Cumae estate, seventy slave children were born, 500 oxen were broken in, a slave was crucified for blasphemy, "ten million sesterces were placed in the money-box because they could not be invested" (*Satyricon* 53.3). For the men whose status Trimalchio identified himself with, there were three places for wealth, in land, out on short-term interest-bearing loans, or in a strong-box. We must of course allow for exaggeration: there was also wealth in ships, urban house property, warehouses, slave-craftsmen and raw materials, but that represented a small fraction of the wealth of the élite and induced no significant difference in the "economic" thinking.

We then speak of their "investment of capital" and of land as the "preferred investment".[56] That phrasing contains some truth, but it is neither the whole truth nor nothing but the truth, because it fails to convey to a modern reader the very large non-economic element in the preference. To begin with, there is the complete absence of the concept of amortization.[57] When the fourth-century B.C. Athenian orator Demosthenes attained his majority, he brought suit against his guardians for the recovery of his inheritance. He itemized to the jury the estate recorded in his father's will, under two headings: (1) the active (*energa*), which included 32 or 33 slave swordmakers, bringing in 3000 drachmas a year; another 20 slaves engaged in the manufacture of furniture, 1200 drachmas annually; and 6000 drachmas on loan at 12%; (2) the inactive: raw materials on hand at his father's death nine years before, worth 15,000 drachmas, the house worth 3000, the furniture and his mother's jewelry, 8000 in cash in a strong-box at home, a maritime loan of 7000 drachmas, and 4600 on deposit in two banks and with a relation. This represents a remarkable conception of "capital", and it becomes all the more remarkable when one pursues in detail the actual claim on the guardians, which ignores amortization and depreciation, and assumes unchanging figures for annual production, rate of profit and income.[58] Yet this was a normal ancient presentation, including the amalgamation of personal, family-household possessions (his mother's jewels) and business property (the raw materials). Demosthenes won his suit.

I deliberately chose as my first test-case an urban business, where one might have expected more sophisticated accounting. If we now look at the text that is regularly cited by modern historians as the most reliable ancient analysis of Italian farm income, the model 7-*iugerum* (4½-acre) vineyard described by Pliny's near contemporary, Columella (3.3.8–10), we discover that though he allows for the purchase price of the land, of the slave vine-dresser, the vines and props, as well as for the loss of two years' income while the new vines are maturing, he forgets the farm buildings, equipment, ancillary land (for cereal grains, for example), the maintenance costs of his slaves, depreciation and amortization.[59] His implied 34% annual return is nonsense, even after allowing for his polemical intention in this section, and we must conclude that this was a merely perfunctory desk exercise, that the large landowners worked from crude empirical knowledge alone, heavily backed by the social-psychological pressures of land ownership in itself. Pliny neither calculated nor claimed that the second Umbrian estate would produce a higher return than the loans he would have to call in to meet the purchase price. He spoke only of the gain in amenity.

Investment in land, in short, was never in antiquity a matter of systematic, calculated policy, of what Weber called economic rationality.[60] There was no clear conception of the distinction between capital costs and labour costs, no planned ploughing back of profits, no long-term loans for productive purposes. The import in this context of the short-term loan (like the short-term tenancy) cannot be exaggerated. From one end of antiquity to another, one can easily count the known examples of borrowing on property for purposes of purchase or improvement. The mortgage was a disaster ("mortgaging the old homestead"), a short-term personal loan designed to "cover deficiencies in the supply of necessities occasioned generally by some emergency which has made unexpected demands upon the resources of the borrower",[61] not a deliberate device for raising money at a low rate in order to invest at a higher rate, the main function of the modern business mortgage. Among the men of property, these demands were either familial (a dowry for a daughter) or sumptuary or political, singly or in combination. Sometimes such expenditures brought large returns, as we have seen, but they were in no sense returns on an investment in property.

It is thus not surprising that there was neither a recognizable real-property market nor a profession of estate agent or realtor. The Greek language, like modern German, lends itself to the creation of compound nouns, and a collection has been made of more than one hundred known combinations incorporating the word "seller": "corn-seller", "perfume-seller", comic inventions like Aristophanes' "decree-seller", but not one attestation of "land-seller", "house-seller", "property-seller".[62] Nor was there a word for "broker".[63] And the same holds true for Latin.

When Pliny was sent to Bithynia in Asia Minor by the emperor Trajan, probably in A.D. 109 or 110, in order to sort out the financial disarray and extravagance of the affluent cities of that province, he reported (*Epistles* 10.54) that, having succeeded in collecting substantial sums owing to one city, probably Prusa, "I fear the money may lie idle, for the opportunity of buying property is non-existent, or nearly so, and people cannot be found who will borrow from the municipality, especially at the 9% which is the rate for private loans." He proposed that the city councillors be compelled to borrow at some lower rate. Trajan promptly rejected the idea as "unjust". Three things are to be noted. The first is the familiar trinity, cash on hand, land, money on loan. The second is that neither the city nor the emperor saw anything improper in allowing the money to lie idle. The third is the unavailability of land for purchase.

It is not altogether clear how Pliny discovered that there was no land to be had. I suggest the answer is that he learned from the small-town gossip of any Mediterranean society, more particularly from the gossip among the very municipal aristocracy on whom he was prepared to impose loans. The Roman equestrian, Gaius Canius, who wished to buy a vacation spot in Syracuse, "let it be known" (*dictabat*), says Cicero (*De officiis* 3.58), that he was in the market. The gossip reached a local banker who proceeded fraudulently to sell Canius his own *hortulus* on the waterfront at an exhorbitant price. The normal purchase of land in antiquity, I further suggest, was windfall purchase (which is not to say that windfalls were rare). Pliny himself was not actively seeking another estate when he became interested in the one in Umbria, and he was certainly not overburdened by idle cash, since he would have to dip into his mother-in-law's money-box to make the purchase. Derelict land, going at a bargain because of neglect, war devastation or someone's bad luck, was one such windfall. A more significant one was confiscated land, such as the Roman *ager publicus*, whether confiscated from individuals by court action or imperial fiat or taken from whole groups and communities in either civil war or conquest. And we must also include, whenever circumstances were propitious, land extorted from peasants through usurious loans, illegal seizure or "patronage".[64]

Political crisis or political pressures could, of course, have the reverse effect of rapidly driving up the price of land. One such instance, the consequence of Caesar's march on Rome in 49 B.C., is discussed briefly in chapter 5. Another occurred at the beginning of the second century A.D., described by Pliny in one of his letters (6.19):

"Have you heard that the price of land has gone up, particularly in the neighbourhood of Rome? The reason for the sudden increase in price has given rise to a good deal of discussion. At the last election, the Senate expressed the very proper opinion that 'Candidates should be prohibited from providing entertainments, distributing presents, and depositing money with agents'. The first two practices were employed without restraint or concealment, and the third was done secretly but was well known to all." The emperor, Trajan, was asked to remedy the evil. "This he has done, by applying the law against bribery to force candidates to limit their scandalously gross expenditure; and he has also compelled them to concentrate a third of their patrimony in realty, thinking it unseemly (as indeed it was) that candidates for office should treat Rome and Italy not as their native country, but as a mere inn or lodging-house for them on their visits. Consequently candidates are rushing about, struggling to buy up anything they hear is for sale, and thus increasing the amount available for sale."[65]

This is a neat instance of a sellers' windfall, as temporary and adventitious as a buyers' windfall. The absence of a real-property market is underscored, not only by the way Pliny describes the scurrying about of the candidates whose political careers depended on a quick purchase, but also by the effect on prices of the requirements of a mere handful of men. The moralizing about the effects of excessive conspicuous (political) expenditure is also notable (and to be taken literally). So is the emperor's aim, not "to interest more persons in promoting Italian agriculture"[66] but to compel the increasingly provincialized Senate to become proper Romans and Italians, befitting their status as the élite of the Empire.

Windfall land is visibly cheap or dear, as the case may be; no more sophisticated investigation is required than what I have already called crude empirical knowledge. Under ancient dry-farming conditions, furthermore, lacking large water installations or expensive machinery, derelict and devastated land recovered very rapidly. Olives, vines and flocks required a few years for replacement, but that merely demanded patience on the part of the landowning upper classes with whom we are now concerned, more than capital, the scale of which is regularly exaggerated in modern accounts.

The purchase of windfall property is a form of investment, to be sure, but only in the restricted sense I have been defining. And it was almost exclusively a private activity. During his great veteran settlement programmes in 30 and 14 B.C., Augustus found his own surplus holdings and his considerable confiscations insufficient for the purpose, and he purchased tracts from cities in Italy and the provinces, at a total cost of about 860 million sesterces on his own reckoning (*Res gestae* 16.1). That was an important, indeed prodigious, accomplishment. His further claim, "Of all those who founded military colonies in Italy or the provinces I was the first and only one to have done this in the recollection of my contemporaries," means that "he was the first to pay it from resources which he could regard as private".[67] He does not go on to specify how he made the purchases, and we may legitimately doubt the free willingness of many sellers.

Be that as it may, it is a fact that, though ancient states all owned land, from which they derived income normally by letting it, in the case of the Roman emperors also by direct exploitation through agents, they almost never bought land. Neither did temples or cult centres, many of which accumulated and hoarded substantial treasures through gifts and dedications. Nor did the innumerable semi-private cult-groups and societies that proliferated in the Graeco-Roman world. They, too, obtained land by gift, sometimes in the form of trusts backed by property (like Trajan's *alimenta* scheme), and their cash was fructified through interest-bearing loans, not through investment in land. Only guardians appear to have constituted an exception, in Rome at least, where the law required them to place a ward's cash either in land or in interest-bearing loans.[68] And even that provision is a far cry from the modern tradition, still by no means dead, which impels charitable and other public trusts to place their funds in the safety of the land.

Of course, windfalls could not have been realized without alertness, a genuine interest in acquisition, and, above all, political influence and status. There were even some men, not many I believe, who actively speculated in derelict property, chiefly in urban buildings. Crassus is the legendary paradigm (Plutarch, *Crassus* 2.1–6).[69] I have not been trying to argue that there was not, in most periods of antiquity, a constant movement of landed property. Without it there could not have been the trend I stressed earlier towards greater and greater accumulation; there could have been no Trimalchios on the one hand, no men, on the other hand, like the occupiers of *ager publicus* who brought about the deaths of Tiberius and Gaius Gracchus, later like Ahenobarbus or Herodes Atticus. What I have been attempting to do is to pinpoint the ancient "investment" concept, to define its character and its limits in both ideology and practice. Ancient writers—we must never allow ourselves to forget—did not describe land as the best investment in maximization of income language; it was profitable, to be sure, if held on a large enough scale, but they ranked it first at least as much on grounds of "nature" and morality, and they had not yet learned to draw a simple one-for-one equation between morality and profits. Even today, it should be remembered, there are important social strata who knowingly accept a low rate of return on investment in farming because there are advantages "other than the direct monetary return . . . the feeling of personal security, the sporting rights, the social position, possibly some taxation advantage".[70]

"With respect to property", wrote the author of the first book of the pseudo-Aristotelian *Oikonomikos* (1343a25–b2), "the first care is that it be according to nature. Agriculture ranks first according to nature, second those arts that extract from the ground, such as mining and the like. Agriculture is the best because it is just, for it is not at the expense of others, whether willingly as in trade or wage-earning or unwillingly as in war. It is also one of the activities according to nature in other respects, because by nature all things receive their nourishment from their mother, and so men receive theirs from the earth." There is more to this painfully naive re-statement of good Aristotelian doctrine but I need not continue. It is also good Cato, and good Cicero. It is, in short, one of many formulations of the landowning ideology of the ancient upper classes. Aristocracies have been known to cling in their practical behaviour to outworn ideologies and to sink with them. That was not their fate in antiquity. By comparison with Weber's "Pro-testant ethic", their mentality may have been a non-productive one; it was in no way a non-acquisitive one. They could permit themselves the luxury of a moral choice and still wax richer, not poorer.

V

Town and Country

THE BACKWARDNESS and brutishness of western
Europeans outside Italy, explained the Greek geographer Strabo,
flow from their hunting, pastoral, raiding way of life. Once they
are converted (or compelled) to a peaceful, settled agricultural
existence, urbanism will develop, and they will become civilized.[1]
Although Strabo was writing at the beginning of our era, he was
repeating good old Greek (as well as Roman) doctrine. Greeks and
Romans never tired in their praise of the moral excellence of agriculture, and simultaneously in their insistence that civilization
required the city. They were not being self-contradictory: Strabo,
it will have been noticed, saw agriculture, not trade or manufacture, as the prelude to stability and urbanism. The true city in
classical antiquity encompassed both the *chora*, the rural hinterland, and an urban centre, where the best people resided, where
the community had its administration and its public cults. The
two were conceptually so complementary that even the absolute
Hellenistic monarchs acknowledged the "freedom" of the *chora*
belonging to the newly created Greek cities of the eastern regions;
city-land was exempt from the royal domanial rights over all land
in the kingdom.

But what is a city? Modern geographers have been unable to
achieve a "standardized definition".[2] Strabo of course did not
bother, not even when he protested (3.4.13) against those writers
who mistakenly called the large villages (*komai*) of the Spanish
peninsula "cities". His audience required no definition. A still

later Greek writer, Pausanias, sneeringly dismissed the claim of a little town in central Greece to be called a *polis*: "no government buildings, no theatre, no agora, no water conducted to a fountain, and where the people live in hovels like mountain cabins on the edge of a ravine" (10.4.1). *His* audience would also have understood. The aesthetic-architectural definition was shorthand for a political and social definition: a genuine "city" was a political and cultural centre, now with a highly restricted autonomy to be sure, in contrast with the proud independence of the old Greek *poleis*, but still a place where the well-born and the educated could live a civilized existence, a life of *urbanitas* in Roman parlance, in which they could dominate municipal affairs if no longer the whole gamut of state activity. Mere size was no test: many genuine cities were no bigger than villages in population or area. And the economy did not enter into consideration at all, apart from the requirement that the material goods indispensable for civilized amenities had to be available somehow.[3]

There were, of course, formal administrative definitions of a *polis* or a *civitas* in antiquity, as there are in all modern countries. Strabo was not concerned with that aspect, nor will the economic historian be. We can readily agree with Strabo that a mere conglomeration of people does not constitute a city. Otherwise Homeric Ithaca, an early medieval cathedral town and, for that matter, a prison or large army base are all cities: there are modern prisons whose inmates outnumber the total population of many Greek "cities". Then we move beyond Strabo (and every other ancient writer) to ask another kind of question altogether. What is the economic relation between town and country? The answer will not be the same for Sparta and for Athens, as in our own day it is not for Rome and Genoa. When Martin Luther thundered in his *Address to the Christian Nobility of the German Nation*, "The Antichrist must take the treasures of the world, as it is written. . . . If we are right in hanging thieves and beheading robbers, why should we leave the greed of Rome unpunished? Here is the greatest thief and robber that has ever come or is likely to come on earth," he, for his own purposes, made an important historical observation. From the time Rome became an imperial city until today she has been a parasite-city, living on gifts, rents, taxes, tribute. That does not make Rome any less a city, only a different kind of city from Genoa.

Hypothetically, the economic relationship of a city to its countryside—we must start with a single city in isolation—can range over a whole spectrum, from complete parasitism at one end to full symbiosis at the other. All residents of a city who are not directly engaged in primary production derive their food and raw materials from the producers in the countryside. All cities are in that sense centres of consumption. The question then is whether ancient cities were, as Max Weber thought, primarily centres of consumption.[4] Stated differently, how did the cities pay for what they drew from the country? The parasitical city paid merely by returning all or part of the rents and taxes it took from the country in the first place; the fully symbiotic relationship would be represented by equal payment in urban production and services. A number of models can be constructed, in which the main variables are the distribution of the population, the quantity of rural production, the quantity of urban production, and the proportion of each transferred to the other. Urban manufactures and services designed solely for urban consumption are excluded: it is economically irrelevant to a tenant-farmer whether his city-dwelling landlord has the wheat he receives in rents converted into bread in his own household or by a baker to whom he pays a fee.

The model must then be complicated because the isolated city-country unit exists only in very primitive societies or in the imagination of Utopian writers. A city may outgrow the food-producing capability of its own hinterland. Anyway, there is scarcely a city which is self-sufficient in timber, metals, salt, spices, not to mention slaves, hides, semi-precious stones and other commodities that have become necessary amenities for civilized society. Even such staunch defenders of the moral advantages of self-sufficiency as Plato and Aristotle conceded that unfortunate fact of life.[5] Again we ask: How did a city pay? And again the answer is a spectrum of possibilities, from Odysseus' raid on

Ismarus, where, he reported (Homer, *Odyssey* 9.39–42), "I sacked the city and killed the men; taking the women and many goods, we divided them," to a perfect balance of trade. Some think, though I do not, that the world of Odysseus was a Never-Never-Land not to be introduced into a serious historical account. But Caesar in Gaul was real and historical enough, as was the empire which produced sixty per cent of the Athenian public revenue in the fifth century B.C. (Thucydides 2.13.3), or the Sicilian corn tithe from which the inhabitants of the city of Rome for a time made much of their bread. The primitive models suitable for the isolated city must therefore be modified by further variables: rents, taxes and tribute drawn from outside the immediate territory of the city; production, both urban and rural, for export; transport facilities. Nor can politics be ignored, even in a "purely economic" analysis. Successful Roman expansion freed Italian land from taxation, a case of one variable, external tribute, cancelling out another, internal levies on the countryside.

There were also certain constants, the ox to begin with. The ox was the chief traction animal of antiquity, the mule and donkey his near rivals, the horse hardly at all. All three are slow and hungry. The transport figures in Diocletian's edict of maximum prices imply that a 1200-pound wagon-load of wheat would double in price in 300 miles, that a shipment of grain by sea from one end of the Mediterranean to the other would cost less (ignoring the risks) than carting it seventy-five miles.[6] A state could afford to engage ox-teams for the extraordinary purpose of shifting marble column-drums for temples, employing on an average thirty yoke for each drum,[7] and it could perform other extraordinary feats, especially if the army required them. But individuals could not move bulky merchandise long distances by land as a normal activity, nor could any but the wealthiest and most powerful communities. Most necessities are bulky—cereals, pottery, metals, timber—and so towns could not safely outgrow the food production of their own immediate hinterlands unless they had direct access to waterways.

Not even the famed Roman roads, built for military and political, not commercial reasons, made any significant difference, since the means of traction remained the same. It was the many rivers of Gaul, not the roads, that elicited comment from Roman writers and facilitated the growth of inland cities.[8] And in Asia Minor, Pliny, on his mission for the emperor Trajan early in the second century, wrote from Nicomedia, a harbour-town on the gulf of Izmit at the eastern end of the Sea of Marmara, proposing a complex canal construction linking the nearby Lake Sophon to the east (with a natural outlet northwards to the Black Sea) to the Sea of Marmara. Across the largish lake, Pliny explained (*Epistles* 10.41.2), "marble, produce and building wood are transported cheaply and with little effort to the highway, but then they have to be taken to the sea by cart with much labour and great expense". The highway was nothing less than the main Roman road running eastwards from Nicomedia, eventually to Ankara and beyond; the short stretch from the lake to Nicomedia and the sea was some eighteen kilometers.[9] That may help to explain how the Antioch famine of 362–3 reached such disastrous proportions when grain was available fifty miles away along another proper Roman road. Hoarding and speculation played their part, no doubt, but the frequent phenomenon of famine amid nearby glut cannot be attributed solely to greed.

It is almost true that, the state apart, the peasantry were, within narrow limits, the chief beneficiaries of the Roman roads. Thus, although the road-building in the Romanized southeast of Britain stimulated the growth of villages, the average distance from the small local market to the edge of its "tributary area" remained at the standard maximum distance to a market preferred wherever means of transport are primitive, namely, four to five miles.[10] Peasants (and not only peasants) are ruled by what economic geographers have called the "law of minimum effort" or the "principle of least effort".[11] And peasants, it need hardly be said, could not rescue a great city in time of famine or supply Nicomedia with its timber and marble.

Anyone in antiquity who forgot these elementary facts of life was quickly ruined. Mark Antony forgot, when he allowed his 200,000 men in western Greece to be blockaded by Agrippa in 31 B.C., with the inevitable consequence of hunger, disease and desertion despite his efforts to commandeer supplies by every possible device, so that in the battle of Actium he was hopelessly outmanned. Roman emperors never forgot. Roman expansion into western and northwestern Europe took the ancient world away from the Mediterranean and its tributaries for the first time. But there were navigable rivers; the main settlements were located on their banks and they were a major factor in all military logistical calculations, as in the creation of the greatest grain-milling complex of the time in the region of Arles.[12] When it was necessary to station armies far away from the rivers or the sea, the local population was impressed into maintaining them, without any concern for the relation between local agricultural production and army requirements. Roman armies could march long distances along the roads; they could neither be fed nor clothed nor armed from long distances by those routes.

Water transport, in short, and especially sea transport, created radical new possibilities for the ancient town. In the first place, imports of food and other bulk commodities permitted a substantial increase in the size of the population, no longer held down by the limiting factor of local agricultural production, and an improvement in the quality of life, through a greater variety of goods, a greater abundance of slave labour for domestic as well as productive work. Both population and amenities would then be further stimulated by the inevitable attraction of a secondary population, craftsmen, entertainers, artists, teachers and tourists. There might also be a feedback effect on the countryside in that imported necessities allowed more efficient exploitation of larger landholdings (though not of peasant holdings) through specialization, not really possible in more or less isolated, self-sufficient communities. One wonders whether the cultivation of roses, violets and peacocks on villas near the city of Rome (Varro, *De re rustica* 3.2) would have been tolerated had the city's corn supply not been looked after by the provinces. The ancient city was reluctant to leave food supply to chance or the free play of the market, at least so long as the city remained a genuine, autonomous community. Even classical Athens made it a capital offence to export home-grown corn, despite its control of the Aegean Sea and therefore of the massive wheat imports from southern Russia (and elsewhere).

One should not rush matters. The dialectics of the town–country–sea relationship are complex, the tempo of development slow and sometimes abortive. Easy access to the sea or a major river was only a necessary condition for growth, not a sufficient condition. The great Athenian harbour, the Piraeus, was a fifth-century B.C. creation, and the original impetus came from Themistocles' navy-building programme for which the sand-beach of Phalerum was no longer adequate. Brundisium (modern Brindisi) failed to grow into a major centre though it was the best port south of Ancona on the east coast of Italy, the side facing Greece and the east. Still further north, Ravenna, at the mouth of the Po, had a splendid harbour said to provide safe anchorage for 250 ships (Dio Cassius 55.33), but it never became a commercial centre.

The city of Rome offers the most striking testimony. Rome is fifteen or twenty miles up the Tiber from Ostia on the sea. Yet Rome had conquered Italy and defeated Carthage before Ostia began to be developed as its commercial harbour.[13] Rome's first interest in Ostia, in the fourth century B.C., was military-defensive. Then came the third-century need for a navy in the wars with Carthage. At that critical moment, Rome, in the slightly exaggerated formulation of an ancient authority, had "no warships at all, not so much as a single galley", no knowledge of ships or ship construction, and no citizens with practice in rowing, sailing or marine fighting.[14] That was more than two centuries after the Carthaginian Hanno had sailed down the West African coast at least as far as Sierra Leone.

Victory over Hannibal at the end of the third century B.C. was a watershed not only in the political history of Rome but also in its urban history. The oligarchic ruling circle, the *nobilitas* as it was soon called, acquired extensive tracts of *ager publicus* and needed slave labour; they also acquired expensive tastes and habits, for

9

political in-fighting and for conspicuous consumption, which leaped in geometric progression. Gladiatorial shows, for example, were originally introduced for funeral games: the first recorded instance, in 264 B.C., involved only three pairs of gladiators, but by 216 we hear of twenty-two pairs, by 174 B.C. of seventy-four pairs in a celebration lasting three days.[15] Meantime, slaves and dispossessed peasants were rapidly pushing up the population of the city, and they had to be fed, clothed and housed (and the free men amused). It was no longer possible to rely, as in centuries past, on the immediate hinterland and on small coasting-vessels coming from the port of Puteoli in the Bay of Naples and then up the Tiber to Rome. So the harbour town of Ostia finally came into being as the only rival to Alexandria and Carthage in scale, to flourish for four centuries before sinking into a malarial marsh.

It is therefore more correct to say that Rome took to the sea because she had become a great city than the other way round. Rome was hardly typical, the complete parasite-city (though she was unique only in scale). No one will pretend that Rome paid in production for even a tiny fraction of her massive imports. But what of the cities which had no provincial booty and tribute with which to balance their accounts? One significant group may be noticed quickly, the cities which by their location were clearing-houses and transfer points, deriving substantial income from tolls, harbour-dues and dock charges, as well as from the services required by transient merchants and ships' crews. Ancient ships usually preferred to take short hops whenever feasible: the peculiar conditions of winds and currents in the Mediterranean, the absence of the compass, the limited ability to tack, shortage of storage space for food and fresh water were contributing factors. Hence the importance of Rhodes, in the Hellenistic period the outstanding example of a port-of-call. When, in the middle of the second century B.C., Rome decided for political reasons to bring Rhodes to heel, she accomplished that by the simple device of declaring the island of Delos a free port and improving the harbour installations there. The Rhodians soon complained that the effect on their public revenues was a reduction from one million drachmas a year to a mere 150,000.[16] That drastic decline in the volume of traffic, eighty-five per cent, from which Rhodian traders would not have been protected, since ancient states took harbour-fees from citizens and foreigners in equal measure, will have hit all the subsidiary services as well, amounting altogether to a most severe blow on the Rhodian economy, private as well as public.

There were other commercial cities: one thinks of Aegina, of Chios, a clearing-house in the slave trade,[17] or of Marseilles, an entrepôt for products transported to and brought from the barbarians of the interior.[18] But these were special cases. Ancient cities in the great majority counted farmers, whether working or gentleman farmers, men whose economic interest lay chiefly and often exclusively in the land, as the core of their citizenry. Not a few important ones were in a sense entirely agrarian, that is to say, the land was their one source of wealth and they paid for their imported metals, slaves and luxuries with their agricultural surpluses: Thebes, for example, or Akragas (Roman Agrigentum), the second city of ancient Sicily, or Cyrene, at a lower level Pompeii. Little more needs to be said about them in the present context, or of cities servicing a more extensive, but continuous, agricultural area than "their own", in Campania, for example; or of those cities in which a large military and imperial administrative personnel swelled the consuming sector in Hellenistic and Roman times, such as Antioch in Syria or Sirmium (modern Mitrovica) on the Save River, a small colony which had a brief period of sensational growth as one of the imperial capitals in the fourth century.

Finally, we come to the interesting, difficult and perhaps most significant group, the cities with an insufficient agricultural base and a genuinely "mixed" economy, agrarian, manufacturing and commercial together. Athens is the test case, not only because it is the one such city we know almost enough about but also because her economic history raises in the most acute form the question: How did an ancient city pay for its necessities, some produced internally, the rest obtained abroad? Not parasitical, imperial Athens, with its large tribute, but fourth-century Athens, which could no longer pass on the costs to subject states.*

We cannot draw up a balance-sheet of imports and exports, not even an approximation; we cannot indeed offer quantities at all; we must therefore resort to models and indicators again. In what is still a widely read reply to the Weber-Hasebroek school, Gomme announced that "the Greeks were well aware that imports and exports must in the long run, somehow, balance".[19] He cited no authority, and the few which are available fall squarely into Schumpeter's class of "prescientific statements" not made to bear any "superstructure". Plutarch's banal observation (*Solon* 22.1) that the Athenian lawgiver encouraged the crafts because he knew that merchants do not like to import into a country—and Athens already required grain imports—from which they cannot take out a return cargo, is immediately followed by a miscellany on Solon's legislation with respect to women and bastards, the etymology of "sycophant" and "parasite" and much else. The famous passages in the elder Pliny (*Natural History* 6.101; 12.84), giving dubious figures of the drain of Roman gold and silver to India and other eastern countries in payment for luxuries, are moral in their implication. Any doubts on that are quieted by the explicitly anti-sumptuary rhetoric of Dio Chrysostom (79.5–6) on the same topic. No economic analysis or economic programme followed, either in the moralist writings or in practice, private or public.[20]

Furthermore, Gomme apparently overlooked the fact that even in our complex economy many cities and towns "are supported exclusively by their role as market centres", as a "cluster of retail and service establishments".[21] He insisted that the "balance" would be found by adding up the exports of wine and olive oil, manufactured goods, and silver together with invisible exports (the profits of shipping and tourism). The catalogue is irreproachable,

---

* In this simpler model, I am deliberately excluding the effect on "balance of payments" of imperial tribute and of armies stationed more or less permanently in outlying parts of an empire.

but unhelpful unless some ratios can be established among the individual items. Remember that we are examining the most populous city of the Graeco-Roman world in its day (for present purposes, non-citizens and slaves have to be counted in as consumers), compelled to import regularly perhaps two thirds of its wheat, all the iron, tin, copper and ship timber it required, all its numerous slaves (other than those bred at home), and all the ivory, semi-precious stones, most of the hides and leather, and a vast miscellany of commodities (including flax for linen and papyrus for writing) essential for a now traditional high standard of civilized living. Athens was self-sufficient only in honey, olive oil, ordinary wine, silver, building stone (including marble), potting clay and fuel; probably in a favourable position, approaching self-sufficiency but no more, in wool, fish and meat. The import bill was clearly an impressive one.

How do we then rank the exports? I cannot, for a start, attach any significance to agricultural products, not even olive oil and wine. Writing about olives in the Greek world generally, one economic historian observed that "in a region in which the production of the commodity was so general, it is natural that we should find only scattered references, and those often dealing with extraordinary circumstances".[22] That, however, is no mere literary convention but a consequence of the realities of Greek production and trade. The Athenians exported some olives and olive-oil throughout their history: that is proved by the Hadrianic law of about A.D. 125 reserving one third of the local production for public use, a law which reminds us forcefully that Greek (and Roman) cities were also large *consumers* of olive-oil.[23] Given this latter fact and given the ubiquity of the olive-tree, where were the external markets for the export of this commodity, *from the important urban communities*, on a scale large enough to weigh significantly in the balance of payments? As for wine exports, the same considerations apply with the added qualification in the case of Athens that its wine was poor in quality. The important foreign trade was in famed regional wines; *vin ordinaire* was normally produced at home.[24]

The situation is very different with two other items in the catalogue. Silver was the most important Athenian resource, exported in substantial quantities; whether in bullion or in silver coin was immaterial. For Xenophon (*Poroi* 3.2), Athens had the great advantage that importers "who did not wish to take out return cargoes" could make a handsome profit simply by taking out silver. Hence he built his programme in the little pamphlet on public revenues on the inexhaustible mines at Laureion and on the presence of numerous metics. The latter created what we call invisible exports, for which Athens had two interlocking advantages. She became, perhaps as early as the tyranny at the end of the sixth century B.C., a commercial centre and clearing-house, and, not much later, a tourist centre. The beginnings are obscure, but the continued growth of the city in both respects is easily followed, as is the way the two interests stimulated each other and the way the empire provided further impetus. We must not be too high-minded and look only at the Greater Dionysia and the Sophists. The Piraeus was an international port, with all that implies, and there were also well paying visitors like the son of the Crimean nobleman, the plaintiff in Isocrates' seventeenth oration, known as the *Trapeziticus*, for whom study (*theoria*) was an elastic concept. The whoremasters of Menander, Plautus and Terence were no comic invention; it is purely contingent that the action of the pseudo-Demosthenic oration against Neaira occurred chiefly in Corinth rather than in Athens. The constant coming and going of tens of thousands of "foreigners", Greeks and others, for whatever purpose, constituted a major, though not measurable, contribution to the Athenian balance of payments.

I have left the export of manufactured goods to the end. That is the capstone of the Gomme model. Perhaps I should say the missing link: evidence for Athenian export of manufactures other than pottery is effectively non-existent, and the Greek taste for fine painted pottery died out rapidly (and mysteriously) in the fourth century B.C., precisely the century we are considering. How much "must there have been" in the way of manufacturing for export, despite its non-recognition in the available sources? On this question there is clear awareness in ancient writers, and I begin with two key texts, both by Xenophon.

The superiority of the meals served at the Persian court, he explains (*Cyropaedia* 8.2.5), is not surprising, given the size of the kitchen staff. "Just as the various trades are most highly developed in large cities, in the same way the food at the palace is prepared in a far superior manner. In small towns the same man makes couches, doors, ploughs and tables, and often he even builds houses, and still he is thankful if only he can find enough work to support himself. And it is impossible for a man of many trades to do all of them well. In large cities, however, because many make demands on each trade, one alone is enough to support a man, and often less than one: for instance one man makes shoes for men, another for women, there are places even where one man earns a living just by mending shoes, another by cutting them out, another just by sewing the uppers together, while there is another who performs none of these operations but assembles the parts. Of necessity he who pursues a very specialized task will do it best."

This is the most important ancient text on division of labour,[25] but my present interest is in something else, in the stress on the low level and inelasticity of demand, on the threat of over-production. Demand stands in a simple arithmetical ratio to numbers: the larger the city, the greater the demand. And even in big cities, Xenophon tells us elsewhere, demand will not stand up to pressure. In defending his proposals in the *Poroi*, which envisaged so large an increase in silver mining that every citizen would eventually draw full maintenance from the state, he argues as follows (4.4–6): "Of all the activities I know, silver mining is the only one in which expansion arouses no envy. . . . If there are more coppersmiths, for example, copperwork becomes cheap and the coppersmiths retire. The same is true in the iron trade. . . . But an increase in the amount of the silver ore . . . brings more people into this industry."

In both passages Xenophon thinks of manufacture only for the local market; otherwise his remarks make no sense.[26] Similarly, when Aristotle in the *Politics* (1291b22–25) gives examples of cities in which the *demos* has unusual opportunity for non-agricultural employment, he specifies fishing (Byzantium and Tarentum), trade (Aegina and Chios), ferrying (Tenedos) and the navy (Athens), but no manufacturing speciality. Strabo explains at length (8.6.20–23) the basis for the great wealth of Corinth, plundered by the Romans in 146 B.C.; he is unaware of any manufacture for export. Among the endlessly varied symbols on Greek coins, favourite agricultural products are not uncommon, manufactured products unknown. When Greek and Roman moralists allow, no matter how grudgingly, that foreign traders have some virtue, unlike local petty shopkeepers, they invariably credit them with public service as importers, not as exporters: I need not repeat the relevant quotations from Aristotle and Cicero. There were exceptional protective measures for domestic agriculture, such as a law of the northern Aegean island of Thasos in the late fifth century B.C., prohibiting the importation of foreign wines into the coastal areas on the Thracian mainland which Thasos controlled.[27] I know of no comparable law protecting a manufacture.

I will not extend the catalogue. These are all arguments from silence, it will be objected, to which I reply that, given the nature of the sources, the issue comes down to how we interpret the silence. Is it, with Gomme, a mere accident of the survival of evidence, literary and archaeological, or a matter of ancient literary taste? Or is it, as I believe, a silence that is explained in the simplest possible way, because there was effectively nothing to speak about? Clearly, there were some manufactures deliberately designed for export, such as the shoes and summer mantles, made we do not know where, which an Athenian brought to Cyrene once a year in such small supply that Bishop Synesius was impatient lest he miss the opportunity to buy. There were the high-grade linen garments from St. Paul's city of Tarsus, famed throughout the Roman empire, which brought the weavers of that city an apparently steady livelihood, but on so low a level that few could afford the 500-drachma fee required for the acquisition of local citizenship (Dio

Chrysostom 34.21–23). There was Patavium (Padua), located in a famous sheep-raising district, with access to the sea by river, which for a time in the early Empire exported woollens to Rome on a considerable scale, especially fine carpets and cloaks (Strabo 5.1.7, 12).[28] There was Arretium (Arezzo), which for a fleeting moment saw substantial fortunes made from dominance in the newly fashionable *terra sigillata*, a position that did not last two generations. Its most important successors, Lezoux and La Graufesenque in Gaul, did, it is true, export their ware for a long period throughout the western empire, but the potters were themselves modest men, not even little Wedgwoods.

David Hume was not seriously mistaken when he could "not remember a passage in any ancient author where the growth of a city is ascribed to the establishment of a manufacture".[29] Linen-weaving did not lay the foundation for Tarsus, nor the production of shoes and summer mantles for Athens; as for Lezoux and La Graufesenque, they flourish only in archaeological manuals, while Patavium was a centre of wool manufacture in (and for) the North Italian sheep-raising area long before the omnivorous city of Rome became one of its markets.[30]

In its relatively brief flourishing period, there were potteries in Arezzo employing as many as fifty-plus slaves. Cephalus's shield factory in fifth-century Athens had more than one hundred. Gomme was right to stress that workshops of such magnitude could not be, and were not, exceeded until the industrial revolution shifted the balance of an entrepreneur's input from labour to equipment, to capital goods. It has been claimed, rather exuberantly, that such excavated districts as the potters' quarter of Corinth evoke, in their physical appearance, "the artisan quarters of medieval cities".[31] But it seems commonly to be overlooked that the excavators of Tarsus have found no Cloth Hall, that all ancient cities lacked the Guildhalls and Bourses which, next to the cathedrals, are to this day the architectural glories of the great medieval cities of Italy, France, Flanders, the Hansa towns, or England. Contrast the Athenian Agora with the Grande Place in Brussels. It was no oversight on the part of Pausanias when he omitted that class of buildings from his sneer about the little town in Phocis.

The clothmakers of Flanders had no difficulty in meeting the financial charges of citizenship; on the contrary, they were an integral section of the ruling oligarchies. The political role of the guilds set the medieval city apart from the ancient, as the political role of the peasantry set the ancient city apart from the medieval.[32] Not only were there no Guildhalls in antiquity, there were no guilds, no matter how often the Roman *collegia* and their differently named Greek and Hellenistic counterparts are thus mistranslated. The *collegia* played an important part in the social and religious life of the lower classes, both free and slave; they sometimes performed benevolent functions, as in financing burials; they never became regulatory or protective agencies in their respective trades,* and that, of course, was the *raison d'être* of the genuine guilds, medieval and modern.[33]

The ancient-medieval contrast is closely linked with the difference in the quantity and significance of production for export in the two worlds. The local peasantry remained a constant: men with the small holdings we have examined, even free citizen-peasants, represent the lowest and most inelastic possible market for urban production. That is why "in most peasant societies, markets are periodic rather than permanent and continuous . . . the per capita demand for goods sold in the market is small, the market area is limited by primitive transport technology, and the aggregate demand is therefore insufficient to support permanent shops."[34] What is true of peasants with respect to level of demand (though not periodicity) is no less true of the urban plebs. Production can therefore leap upward to the extent, and only to the extent, that there are export markets, in antiquity markets accessible to water-borne traffic. The widespread prevalence of household self-sufficiency in necessities was enough to put a brake on extensive production for export.

That is what Max Weber meant when he labelled the ancient

* In the late Roman Empire some became compulsory agencies of the state, but that is a quite different function.

city a centre of consumption, not of production. He was not ignorant of the hundreds of craftsmen, making an infinite variety of things, equally varied in quality. But he located them correctly within the structure of the city. The level of consumption increased in the course of ancient history, at times to fabulous proportions. The evidence is too well known to require repetition. From time to time the authorities tried to curb excesses: sumptuary laws are associated with the names of such widely different figures as Solon, Demetrius of Phalerum, Sulla, Julius Caesar and Augustus. The younger Pliny was despatched to Bithynia by Trajan early in the second century in order to check extravagance and waste in the deployment of municipal funds. Always the goal was the same, prevention of the self-destruction of the social élite, caught up in the powerful pressures created by status requirements, an objective wholly unrelated to that of Colbert, for example, when he reduced the number of holy days in order to increase the productivity of French workers and peasants.

To sum up: essentially the ability of ancient cities to pay for their food, metals, slaves and other necessities rested on four variables: the amount of local agricultural production, that is, of the produce of the city's own rural area; the presence or absence of special resources, silver, above all, but also other metals or particularly desirable wines or oil-bearing plants; the invisible exports of trade and tourism; and fourth, the income from land ownership and empire, rents, taxes, tribute, gifts from clients and subjects. The contribution of manufactures was negligible; it is only a false model that drives historians in search of them where they are unattested, and did not exist.

It will have been noticed that I also failed to include the size of the city as a significant variable. In this respect, too, the ancient trend was very much upward, culminating in the first two centuries of the Roman Empire which saw not only the few great metropolises, led by Rome itself, but also a series of cities, especially in the eastern half, in the 100,000 class. The new dimension was visible all along the line: even a minor town like Pompeii had, at the time of its destruction in A.D. 79, some 20,000 inhabitants, a total exceeded by no more than a dozen Greek cities of the classical period. Partly, this urban growth was the consequence of a general population increase; partly, it reflected the increased volume of trade and increased wealth in the hands of the upper classes. But mainly it was a response to the new political pattern, the replacement of the city-state by a great bureaucratic empire. Larger cities (or army centres) then meant increased demand for urban trades for internal services, and, in some cases, notably Rome, there was also an impact at considerable distances in the countryside beyond the immediate hinterland, for example, to provide the wine and pork for Roman consumers. What is not to be perceived, however, is any notable effect on urban production for export.

It is not very relevant that the cities had largely lost the taxes and tribute which had contributed so much to the earlier city-states. Although technically that income now went to the imperial treasury instead, a major share found its way into many cities other than Rome, through the wages, perquisites and largesses paid out to a growing number of imperial officials and their staffs, and through the armies. For the rest, larger urban incomes, especially in that sector of the population who were the large consumers, were derived from the same sources as before, from the land, from government service, and from invisible exports. They were ample incomes, for reasons previously indicated: it is perhaps not coincidental that this period of growing urbanism, of an absolute and relative increase in the numbers of the economically parasitical classes, of sumptuary life-styles, was also the period during which the distinction came into full force between *honestiores* and *humiliores*, a symptom of depression in status of the free poor, craftsmen as well as peasants. Any notion of seeking to increase urban revenues through manufacture was not on the agenda: there were neither financial incentives nor market opportunities for those who possessed the potential capital, and there were the powerful social-psychological pressures against it. By contrast, the agrarian European feudal world provided the medieval cities with the external markets the ancient cities lacked.

The kings, lords and church dignitaries, living on their manors or in small agglomerations, created a fundamentally different town-country relationship from that of their highly urbanized land-owning predecessors.[35]

The same pattern of disincentive underlies another feature of the ancient economy that I have noticed several times, the condition of what may loosely be termed their business practices. This was a world which never created fiduciary money in any form, or negotiable instruments. Money was hard coin, mostly silver, and a fair amount of that was hoarded, in strong-boxes, in the ground, often in banks as non-interest-bearing deposits.[36] Payments were in coin, only under special conditions by a transfer within a particular bank or within the coffers of a Roman tax-farming corporation. In Greek law sales were not legal and binding until the sale price had been paid in full; credit sales took the form of fictitious loans (and are therefore normally impossible to detect in the sources). There was endless moneylending among both Greeks and Romans, as we have seen, but all lenders were rigidly bound by the actual amount of cash on hand; there was not, in other words, any machinery for the *creation of credit* through negotiable instruments.[37] The complete absence of a public debt is in this context a meaningful indicator. No Greek or Roman could have comprehended a modern definition of the money supply as "the total of bank liabilities plus currency held by the nonbank public".[38]

A recent, thorough study of Greek banking and moneylending has failed to turn up more than two actually attested instances (one a dubious one) of moneylending for business purposes, whether for agriculture, for trade, or for manufacture, in the sources from any period, apart from maritime (or bottomry) loans, an exception to be explained by the function of that type of loan as an insurance policy rather than as a form of credit.[39] (What we choose to call "banks" in antiquity are scarcely visible in the bottomry business.[40]) Certainly there were transactions which have failed to creep into our sources, but the pattern of Greek moneylending for non-productive purposes is indubitable.

The Roman citizenship structure did not create the legal wall characteristic of the Greek city-state between land and credit that I examined earlier. Cicero turned to *faeneratores* for the money with which to purchase an urban villa (*Letters to his Friends* 5.6.2). But when Pliny contemplated the purchase of a large estate in Umbria (*Epistles* 3.19), far from intending to apply to a professional money-lender for a mortgage, he planned the opposite, to call in his own interest-bearing loans and then, if necessary, to make up any deficit by dipping into his mother-in-law's cash-box. Whose behaviour was the more typical, Cicero's or Pliny's? Until a study is made of Roman moneylending comparable to the work on Greek banking I have just mentioned, we are restricted to hypotheses. Mine is that among the Romans, too, large-scale borrowing, borrowing among the men of means, was for non-productive, consumers' purposes, under which heading I of course include loans for political ends.[41] Short-term loans, rudimentary bookkeeping (including the common practice of not issuing receipts for private payments), the absence of a concept of amortization—I need not repeat what I have already said on these topics—were all by-products of this fundamental phenomenon. So, for that matter, was the pawnbroking and petty usurious moneylending that flourished at the expense of the poor.

In consequence, not only were the ups and downs in production always attributable to natural catastrophe or political troubles, not to cyclical crises, but so-called "credit crises" turn out to have had the same roots, not in supply-and-demand operations in a normal "money market". Attributable and attributed: Cicero was painfully aware of the effects of a sudden shortage of coin on interest rates and land prices, and nearly three centuries later the historian Dio Cassius revealed similar awareness of the reverse, when Augustus brought the captured Egyptian treasure to Rome.[42] However, it has been observed that not one ancient commentator, no matter how "attentive to the particular circumstances in which he found himself from day to day, or which he described as an historian, offers any reflections on what we call long-term movements, on the secular movement of prices".[43]

One rudimentary, but exemplary, instance of a credit crisis growing out of military catastrophe is known from the chance preservation of a long, complicated decree of the city of Ephesus at the beginning of the third century B.C., laying down temporary palliative measures respecting payments on mortgage-loans on farmland, dowries and other types of obligation.[44] Behind that emergency legislation lay years of continual warfare among the successors of Alexander the Great. Ephesus was within one of the main arenas of fighting and was devastated. Hence there was a crisis.

Or, the civil war that brought Julius Caesar to power instilled a fear in Roman moneyed circles of a "demagogic" measure to cancel debts. Interest rates were lowered by the tribunes; creditors called in their loans; debtors were unable to pay; their land was seized and became a glut on the market, with coin literally running out. Caesar's efforts to deal with the situation included a futile attack on the shortage of coin, a chronic problem, certain revisions in property assessment procedures and perhaps in the law on property transfers.[45] Another, rather mysterious outbreak occurred in the city of Rome in A.D. 33, under Tiberius. This crisis, according to a very brief but not very lucid account of Tacitus (*Annals* 6.16–17), began with a popular outcry against widespread irregularities by the moneylenders, to which they again responded by calling in their loans, again threatening the landed holdings of many respectable men. The emperor intervened with an interest-free loan-fund of one hundred million sesterces for worthy debtors and the excitement soon died down.[46] Tiberius' concern was for "those whose *dignitas* and *fama* were threatened";[47] so was Cicero's in his ferocious denunciation (*De officiis* 2.78–84) of debt-relief measures, in general and in particular. They are an attack on property and the propertied classes, he says in no uncertain terms, but he knows nothing about a threat to economic growth or *to the economy*, except for the rudimentary "prescientific" observation (Schumpeter's phrase again) that more money is loaned in periods in which the collection of debts is not threatened by demogogic interference.

One more negative has to be introduced into this long tale of the qualitative stability, the "fixity", of business practices after the end of the fourth century B.C.[48] I refer to the absence not only of the corporation but even of the long-term partnership. Under the Roman Empire, there were merchants who had their permanent representatives or agents in certain large ports, as there were representatives of such informal "collectivities" as the ship-owners (*navicularii*) of Arles, with their agent in Beirut.[49] However, that relatively simple and restricted operation did not lead, in private business affairs, to long-term partnerships, let alone to the extensive, powerful and durable organizations created earlier, under the Republic, by the tax-farming corporations, except perhaps among the merchants and shippers responsible for the imperial corn supply.[50] Here we have proof—I use the word deliberately—that we are not faced with an intellectual failing. Since the idea of a corporation was a familiar one, its non-extension to other spheres of activity reflects the absence of a need, specifically of the need to pool capital resources, to transcend the financial capacity of any individual to produce marketable commodities, to carry on commerce, to lend money.

In short, the strong drive to acquire wealth was not translated into a drive to create capital; stated differently, the prevailing mentality was acquisitive but not productive.* That brings me back, at the risk of being repetitive, to the role of metics, freedmen and slaves in the business life of the ancient world. It is irrelevant to insist that metics were as Greek as the Greek landowners who demeaned trade. No one is claiming the existence of racial attitudes. What is being claimed is the existence of powerful social and political attitudes, and of important economic consequences. Much of the daily buying and selling of processed foods and other raw materials and of manufactured goods in all the cities of antiquity—I should even guess the largest quantity—was carried on without middlemen, through direct sale by individual craftsmen to individual consumers. In the Greek world, paradoxically,

* Similarly, ancient Utopian schemes concentrated on consumption, not production, as in the "communism" satirized in Aristophanes' *Ecclesiazusae*.

these craftsmen-sellers were for the most part citizens of their respective communities, and even in much of the Roman Empire, too, except where the Roman freedman system prevailed—mostly poor citizens at that, politically impotent except in such untypical communities as classical, democratic Athens, socially inferior, but citizens nonetheless, not metics, not outsiders. The entrepreneurs, the men who managed the large-scale maritime trade or who were the moneylenders to the wealthy, Rostovtzeff's *bourgeoisie*, were mostly free from the obligations and distractions of municipal or imperial administration; they were the men who might have been expected to develop and create new techniques of capital formation—and they did not do so. Actually, these were not the men with the greatest accumulation, with the greatest potential. For that we look to the landholding élites, and their disincentive was decisive.

Nothing I have been saying should be taken to deny the absence of experts and expertise in all the fields that contributed to manufacture, engineering, food processing and navigation. There was extensive writing on these subjects in antiquity, nearly all of it now lost, with one outstanding exception, the *De architectura* of Vitruvius, written probably in the reign of Augustus, the standard work on the subject for the next 1500 years or so.[51] When Vitruvius decided to write a complete text-book, he came with impeccable credentials; his literary and scientific education was considerable, he had himself practised both as engineer and as architect and he was immersed in the far from negligible Hellenistic literature. His book is therefore the highest example available from antiquity of the knowledge and thinking of a man who was a do-er, not just a know-er, and who combined the best practice of both Greeks and Romans.

In sequence, the *De architectura* deals with the following topics: architecture in general and the qualifications of the architect, town-planning, building materials, temples, other civic buildings, domestic buildings, pavements and decorative plaster-work, water supply, geometry, mensuration, astronomy and astrology, and, finally, "machines" and siege devices. Vitruvius is a discursive

10

writer. He has a great deal to say, for example, about the ethics of his profession. In the preface to the tenth book there is the suggestion that the carelessness of architects could easily be remedied by universal adoption of a law of Ephesus holding the architect personally responsible for all costs exceeding twenty-five per cent above his original estimate. Scattered through the prefaces are stories drawn from the history of inventions: invariably the circumstances, and therefore the explanation, are either accidental (as in the discovery of the marble quarries at Ephesus when two fighting rams chipped a bit of the hillside) or frivolous (as in Archimedes' discovery of the principle of specific gravity in response to a royal request for a way to unmask a dishonest silversmith).

Like, say, Aristotle in the fourth century B.C., Vitruvius saw neither a virtue nor a possibility in the continued progress of technology through sustained, systematic inquiry. Now that the essential "machines"—the ladder, pulley, windlass, wagon, bellows and catapult—were known, Vitruvius, like Xenophon, stressed the qualitative benefits of expertise and technique, not their quantitative, productive possibilities, though he was an engineer and builder, whereas Xenophon was merely explaining the excellence of the food at the Persian court. It is therefore consistent that one brief, quiet paragraph (10.5.2) is sufficient for the important recent invention of the water-mill, and that in the whole of the *De architectura* there is just one passage which considers the achievement of greater economy of effort or greater productivity. Vitruvius recommends (5.10.1) that in public baths the hot-water room for men be placed next to the one for women, so that they can be fed from a single heat source. It will be conceded that this is not a very impressive instance.

The Greeks and Romans inherited a considerable body of techniques and empirical knowledge, which they exploited well insofar as it suited their particular values, and to which they added the gear and the screw, the rotary mill and the water-mill, glass-blowing, concrete, hollow bronze-casting, the lateen sail, and a few more. There were refinements and improvements in many spheres. But there were not many genuine innovations after the fourth or third century B.C., and there were effective blocks. These latter are for some strange reason argued away by many historians, but there are two which resist absolutely, and they both affected essential and profitable activities. The first was in mining, especially in the western and northern provinces where the ground-water line often created great difficulties; no one found a way to improve on hand bailing, the water-wheel operated by a foot treadle and perhaps the Archimedian screw for drainage devices: so technically simple a device as the chain-pump with animal power is unattested.[52] The second instance is a more generalized one. Power in antiquity was muscle power, human and animal; the ancients sailed with the wind and made complicated weather-vanes, but never a windmill.

There is a story, repeated by a number of Roman writers, that a man—characteristically unnamed—invented unbreakable glass and demonstrated it to Tiberius in anticipation of a great reward. The emperor asked the inventor whether anyone shared his secret and was assured that there was no one else; whereupon his head was promptly removed, lest, said Tiberius, gold be reduced to the value of mud. I have no opinion about the truth of this story, and it is only a story. But is it not interesting that neither the elder Pliny nor Petronius nor the historian Dio Cassius was troubled by the point that the inventor turned to the emperor for a reward, instead of turning to an investor for capital with which to put his invention into production?[53] My answer to that rhetorical question is more 'No' (it is not very interesting) than 'Yes'. We must remind ourselves time and again that the European experience since the late Middle Ages in technology, in the economy, and in the value systems that accompanied them, was unique in human history until the recent export trend commenced. Technical progress, economic growth, productivity, even efficiency have not been significant goals since the beginning of time. So long as an acceptable life-style could be maintained, however that was defined, other values held the stage.

The behaviour of governments provides the final test. Ancient states were capable of mobilizing extensive resources for amenities and for military purposes, and the trend was upward in a kind of megalomania, from the Golden House of Nero to Diocletian's nine-acre palace in Dalmatia in the private sphere, or from Augustus' conversion of Rome into a city of marble to Diocletian's thirty acres of public baths in the public sphere. Even quite modest cities could achieve the Pont du Gard, which supplied fresh water to a not very important provincial town in southern Gaul, or the vast amphitheatre of Puteoli. But what did they do otherwise? In the century following Alexander's conquest of Egypt, the Ptolemies thoroughly reconstructed that country. They reclaimed great quantities of land, they improved and extended the irrigation system, they introduced new crops, they moved Egypt belatedly from the bronze age into the iron age, they made administrative and managerial changes—all in the interest of the royal revenue, and all amounting to nothing more than giving Egypt the advantages of already existing Greek technology and Greek processes. Simultaneously, the Ptolemies founded and financed the Museum at Alexandria, for two centuries the main western centre of scientific research and invention. Great things emerged from the Museum, in military technology and in ingenious mechanical toys. But no one, not even the Ptolemies themselves, who would have profited directly and handsomely, thought to turn the energy and inventiveness of a Ctesibius to agricultural or industrial technology. The contrast with the Royal Society in England is inescapable.

So is the contrast between the later Roman emperors and Louis XIV, whose armies within what had been a single Roman province, as Gibbon pointed out, were greater than those any ancient emperor could muster. From the middle of the third century, the numerical inadequacy of the armies who had to resist continuing and growing Germanic and Persian incursions could not long have escaped the notice of those responsible for the empire. Nothing could be done: neither the available manpower nor food production nor transport could bear a burden greater than the one imposed by Diocletian when he doubled the army's strength, at least on paper. Taxes and compulsory services were increased, the burden falling largely on those least able to bear it. Men and means were shifted to the main danger points, sometimes benefiting frontier provinces at the expense of the others. But nothing could be done to raise the productivity of the empire as a whole or to redistribute the load. For that a complete structural transformation would have been required.

VI

The State and the Economy

AT THE very end of the fifth century B.C., a wealthy defendant, charged with some serious offence against the Athenian state but otherwise unknown, began his address to the court in this revealing, though legally irrelevant, way (Lysias 21.1–5):

"In the archonship of Theopompus [411/10 B.C.], having been designated a *choregos* for the competition in tragedy, I spent 3000 drachmas, and another 1200 two months later when I won the prize with the men's chorus at the festival of the Thargelia." The following year "I spent 800 drachmas on the Pyrrhic dancers in the Greater Panathenaea, and at the Dionysia I was victor with a men's chorus which cost me 1500 drachmas, counting the dedication of a tripod." The next year, "300 for the cyclic chorus at the Lesser Panathenaea, and all that time, I was trierarch for seven years and laid out six talents [36,000 drachmas] for that. . . . Hardly had I disembarked when I became gymnasiarch for the festival of Prometheus. I was the victor and spent 1200 drachmas. Then I was *choregos* for a boys' chorus which cost me 1500 drachmas." The next year "I was the victorious *choregos* for the comic poet Cephisodorus and I spent 1600 drachmas, counting the dedication of the props, and I was also *choregos* for beardless Pyrrhic dancers at the Lesser Panathenaea, at a cost of 700 drachmas. I was also victor with a trireme in the Sunium race, spending 1500 drachmas," and there were various minor rituals, too, the cost of which came to more than 3000 drachmas.

The technical Greek term for these expensive public activities was *leitourgia*, an old word from which our ecclesiastical word "liturgy" eventually emerged by an easy development (work for the people → service to the state → service to the divinity).[1] The Greek liturgy was rooted in the age when the community was still inchoate, when the aristocratic households performed essential public services, such as the construction of a temple, by expending labour and materials at their private disposal. In the classical city-state the liturgy had become both compulsory and honorific at the same time, a device whereby the non-bureaucratic state got certain things done, not by paying for them from the treasury but by assigning to richer individuals direct responsibility for both the costs and the operation itself.

The honorific element was underscored in two ways. First, the chief sphere of liturgical activity was always religion: in Demosthenes' day there were at least 97 annual liturgical appointments in Athens for the festivals, rising to over 118 in a (quadrennial) Panathenaic year.[2] In Athens and some other cities (though the evidence outside Athens is very thin), the trierarchy, personal command of a naval vessel for one year, was the other main liturgy. But there were as yet no liturgies for wall-building or street-cleaning. Second, there was a free, competitive element, what the Greeks called an *agon*: the holder of a liturgy was not taxed a specific sum but assigned a specific task, which he could perform more or less effectively, at greater or smaller personal expense. Our man boasted that in eight years his contribution exceeded the legal requirement by more than three times. No one could check that claim, but we can feel confident in the string of victories. Even after due allowance for exaggeration, the outlay was enormous: the total alleged for the eight years, war years at that, was about nine and a half talents, more than twenty times the minimum property requirement for hoplite service.

No one today boasts in a persuasive way of the size of his income tax, and certainly not that he pays three times as much as the collector demands. But it was standard practice in the Athenian courts, and sometimes in the popular assembly, to boast about one's own liturgies and to accuse one's opponent of dodging his. A *topos*, a rhetorical commonplace, we are often told. No doubt, but skilled orators did not employ *topoi* that did not strike a responsive chord in the audience. The honorific element was meaningful, a reflection of the complexities of the Greek notion of "community". It is often overlooked that Aristotle defined man as being not only a *zoön politikon*, a *polis*-being, but also a *zoön oikonomikon*, a household-being, and a *zoön koinonikon*, a being designed by nature to live in a *koinonia*. That word is not easily translatable, except in very narrow contexts; here we may say "community" provided that the word is understood more broadly than in current popular usage, in the spirit, for example, of the early Christian communities.

The obvious difficulty with the city-state as a community, with its stress on mutual sharing of both burdens and benefits, was the hard fact that its members were unequal. The most troublesome inequality was not between town and country, not between classes, but simply between rich and poor. How did one overcome that in a true community? The democratic answer was, in part, through the liturgy-system, whereby the rich carried a large financial burden and were recompensed by corresponding honours. "Expending my resources for your enjoyment" was how one fourth-century orator summed up the liturgy principle (Aeschines 1.11). Those who disapproved of democracy placed the accent differently: "the common people," wrote an anonymous fifth-century pamphleteer, "demand payment for singing, running, dancing and sailing on ships in order that they may get the money and the rich become poorer" (Ps.-Xenophon, *Constitution of Athens* 1.13).

The duality inherent in the liturgy system—the honour of being a public benefactor on the one hand, the financial expenditure on the other hand—came to an end in the later Roman Empire. By then the liturgies (*munera* in Latin) were performed solely because men were compelled to take them up, which meant, in practice, that membership of certain key bodies, the municipal senates and the appropriate *collegia*, was now compulsory and, more than that, compulsory in successive generations, hereditary.[3] That is a familiar story, but we must resist the view that it was nothing more than another brutal innovation by the military absolutism of the late Empire.[4] On the contrary, it was the irresistible end of a long development that can be traced (but has not been) in stages, though not in graphs.*

The moment Alexander's successors established their autocratic, bureaucratic monarchies, liturgies proliferated, their range was extended and they grew increasingly burdensome. The Roman emperors then took over the Hellenistic practice, universalized it and slowly schematized it. The imperial upper strata, Roman citizens of senatorial or equestrian rank, were exempt (and veterans were partially so). The propertyless made their contribution in corvée labour. That left the provincial landowning aristocracy, the so-called curial class, with the main burden insofar as they were unable to pass it to *coloni*. One group of important liturgies in fact came to be classified as "patrimonial": they were assigned not to persons but to specific landed estates as a permanent charge which was transferred with change of ownership. Among these, in the later Empire, I cannot resist singling out membership in the *corpus naviculariorum*, the body of shipowners responsible for the transport of government corn.[5]

Municipal magistrates throughout the Roman empire, unpaid unlike the privileged holders of imperial posts, were expected to offer *summae honorariae*, donations for games, civic buildings, baths and other amenities. By the first century A.D. these *summae*, which were instituted in the late Republic, became a regular obligation. The conventional minima varied from city to city; the generosity of office holders varied enormously from individual to individual; the old honorific element remained fairly strong, as the competition for offices shows.[6] But the honour for most men lay in the

---

* Here and elsewhere I ignore the "free" and "immune" cities in the Roman Empire. Despite their own pompous and noisy claims, echoed in modern books, they were a negligible element in the imperial structure.

office as such and in the benefaction to their local community, whereas the mounting liturgies were another matter, in particular the large and increasingly costly group linked with the mainten-ance of the imperial roads,[7] the imperial post and transport system, the army corn supply and army billeting. Hence com-pulsions began to show themselves in the reign of Hadrian, long before the end of the conventional Golden Age.[8]

The history of liturgies thus documents the not new point that "state" is too broad a category. Any inquiry into the relationship between the state and the economy will have to differentiate not only between the autonomous community, the city-state, and the autocratic monarchy, but, in the latter type, also between the Hellenistic monarchies and the Roman. Essentially, the Hellenistic monarchies, whether Ptolemaic or Seleucid or Attalid, were self-contained territorial units ruled from within, whereas the Roman emperors, at least into the third century of our era, continued to differentiate sharply between a minority of Roman citizens and the majority of subjects who were not, between Italy and the provinces. In both types there were internal distinctions based on order and status, between a Greek citizen of Alexandria and an Egyptian peasant in Kerkeosiris, as between *honestiores* and *humiliores*, and the Hellenistic rulers had foreign possessions from time to time. Nevertheless, the main distinction remains valid, and, though it does not follow automatically that there were con-sequent differences in their impact on the economy, the possibility must always be kept in mind.

For analytical purposes, however, there was one common element that cut across the structural differences. The authority of the state was total, of the city-states as of the autocracies, and it extended to everyone who resided within the territorial borders (indeed to everyone who resided wherever its writ ran). Classical Greeks and Republican Romans possessed a considerable measure of freedom, in speech, in political debate, in their business activity, even in religion. However, they lacked, and would have been appalled by, inalienable rights. There were no theoretical limits to the power of the state, no activity, no sphere of human behaviour, in which the state could not legitimately intervene provided the decision was properly taken for any reason that was held to be valid by a legitimate authority. Freedom meant the rule of law and participation in the decision-making process. Within that definition there was infinite room for state intervention, as much as there was under Greek tyrants, Hellenistic monarchs or Roman emperors. Only the methods varied. Therefore, if a Greek state failed to set maximum interest rates, for example, that has to be explained in some concrete way, not by reference to rights or to private spheres beyond the reach of the state.

Nor, I need hardly add, can any specific instance of non-interference in the economy be explained by a theory of *laissez faire*. Neither that doctrine nor any other can exist without the prior concept of "the economy", on the absence of which I surely need not repeat myself at this late stage. There was of course enough empirical knowledge, without generalized concepts and theories, for *ad hoc* decisions in one or another situation. And there were economic consequences of actions taken for other reasons, some foreseen, others not. Economic policy and unintended economic consequences are difficult to disentangle, especially in a society in which "economic elements are inextricably joined to political and religious factors",[9] but we must make the attempt.

Let me illustrate. When Rome punished Rhodes by establishing a free port at Delos, Roman senators would not have been unaware that economic benefits would follow for the merchants trading through Delos. Did that weigh in the decision, which was basically political, or was it a consequence of incidental significance, even though not an undesirable one? May we say, with one economic historian, that this was an outstanding instance of the "economic penetration" that followed all Roman conquests, "that the Rhodian circulation of goods steadily declined and passed into the hands of Roman competitors"?[10] The fact that Polybius is satisfied with a purely political explanation may not count for much, but it is surely decisive that most of the beneficiaries at Delos were not Romans but men from other Italian communities, including the old Greek colonies of southern Italy, whose mercantile interests were not a factor in Roman decision-making in the mid-second century B.C.[11]

Or, where should we place the stress in the universal Greek restriction of land ownership to citizens, or in the two second-century attempts to compel newly created Roman senators from the provinces to acquire estates in Italy? These laws and measures had economic ramifications, but what was the intent? In a society as complex as the Greek or Roman, it is hard to conceive of any action by a state which lacked an economic component, which neither involved disbursements, public or private, nor had an impact on one or another aspect of the economy. In that sense, all public acts are also economic acts, a meaningless statement. To appreciate how the ancient state made its mark on the economy (and vice versa, the economy on the state), it is necessary not only to differentiate aims and consequences but also to place the accent correctly (I avoid the word "cause"), to pinpoint the interests as precisely as possible. Thus, in 67 B.C. Pompey cleared the eastern Mediterranean of a considerable infestation of pirates based in Cilicia in southern Asia Minor. An uncomplicated action, it would appear, yet one is entitled to ask how Pompey succeeded in a few months when no Roman had made any impact in the preceding hundred years. The answer reveals the existence of a familiar conflict of interests. The pirates had been the chief suppliers of slaves for the Italian and Sicilian estates, a Roman interest which was paramount until two new factors entered the picture: Roman magistrates and Roman revenues were now subject to attack, and piratical activity in the Adriatic was beginning to imperil the corn supply of the city of Rome. Then, and only then, did Rome take effective action.[12]

War and empire provide the best test case. Underneath lay an openness about exploitation, characteristic of any society in which slavery and other forms of dependent labour are widespread, an openness that required no justification, no ideology of conquest or empire. In a passage in the *Politics* (1333b38–34a1) that is quoted less frequently in histories of ethics than some others, Aristotle included among the reasons why statesmen must know the art of warfare, "in order to become masters of those who deserve to be enslaved". Few, if any, would have disagreed. We should not forget that no Athenian or Roman is known who proposed the abandonment of the empire. There were disagreements over tactics and timing, not over empire as such.

Nevertheless, the history of ancient warfare runs a great gamut in this respect. In the archaic period there were local wars enough which were nothing more than raids for booty; occasionally in later times, too, as when Philip II, Alexander's father, is said to have mounted a successful invasion of Scythia in 339 B.C. for the sole purpose of replenishing his treasury.[13] When Caesar went off to Gaul, his aim was not merely to gain glory for himself and un-developed territory for his country. On the other hand, not a single conquest by a Roman emperor was motivated by the possibility of imperial enrichment; they were all, without exception, the result of political-strategic calculations, and, though the armies picked up what booty they could and the emperors added some new provinces to the empire, the economic element was incidental and insignificant, except normally on the debit side, in the costs to the treasury and in the losses of manpower. As early as 54 B.C. Cicero wrote to his friend Atticus (*Letters to Atticus* 4.16.7) that Caesar's second expedition to Britain was causing concern in Rome; among other things, it was now clear that there was no silver on the island and "no hope for booty other than captives, among whom I believe you cannot expect any highly qualified in literature or music". There was no change of heart in subsequent generations—conquest still led to exploitation—but a change in the conqueror's circumstances, in the Roman capacity to conquer, and then to hold, beyond the distant frontiers already reached.

"Exploitation" and "imperialism" are, in the end, too broad as categories of analysis. Like "state", they require specification. What forms did they take, and not take, in the Roman empire, the greatest and most complex in ancient history? For the Roman state, the provinces were a main source of revenue through taxes. A small number of Romans made large fortunes as provincial governors, tax-collectors and moneylenders in the provinces during the Republic, in the imperial service under the emperors. There were rich Romans who acquired extensive domains in the provinces, which they normally held as absentee landlords; there were also poorer Romans, especially veterans, who were re-settled in the provinces, and the poorest of all, the plebs of the city of Rome, received the crumbs of *panem et circenses*. However, Romans neither monopolized the provincial soil nor denied local people the opportunity to become, or to continue as, wealthy landowners themselves. On the contrary, the trend was towards a provincialization of the imperial aristocracy, as more and more wealthy provincials also profited from the *pax Romana*, gained Roman citizenship, and, in not a few cases, even senatorial status.

What is missing in this picture is commercial or capitalist exploitation. The ancient economy had its own form of cheap labour and therefore did not exploit provinces in that way. Nor did it have excess capital seeking the more profitable investment outlets we associate with colonialism. The expanded commercial activity of the first two centuries of the Empire was not a Roman phenomenon. It was shared by many peoples within the empire and was no part of imperial exploitation; there was no competition between Romans and non-Romans for markets.[14] Hence, there were no commercial or commercially inspired wars in Roman history, or at any time in antiquity. They exist in our books, to be sure: the seventh-century B.C. war over the Lelantine Plain in Euboea, the Peloponnesian War, Rome's wars with Carthage, even Trajan's badly miscalculated and expensive assault on Parthia have all been attributed to commercial conflicts by one historian or another. On investigation, however, it becomes evident that these historians have been bemused by the Anglo-Dutch wars; they have failed to face up to the critical question put to one of them some years ago: "I wonder whether the author means the competition for markets or for the supply of commodities. In either case, what does this mean in the context of Greek technique and psychology about 430 B.C.? As long as these preliminary questions are not even posed, the high-sounding 'explanation' is a mere phrase."[15] When they are posed, the evidence demonstrates that the "high-sounding explanation" is unwarranted and false.

In a recent, massive monograph on maritime commerce in the Roman Empire, we read the following: "Favourable as they were to economic activity, the emperors, whether a monster like Nero or a wise man like Trajan, accomplished all sorts of great works in its favour: the creation or enlargement of harbours, the cleaning and restoration to service of the canal connecting the Pelusiac arm of the Nile with the Red Sea. . . . the erection of lighthouses at port entrances and dangerous points. . . . We have already seen, furthermore, how, because of the requirements in feeding the city of Rome, the same emperors were led to adopt certain measures in favour of those who devoted all or part of their activity to this need. Stated differently, . . . the Empire was preoccupied with economic problems: does that mean that it placed its hands on trade, that the almost total freedom at the beginning of the Empire was now giving way to the beginning of state control? Benefit does not mean control—trade retained its freedom."[16]

Putting aside the recurrent inability to separate the problem of feeding the populace of Rome from economic activity in general, and the touchingly old-fashioned conception of "freedom of trade" —the failure I stressed earlier to distinguish between non-interference and a doctrine of *laissez faire*—we may ask just what M. Rougé is saying about economic policy. He might have added a second category of state activities, the extensive police activity devoted to enforcing the criminal law with respect to sales in general and market regulations in particular. He might then have remembered his own account of the imperial harbour-taxes, usually but not always $2\frac{1}{2}$ per cent *ad valorem*, collected in probably every major port in the Mediterranean, and of the frequent municipal tolls, from which only the imperial *annona* (corn supply), army supply and exceptionally favoured individuals were exempt.[17]

The first point to be noticed is that, apart from scale, nothing in this catalogue of great works in favour of commerce is either new or peculiarly imperial. Under the Empire, there were private benefactors and municipal governments who were also concerned

with harbour installations and the rest. Earlier, every city-state did
what it could in that direction—no emperor was required to
develop the Piraeus—as it policed the markets and then collected
tolls and taxes from all and sundry, on exports as on imports, with
the same narrow range of largely honorific exemptions. Ancient
society was, after all, civilized and required amenities. That they
improved their harbours in order both to meet their naval requirements and to satisfy their material wants is no great cause for
congratulations. We should rather ask what else they did (or did
not do), and particularly what Roman emperors, with their un-
precedently greater power and greater resources, their control
over nearly two million square miles, did or did not do that was
significantly different from what little Athens or Corinth had done
in the fifth century B.C.

"Satisfaction of material wants" is the key concept, not synonymous with the needs of the economy, of trade as such, or of a
mercantile class. Sometimes the latter was a beneficiary (though
not always), and when that happened it was as a by-product.
When other interests cut across, and not infrequently disturbed,
the satisfaction of material wants, they were political-military
interests, among which I include the interests of the public
treasury. The most dramatic example is the late Roman one of the
elimination of "the private contractor and the merchant" from
"a considerable sector of the economy".[18] Again we must not think
of a sudden innovation by Diocletian. When Sicily became a
Roman province in the third century B.C. and paid levies in kind,
the first important step was taken on the long, tortuous path of
withdrawing the corn supply for the city of Rome and the armies,
and eventually of many other imperial requirements, primarily
but not exclusively military, from the play of the market.[19] The
emperors thus created their military-industrial complex, in which
the balance of forces was the precise opposite of ours, for the profits, insofar as that word is applicable, went to the government and
its agents.[20] Such measures entailed not only a heavy burden on
the lower classes but also a reduction in the economic potential of
the wealthy class just below the political and social élite and an

artificial regional imbalance in costs and benefits. These effects were again a by-product, not a policy or an objective. And the élite finally responded by retiring to their estates into a condition of maximum self-sufficiency, withdrawing their custom from the industrial producers in the city and adding to the damage already wreaked by the government.[21]

The distinction between satisfaction of material wants and economic policy was revealed in another way during the long period when the Mediterranean world was fragmented. Strictly speaking, access to due process of law was a prerogative of the members of each individual community, and, though outsiders were *de facto* not normally denied lawful relationships, some more formal *de iure* procedures were obviously desirable, and sometimes required, once trade and movement beyond the boundaries of the community became common and essential. It was necessary to *assure* those who bought and sold abroad that their private contracts would be honoured, that their persons and goods would be protected by law, that their communities would be immune from reprisal in the case of unpaid debts or unsettled disputes. The early Romans achieved this end in two ways, by mutual agreements with their neighbours, first the Latins and then other Italic peoples, and by repeating the Etruscan precedent and entering into a series of commercial treaties with Carthage, defining conditions and delimiting spheres of trade in brief formulations.[22] There is no reason to believe, however, that the expanding Roman state extended and developed these methods outside Italy, and indeed no reason why it should have. Henceforth, the conqueror made and enforced the rules unilaterally.

As for the Greek city-states, they emerged in an ethnic, political and "international" environment different from the Roman, and they developed a different practice. In the fifth century B.C., they began to contract rudimentary agreements, called *symbola*, between pairs of states, providing for lawful procedures in disputes (of any type) between individuals.[23] Although traders were beneficiaries, they were not the only ones. The existing documentation, admittedly thin, is marked by a complete absence of anything

11

we can recognize as commercial clauses, or even references. This is not to say that commercial agreements were never entered into. Aristotle (*Rhetoric* 1360a12–13) included food supply (*trophē*) — his choice of words is noteworthy — among the subjects on which a political leader must be proficient so as to negotiate inter-city agreements.[24] Yet concrete examples are hard to find in the sources. In the fourth century B.C., the rulers of the half-Greek, half-Scythian kingdom in the Crimea, known as the kingdom of the Bosporus, granted Athens what we should call favoured-nation status. The Crimea was then the centre for the distribution of south Russian grain to Greece, and ships destined for Athens, the largest customer, were given priority of lading and a reduction of harbour-taxes. The grateful city repaid the royal family with honorary citizenship. But it is far from certain that this very important, and relatively long-standing, arrangement was ever formalized by treaty.[25]

"Ships destined for Athens", not "Athenian ships" — the concern was *trophē*, not the interests of Athenian merchants, exporters or shipowners. In the middle of the fourth century B.C., Athens took a new step to facilitate, and therefore to encourage, the activity of foreign traders. A new action at law was introduced, called literally a "commercial action", *dikē emporikē*, for the speedy settlement of disputes arising from commercial transactions in Athens (and those alone) during the sailing season. The magistrates in charge were instructed to bring the cases before the normal juries within one month, to admit citizens and non-citizens on an equal footing, whether or not there were *symbolai* with the cities of origin of the foreigners involved.[26] Athens thus guaranteed any outsider who brought commodities to Athens full protection of the law and speedy jurisdiction. Three points are to be noticed. The first is the public need for non-Athenian merchants, so powerful that Athens did not demand reciprocal guarantees for her own merchants abroad. The second observation is that there is no trace of the spread of these specifically and explicitly commercial actions to any other Greek state, classical or Hellenistic; the others continued cheerfully with their reliance on unilateral good faith and their primitive mutual agreements against reprisal, until Roman conquest ended the political autonomy which made them necessary.[27] And the third point is that the encouragement of metics stopped short at clearly demarcated lines.

Xenophon's *Poroi*, to which I have referred repeatedly, was written in precisely the period, and the atmosphere, when the Athenian commercial actions were introduced. It is no coincidence that his proposals in that pamphlet for increasing the public revenues were based on two groups in the population, the slaves in the silver mines and the metics, chiefly in the Piraeus, the harbour-town. His scheme opens with six suggestions for increasing the number of metics in Athens: (1) release them from the burdensome obligation of service in the infantry; (2) admit them to the cavalry, now an honorific service; (3) permit "worthy" metics to buy building-lots in the city on which to construct houses for themselves; (4) offer prizes to market officials for just and speedy settlement of disputes; (5) give reserved seats in the theatre and other forms of hospitality to deserving foreign merchants; (6) build more lodging-houses and hotels in the Piraeus and increase the number of market-places. Hesitantly he adds a seventh, that the state might build its own merchant fleet, and that is all.

The practicality or impracticality of the proposals do not interest me, nor do I suggest that Xenophon was the beginning and end of ancient wisdom, but it is notable that all this comes under the heading of "public revenues"—metics are one of the best sources, he says explicitly—and that Xenophon's ideas, bold in some respects, never really broke through the conventional limits.[28] It was bold to propose a breach in the land-citizen tie to the extent of allowing metics to own house property (for their own use only), but it is significant that he went no further than that. Nor did he touch the head-tax, the *metoikion*, a drachma a month for males, half a drachma for females, imposed on every non-citizen who resided in the city beyond a very short period, perhaps no more than a month.[29] Not only would such a proposal have defeated his purpose of bringing more metics into the city in order to increase the public revenues but it would have had an unacceptable political overtone: any form of direct tax on citizens was condemned as tyrannical (except in war emergencies), and the *metoikion*, a poll tax, the direct tax *par excellence*, was thus the degrading mark of the outsider.

It was a common practice among Greek cities, increasingly so in the Hellenistic period, to honour foreign "benefactors" by reserved seats in the theatre (precisely as Xenophon proposed), by equality of taxation, *isotelia*, which meant exemption from the *metoikion*, and sometimes by exemption from harbour-taxes. The numerous brief epigraphical texts at our disposal rarely inform us about the grounds for being hailed a "benefactor". It is certain, however, that in the great majority of instances the services were political or philanthropic, not services to trade and industry, and certainly not to export. Not infrequently, indeed, the exemption was specifically restricted to goods acquired and taken abroad for personal use.[30]

In any event, the very existence of honorary personal tax exemption tells us much of itself. It tells us that what we should call the impact of the tax system on the economy was not within the Greek conceptual world. Never is there a hint that exemption from harbour-taxes was conceived as a contribution (fair or unfair) to the recipient's competitive position in trade or manufacture; it had the same standing as reserved seats in the theatre. Taxes were not used as economic levers; they were not even reexamined when they were obvious brakes on the economy (again, as always, with due allowance for commonsense limits). Just consider the implications of a universal harbour-tax, levied at the same rate on all imports and all exports. There was no idea of protecting home production, or encouraging essential imports or looking after the balance of trade; there was not even an exemption normally made for the corn supply,[31] to which so much effort, legislative and sometimes military, was directed.

Nor is there evidence of calculation leading to a choice among alternative sources of revenue, as to which might be better or worse for the economy. Xenophon's argument about the limitless demand for silver is a rare and rudimentary exception. Choices were made by tradition, convention and considerations of social psychology, notably in the combination of the avoidance of a property tax with the imposition of liturgies. Sometimes the system failed—either revenue fell far too short or a powerful group felt itself, rightly or wrongly, to be squeezed beyond the (to them) acceptable maximum. Then there was *stasis*, civil war, with ensuing confiscations and sometimes new legislation—and the cycle began all over again: political overturn did not lead to a reconsideration of taxation and public expenditure in any but the narrowest power and social-structure terms.

And what, to return to a question I asked earlier, did the Roman emperors contribute that was new? The answer is, Virtually nothing. Both the imperial harbour-taxes and the local municipal tolls were purely revenue devices, levied in the traditional way on everything passing through in either direction. Only grain destined for the city of Rome and commodities destined for the army were exempt. The whole tax structure was regressive, and became increasingly so as the years went on.* Roman emperors were as far from Thomas Mun and the kings of his day in their thinking as were the small Greek city-states. Meeting food shortages, army needs or senatorial consumers' wants by imports —that was not what Mun meant by "treasure by foreign trade". Had someone brought Charles I the invention for unbreakable glass I mentioned in my previous chapter, he might well have asked for a patent. The Roman inventor merely asked for a reward because none of the standard mercantilist devices, whereby the royal treasury profited while encouraging enterprise —patents, charters, monopolies, subsidies—was employed in antiquity.

Not that emperors had any aversion either to favouring individuals materially or to monopolies as such. All ancient states retained at least regalian rights over mineral resources. Beyond that, monopolies in the Greek city-states were rare emergency measures. The Hellenistic kings, however, quickly

* The liturgies might be thought to redress the balance were it not for the exemption of the aristocracy.

followed the Near Eastern precedent of monopolizing a wide range of economic activities—again usually by regulation rather than by direct operation—and the Roman emperors followed suit.[32] But the motive was strictly fiscal. There was no claim that imperial monopoly enhanced production or productivity, no more interest in such matters in this respect than in the attitude to technology.

One monopoly which all ancient states retained, city or empire, was the right to coin. They did not, however, accompany that prerogative with an obligation to maintain a sufficient supply of coins, except when the state itself needed them for payments, usually to troops.[33] Money was coin and nothing else, and shortage of coins was chronic, both in total numbers and in the availability of preferred types or denominations. Yet not even in periods of so-called credit crisis, as we have seen, did the state make any serious effort to relieve the shortage beyond occasional, doomed efforts to compel hoarders to disgorge their stocks. Again the emperors, Hellenistic and Roman, showed no tendency to move beyond city-state thinking. Indeed, the time came, early in the Roman Empire, when the emperors could not resist taking advantage of their power and their coining monopoly to enrich themselves by debasing the coinage, a procedure that hardly contributed to healthy coin circulation.

One problem the emperors no longer had to face was the coexistence of a large variety of independent coinages (apart from purely local bronze coins), minted on different standards and with uneven skill by the innumerable independent authorities of the Greek world. The Greek passion for coins, and for beautiful coins at that, is well known and sometimes misunderstood. For a long time this passion was not shared by many of their most advanced neighbours, Phoenicians, Egyptians, Etruscans, Romans, because it was essentially a political phenomenon, "a piece of local vanity, patriotism or advertisement with no far-reaching importance" (the Near Eastern world got along perfectly well for millennia, even in its extensive trade, with metallic currency exchanged by weight, without coining the metal).[34] Hence the insistence, with the important exception of Athens, on artistic coins, economically a nonsense (no money-changer gave a better rate for a four-drachma Syracusan coin because it was signed by Euainetos). Hence, too, the general avoidance among the Greeks of official debasement and the ferocity of the penalties for counterfeiting or plating coins, linked with treason, not with paltry market offences.*

A large variety of coin is a nuisance, profiting only the ubiquitous money-changers, though we should not exaggerate, as anyone familiar with Renaissance trade will know. The extent of the nuisance varied according to the metal. Bronze gave no trouble since it was reserved for small denominations for local use. Silver and gold had fairly well established, traditional ratios that changed slowly, and the money-changers were capable of testing weight and purity.† Only the gold-silver alloy, white gold or electrum, was beyond control: whether minted from a natural alloy or alloyed artificially, the popular electrum staters of Cyzicus in Asia Minor could not be assayed before Archimedes' discovery of specific gravity, and they therefore circulated at a conventional value.[35]

Given the political sense of coinage, it is not surprising that the autonomous Greek states made no substantial effort to abate the nuisance. Agreements between states about exchange ratios, for example, were so rare as to be effectively non-existent.[36] What is significant in the present context is the persistent failure to provide coins of sufficiently large denomination to be adequate for large payments. In his lawsuit against his guardians, Demosthenes at one point (27.58) said to the jury, with a rhetorical flourish, "Some of you" saw Theogenes "count out the money in the Agora." The reference is to a payment of 3000 drachmas, and counting that amount out before witnesses in four-drachma

---

* The Romans maintained this severe attitude to counterfeiting once they began to coin.

† Before Alexander, gold was minted primarily by the Persians but circulated among the Greeks as well. Later it was also minted by Macedon and the Hellenistic kings.

pieces, the commonest and largest normal Greek silver denomination, would have been quite an operation, especially if the payee challenged the weight or purity of many of the pieces. That, I suggest, is why Persian gold darics and Cyzicene electrum staters, each worth more than twenty silver drachmas, were so popular in the fifth and fourth centuries B.C.[37]

Individuals were thus left to make out as best they could, unaided by the state, relying on their accumulated experience and on the money-changers and, to a limited extent, giving preference to certain coins, such as Athenian owls and Cyzicene staters.[38] A fourth-century B.C. decree from the Greek city of Olbia on the north shore of the Black Sea pretty well sums up the pattern.[39] It lays down four basic rules: (1) only Olbian silver coins may be used for transactions within the city; (2) the exchange ratio between electrum and local silver coins shall be fixed by the state; (3) other coins may be exchanged "on whatever basis the parties agree"; and (4) there shall be an unlimited right to import and export coins of all kinds. Apart from the understandable intervention in the difficult electrum case, the rule was thus total non-interference by the state in monetary matters, save for the political insistence on the employment of local coins. No preference was given to Olbians over foreigners: all parties were bound by the same rules; an Olbian who went abroad to sell wheat and brought back foreign coins had to pay the same discount to the money-changers before he could spend his money in Olbia as a foreigner who came to Olbia with his native, or any other, coins.

Equally political was the fifth-century B.C. Athenian decree which laid down the rule that Athenian coins alone were to be current for all purposes within the Athenian empire.[40] The precise date of the decree is disputed; one day it may be decided on epigraphical grounds (with perhaps the help of numismatic analysis), but not, as has been attempted, by injecting complex policy considerations into the discussion, such as the argument that it smacks of Cleon rather than Pericles. The political element is unmistakable: the unprecedented volume of Athenian military and administrative payments, at a time when foreign tribute was the largest source of public revenue, was much facilitated by a uniform coinage, and Athens was now able and willing to demonstrate who was master within the empire by denying the subject-states the traditional symbol of autonomy, their own coins. The Athenians may also have aimed at mint profits, but we shall not know until the missing bit of the text stating the mint charge for re-coining is found.

It is also held that there was a commercial motive, a desire to give Athenian merchants the advantage over others. The logic escapes me. Everyone had been equally the victim of a profusion of mints; had the Athenians been able to enforce their decree for a sufficient number of years, everyone within the empire would have benefited slightly but equally, the Athenians no more than the others, questions of pride and patriotism apart. Only the money-changers would have been the losers, and no one has yet suggested that such a powerful decree was passed just to hurt them. The decree was anyway a failure, even before the empire was destroyed by the Athenian defeat in the Peloponnesian War. Its aims were not, and could not, be achieved until the emperors, Hellenistic and Roman, abolished the political autonomy of the cities and thereby removed the basis of the multiple coinages.

The Athenians were equally ruthless, and more successful, in employing their imperial power, while it lasted, to secure their food and timber supplies.[41] The ancient world, with its low level of technology, limited methods of distribution, and restricted ability to preserve foodstuffs, lived with the permanent threat of famine, especially in the cities. In Aristotle's day, long after the empire was gone (and no doubt earlier although we do not know how much earlier), the Athenian *kyria ekklesia*, the principal Assembly meeting in each prytany, was required to consider "corn and the defence of the country", a most interesting bracketing (*Constitution of Athens* 43.4). By that time, too, there were thirty-five *sitophylakes*, corn-guardians (increased from an original total of ten), an unusually large board whose duties, as defined by Aristotle (*ibid.* 51.3), were "to see to it first that the grain was sold in the market at a just price, then that the millers sold meal in proportion to the price of barley, that the bakers sold bread in proportion to the price of wheat, that the bread had the weight they had fixed." Just price was a medieval concept, not an ancient one, and this interference by the state, altogether exceptional in its permanence, is a sufficient measure of the urgency of the food problem. And when this and all the other legislative measures I have mentioned on other occasions failed, the state, as a last recourse, appointed officials called *sitonai*, corn-buyers, who sought supplies wherever they could find them, raised public subscriptions for the necessary funds, introduced price reductions and rationing.[42]

The institution of *sitonai* was originally a temporary measure, but from the late fourth century B.C. there was a growing tendency to convert them into permanent officials. The widespread shortages of 330–326 B.C. perhaps provided the stimulus.[43] It was probably in the same period that Cyrene distributed 1,200,000 Attic medimni of corn, equivalent to a year's rations for some 150,000 men, to forty-one communities scattered over the Greek mainland and the islands: 100,000 medimni to Athens, 50,000 each to Corinth, to Argos and to Larisa in Thessaly, 30,000 to Rhodes, 72,600 to Alexander's mother Olympias, 50,000 to his sister Cleopatra, and so on. The text of the inscription recording this action says that the city of Cyrene gave (*edoke*) the grain.[44] Some scholars are sceptical, but there are authentic cases of gifts of grain, one from the Egyptian Pharaoh to the Athenians in 445 B.C. Then there was no question of sale at reduced prices. The gift was distributed gratis, but only to citizens, all of whom were eligible, in a survival of the old principle that the goods of the community belonged to its members and should, under certain circumstances, be shared out among them.[45]

The "certain circumstances" came about when there were windfalls or when conquest and empire brought in booty and tribute. When, in 58 B.C., Rome embarked on its long history of distributing free corn (and later other foodstuffs) within the city, resident citizens were eligible regardless of means, and no one else. That principle was maintained until the Severi, early in the third century of our era, converted the food distribution into a dole for the Roman poor, regardless of political status, thus marking the effective end of citizenship as a formal status within the empire.[46] When Constantinople became the eastern capital in the fourth century, the poor of that city joined the Roman poor as recipients. There the emperors' interest stopped.[47] Although there are traces of food distributions in other cities of the empire, Alexandria or Antioch for example, they were irregular, and, more to the point, they were more often the gift of individual benefactors than the responsibility of either the emperor or the local municipality.[48]

Inevitably, the surviving Roman literature repeats malicious stories about rich men accepting their share of the free corn and about others who freed their slaves in order to pass the maintenance costs to the state. Some of these stories are probably true, but there can be no doubt that free corn was always conceived primarily as a welfare measure for the poor. What else was done? There was the spasmodic income from public works, the irregular or indirect gains from war and empire, the benefit to the peasants of the absence of a land tax (wherever that was the case), the occasional dole to the physically incapacitated. Primarily, however, one dealt with the poor, when circumstances made it essential to deal with them, by getting rid of them at someone else's expense.

The story of what we call "colonization" in antiquity, an imprecise term, was long and complex. The centuries-long expansion of the Greek world, beginning before 750 B.C., which led to the establishment of Greek communities all the way from the eastern end of the Black Sea to Marseilles in France, was a hiving-off of surplus citizens to foreign lands, sometimes by conquest, and not always with the consent of those sent away.[49] By the fifth century B.C., such possibilities were being closed down, but opportunities were still quickly seized when they arose. There are the examples of the military colonies (cleruchies) established by Athens on land taken from rebellious members of her empire; of the perhaps 60,000 migrants brought to Sicily, with the co-operation of their home-cities, by Timoleon in the fourth century B.C. after he had conquered half the island; of the large, but incalculable, number of Greeks who migrated to the east under Alexander's successors. The Roman practice of establishing "colonies" in conquered territory needs no detailed examination: it, too, was a hiving-off of the poor at the expense of others. But colonization is an evasion, not a solution, of the needs of the poor, and there came a time when settlement land was no longer available.

During much of the history of Roman colonization, veterans were the predominant element. That is a reflection of the complex history of the Roman army, specifically of its slow professionalization. Traditionally, military service in the city-states was an obligation of the wealthier sector of the citizenry, those who could afford the requisite heavy armour; and though the state tried to pay them enough for their maintenance while they were on active duty, it could not always do so.[50] They were not relieved of their obligations by non-payment, and they expected no material rewards for their services afterwards, only glory. Athens and some other cities supported war orphans until they reached their majority, at a pittance, but that hardly comes under the heading of welfare for the poor, given that their fathers were by definition men of some means.[51]

The Athenian navy, however, was a fully paid service. Except in times of financial strain, the navy provided regular employment, at what was then good pay, for many thousands of Athenian rowers (and many thousands of non-Athenians as well) and for hundreds of shipwrights and maintenance men. Although we cannot specify how many thousands, they were a significant fraction of the total citizenry, and particularly of the poorer section, or the potentially poorer, such as the sons of smallholders.

In a notorious passage (*Constitution of Athens* 24.3), Aristotle wrote that, thanks to the empire, "Athens provided the common people with an abundance of income. . . . More than 20,000 men were maintained out of the tribute and the taxes and the allies, for there were 7000 jurymen, 1600 archers, 1200 knights, 500 members of the Council, 500 guards of the arsenals, 50 guards of the Acropolis, about 700 other officials in the city and another 700 abroad. Besides, in wartime there were 12,500 hoplites, 20 coast-guard vessels, ships collecting the tribute with crews of 2000 chosen by lot, the *prytanes*, war orphans and jailers." The arithmetic is preposterous; not all the categories comprised Athenian citizens or even free men; the navy is surprisingly omitted; hoplites more often than not found themselves out of pocket; not all 6000 empanelled jurymen were in session every day. Nevertheless, Aristotle had the key to the unique Athenian system, the principle of payment to citizens for public service, for performing their duties as citizens. Except for the navy, no regular income was involved: most public offices were annual and not renewable, and jury service was unpredictable. Yet, all political implications apart, this supplementary income, like occasional sallies into public works, had a buttressing effect, particularly when the occasional or temporary pay was added to the normal household income, by the elderly, for example. That is the reality behind Aristophanes' *Wasps*.

Now it is a remarkable fact that pay for a whole range of public offices is not attested for any city other than Athens, nor did any other city operate a navy of comparable size for so many decades. It is no less remarkable that Athens was free from civil strife, barring two incidents during the Peloponnesian War, for nearly two centuries; free even from the traditional harbinger of civil war, demands for cancellation of debts and redistribution of the land. I have no doubt, first that the widespread distribution of public funds was the key; second that the empire lay behind the financial system. After the loss of the empire at the end of the fifth century B.C., the Athenians succeeded in preserving the system, despite great difficulty and financial stresses. That is another story, about the tenacity of democracy in Athens.[52] What is important here is that, lacking imperial resources, no other city imitated the Athenian pattern. Later, Rome acquired tribute on an incomparably greater scale, but Rome was never a democracy and the Roman distribution of the profits of empire took a different path.

The precise ways in which fourth-century B.C. Athenian statesmen, such as Eubulus, Demosthenes and Lycurgus, struggled to supply the finances required by the political system, which I need not go into,[53] reveal the narrow limits within which an ancient state was compelled to manoeuvre financially. It is a commonplace that ancient states did not have budgets in the modern sense. However, Greek and Roman statesmen had a fair empirical knowledge of annual revenues and expenditures, and they could subtract one from the other. In that sense, they budgeted; it is again necessary to remind ourselves that these were not simple societies, and that states could not have functioned at all without some budgetary predictions. The limits are what must be examined.

To begin with, the state was as tied as any private individual to hard cash on hand (occasionally, to short-term, often compulsory loans). In the second century B.C., the affluent temple of Apollo at Delos stored both its own savings and those of the city-state of Delos in its divinely protected strong-room, as the temple of Athena did in classical Athens.* The two treasuries were called the "sacred chest" and the "public chest", respectively, each consisting of a number of jars "on which was indicated the provenience of the contents or the purpose for which it was earmarked".[54] Delos actually had substantial savings—one series of jars containing more than 48,000 drachmas was unopened at least from 188 to 169 B.C.—and altogether, because of its small size and its peculiar character as an international shrine, it is not a model for ancient states in general. Yet the principle of cash in a strong-box restricted Roman emperors just as closely, scattered though the chests may have been in many centres of the empire: when it became the custom for a new emperor on his accession to distribute cash gratuities to his soldiers, the size of the donative

* I refer here to coined money only, not to the infinitely larger quantity of uncoined treasure sterilized in this temple as in so many others.

was largely determined by the amount available in the jars. Most Greek city-states, on the other hand, had early achieved an equilibrium between revenues and expenditures, had little or no accumulated savings, and therefore had to finance any extraordinary activity, a war, famine relief, even construction of a new temple, by temporary *ad hoc* fund-raising measures.

For many centuries, indeed for so long as the self-governing city-states survived, the temporary measures remained temporary. Athens was never tempted, at least she resisted any temptation, to convert the irregular wartime capital levy on wealth, the *eisphora*, into a regular land tax. The Romans did the same, and were eventually helped by being able to finance all wars externally. "Tempted" has·no moral connotations: the choice did not exist in reality. Direct taxes, whether on income or on land, were politically impossible; inelastic markets and traditional methods of technology and agricultural organization blocked any significant growth in productivity, in what we should call the gross national product, and therefore any steady increase in the yield from indirect taxes. When, for whatever reason, the demands on the available food, on the public treasury and on the contributions of the wealthy through such institutions as the liturgy system outran public resources too far, the ancient world had only two possible responses: one was to reduce the population by sending it out; the other was to bring in additional means from outside, in the form of booty and tribute. Both, as I have already said, were stop-gaps, not solutions. Greek colonization brought about no change in the structure of the original Greek settlements in the Aegean, and therefore no permanent solution to their problems, including those of public finance.

The change came with Roman conquest and the creation of the vast Roman empire, and that was a fundamental political change in the first instance. In the fiscal field, the change can be identified in two principal ways: the land tax became the largest source of revenue throughout the empire (though one should not underestimate the ubiquitous harbour taxes); and the greater share of the fiscal burden passed from the wealthier sector of the population to the poorer, with an accompanying depression in the status of the latter.* None of this was completed overnight, and we can not trace the process decade by decade, but in the third century A.D. it had visibly happened. Meantime the possibilities of further external solutions, of still more conquests followed by colonization, gradually came to an end: the available resources simply did not permit any more, as Trajan's disastrous Parthian expeditions demonstrated, if demonstration were required. In the half-century after Trajan, there was an appearance of stability and equilibrium, Gibbon's Golden Age. Hypothetically, had the Roman Empire encompassed the civilized world, as the panegyrists said, there is no obvious reason why Europe, western Asia and northern Africa should not still, today, be ruled by Roman emperors, America still belong to the red Indians.

However, before the end of the second century, external pressures began, which could not be resisted forever. The army could not be enlarged beyond an inadequate limit because the land could not stand further depletion of manpower; the situation on the land had deteriorated because taxes and liturgies were too high; burdens were too great chiefly because the military demands were increasing. A vicious circle of evils was in full swing. The ancient world was hastened to its end by its social and political structure, its deeply embedded and institutionalized value system, and, underpinning the whole, the organization and exploitation of its productive forces. There, if one wishes, is an economic explanation of the end of the ancient world.

---

* The exemption of Italy does not affect the argument.

VII

Further Thoughts (1984)

1 *The Ancient Economy*

IN THE final quarter of the sixteenth century, years for which the necessary figures happen to be available, there was a high correlation between the price of grain in Amsterdam and the price in Danzig.[1] Western Europe was then a regular market for Polish grain, with Amsterdam the main clearing centre, but the notion of economic interdependence means more than that. It means what the sixteenth-century statistics reveal, namely, that there was a direct link between production and prices in *both* producing and consuming centres, shown in the positive correlation and also in the moments when that correlation broke down for reasons that can be understood and explained. The mere presence of trade over long distances is of course a necessary condition for interdependence but it is not a sufficient condition. After all, long-distance trade has existed ever since the Stone Age.[2] That trade of itself does not warrant such jargon as "a large unified economic space"[3] unless it can be demonstrated, or at least suggested with some measure of reasonableness, that the kind of reciprocal relationship that existed between Polish grain production and Dutch grain imports was present, for instance in the case of glass from Roman Cologne exported to Egypt. Otherwise, "a large unified economic space" is no more than a fancy way of saying that goods were exchanged within that area, and then I see no reason for not including China, Ceylon and Malaysia in the same economic space as Rome because the latter received its silks and much of its spices from eastern Asia.

Unfortunately, the problem of interdependence will never be resolved statistically; it is a Utopian notion that a more complete collection of available prices might prove sufficient to show anything.[4] One need only examine the painstaking collection Duncan-Jones has made of figures from imperial Italy and North Africa—of the costs of statues, temples, tombs, funerals, *anything except commodities*, for which "explicit prices are lacking".[5] The only alternative is to analyse the factors involved in the trade and to draw whatever inferences seem legitimate.

The grain trade offers a fair test.[6] Grain prices fluctuated considerably and rapidly, with an almost instantaneous response to changes in supply (e.g. pseudo-Demosthenes 56.9), except when the state intervened directly to regulate supply and prices. Grain producers and shippers tried when they could to aim for markets known to be more favourable to the seller. Although they were hampered by the rudimentary technology in both the transmission of information and the movement of bulk goods, they were sometimes able to cause shortages and even a food crisis in importing communities. The network of informers and agents set up in the Aegean by Cleomenes, governor of Egypt under Alexander, is a neat example.[7] Producers and shippers also tried to influence local selling prices by cornering supplies, withholding goods from the market for periods, and other such devices.[8] However, none of these manoeuvres amounted to anything more than the creation of a temporary imbalance between supply and demand; of themselves, they had no structural effect on grain production and not necessarily even on the profits of the producers. In the case of Athens, to continue with that example, there is no evidence known to me, or even any likelihood, that the grain production of the south Russian steppes or of Egypt was affected by the grain-dealers against whom Lysias inveighed or by the activities of Cleomenes' agents in the Aegean. Economic interdependence requires something more (qualitatively) than what we are able to discern in this particular field.

Any attempt to argue for interdependence in the ancient economy starts with an initial difficulty: at the production end of the supposed relationship there was not one but a variety of ways in which production was organized. It is essential, in my view, to lay the ghost once for all of the slave mode of production as the hallmark of the ancient economy.[9] In the first place, large sectors (in both time and space) of the Graeco-Roman world never employed productive slave labour on any significant scale. That is now clear of the archaic periods, both Greek and Roman,[10] and it was always certain for the eastern regions brought into the Graeco-Roman sphere by the conquests of Alexander. In the latter, the relatively small number of genuine Greek cities, some such as Alexandria and Antioch very large indeed, seem to have had numerous slaves in domestic and administrative service, and up to a point in production, but the countryside remained as it had been for millennia, a preserve of either small independent peasants, or, more important, of one or another form of dependent labour, tied *de facto* to the land but in no correct sense of the words either slaves or serfs. The Greeks found a functioning regime of land tenure and agricultural labour, and, as I noted (pp. 69–71), there was no reason for them to change that system; nor is there any evidence that either they or the Romans after them in fact made any significant changes.[11] I now also believe that in North Africa certainly, and in Spain and Gaul probably, local varieties of dependent labour survived the Roman conquest as they had done in the east.[12] And in the later Roman acquisitions in central Europe, independent smallholders were the rule.[13]

The second difficulty with the concept "slave mode of production" is that chattel slavery has in the past been integrated into other modes of production, most obviously capitalism. Marx himself put the matter simply: "The fact that we now not only call the plantation owners in America capitalists, but that they *are* capitalists, is based on their existence as anomalies within a world market based on free labour."[14] That kind of anomaly is a major reason for the introduction into contemporary Marxism of the concept of "social formation" (or one or another variant on that term), in which one mode of production is said to co-exist with others over which it is dominant. The problem then is that the secondary modes—slavery in the case of American capitalism—are not merely "dominated" by the main mode but are incorporated into it, so that "mode of production" loses any meaning other than as a synonym for a particular category of labour.[15] When that labour was employed, as were American slaves, to produce for a capitalist world-market, it is meaningless and indeed misleading to speak of a slave mode of production in that context.

None of this is to suggest that there were not a variety of social relations of production in classical antiquity, as in every other long historical period. My objection is directed solely at the effort to "codify" the situation by use of the label "mode of production".[16] Perhaps it is worth adding a third objection to the two I have already raised: if one is not to falsify the situation grossly, no scheme based on modes of production can avoid injecting long periods of transition, a notion that Wallerstein has rightly dismissed as "a blurry non-concept with no operational indicators".[17] It is enough to direct attention to the "transition" from antiquity to feudalism. On any account, chattel slavery ceased to be dominant even in Italy by the fourth or fifth century whereas it is improper to speak of feudalism before the time of Charlemagne, leaving a "transition" lasting no less than three or four hundred years.[18] For those who, like the Carandini school, consider the "slave mode of production" to have come to an end by the middle of the second century, the transition lasted at least six centuries: to fill it with a presumed "*latifundia* mode" is a desperate effort.[19]

No less desperate is the recent flurry, again under the lead of Carandini, of publications that borrow the notion of a "bisectorial economy" from Kula's *Economic Theory of the Feudal System*.[20] Although Kula writes at one point (p. 24) that his model "represents the point of departure for the economic analysis of all pre-industrial societies", it is obvious that his account refers to feudal societies alone, in which the two sectors of the economy, one producing goods for subsistence only, the other producing for the market, were both parts of *a single domain belonging to the lord in which there were no labour costs in the market-producing sector*.[21] Carandini's attempt to transfer a feudal lord's calculations to first-century Italy, in the effort to rescue Columella's notoriously faulty vineyard calculations (3.3.8–10), founders on the elementary fact that Columella's vine-dressers were slaves who had to be maintained, not serfs who had to maintain themselves. "Once," Carandini writes (pp. 194–5), "the original nucleus of vine-dressers has been created, they will both plant the vineyard and train slaves on the estate, and the future requirement of vine-dressers will enter into the domestic sector, outside of the accounts of the capital sector (*vitis ratio*)." The items "which are quite properly absent . . . belong to quite another set of books, that of the natural sector".

For all this there is neither a shred of evidence nor a shred of probability. Graeco-Roman bookkeeping was exceedingly rudimentary, essentially restricted to a listing of receipts and expenditures, from which it was impossible to determine the profitability or otherwise of any single activity in a polyculture; hence the familiar maxim stated flatly by Cato: Sell, don't buy.[22] Carandini is moved to flights of rhetoric by the supposed absurdity of thinking this of the sophisticated Romans with their hunger for profits: "It appears that there exists a tradition from Young through Mickwitz to Finley which passes negative judgment on the Roman economy because the Romans were not English and did not live in the eighteenth century" (p. 179). But Kula points out that his equally voracious Polish feudal landowners of the seventeenth and eighteenth centuries were unable to judge any better: "It was not possible . . . to determine objectively whether *dezolacja* [literally "devastation"] had actually occurred and to what extent".[23]

All this brings me back to the point with which I closed my first chapter in the original edition, namely, that we may speak of "the ancient economy" only for reasons which have little or nothing to do with the economy, because of the political and cultural history of Graeco-Roman antiquity. That it is proper to conceptualize and discuss the ancient economy in that special sense seems to me to remain a valid proposition despite objections that have been raised by several critics.[24] It is not a serious objection, for example, to evoke in opposition a particular passage in an ancient author or a specific case of economic behaviour unless it can be reasonably argued that the passage or the case represents more than a passing exception.[25] Any analysis of the ancient economy that pretends to be more than a mere antiquarian listing of discrete data has perforce to employ models (Weber's ideal types). A model has been defined as "a simplified structuring of reality which presents supposedly significant relationships in a generalized form. Models are highly subjective approximations in that they do not include all associated observations or measurements, but as such they are valuable in obscuring incidental detail and in allowing fundamental aspects of reality to appear."[26] Or, as Weber wrote, "In its conceptual purity, this mental construct cannot be found empirically in reality. It is a *utopia*. Historical research faces the task of determining in each individual case, the extent to which this ideal-construct approximates to or diverges from reality, to what extent, for example, the economic structure of a certain city is to be classified as a 'city-economy'."[27]

A good example of the proper way to employ models in the study of the ancient economy has recently been provided by two alternative models of trade in the Roman Empire. Keith Hopkins has produced an elaborate model showing a very considerable increase in the volume of trade during the three or four centuries and a consequently significant economic growth in the empire in that period.[28] The alternative model by Thomas Pekáry denies any significant change in the volume of trade and therefore the existence of any significant economic growth. The elements of his model are 1) the small size of the "consumer stratum", 2) the low volume of coinage (a point on which he clashes directly with Hopkins), and 3) the high cost of transport, especially by land.[29]

To choose between these two models (or to propose yet another one) would require a lengthier analysis than is possible here. That this is the way to advance our understanding of the ancient economy, and not the continual evocation of individual "facts", is clear to me. Perhaps I should say that at present I prefer the Pekáry model to the Hopkins one because the latter seems to me to overlook the possibility of exploitation without any increase in productivity, that the Roman "provinces were simply being systematically exploited and (that) no trade balance needs to be assumed to have provided provincials with their tribute money".[30]

In that context something should be said about the criticism that I have ignored the Hellenistic world, even that I have done so "because it does not fit the concepts so neatly".[31] The term "Hellenistic" was invented by the great German historian J. G. Droysen in the 1830s to define the period in Greek history between the death of Alexander the Great in 323 and the death of Cleopatra in 30 B.C. It has been accepted almost universally, and yet for the study of the ancient economy it is seriously misleading because in those three hundred years there were two basically distinct "Greek" societies in existence.[32] On the one hand, the old Greek world, including the "western" Greeks, underwent no changes in the economy that require special consideration despite all the political and cultural changes that undoubtedly did occur.[33] On the other hand, in the newly incorporated eastern regions—much of Asia Minor, Egypt, Syria, Mesopotamia—the fundamental social and economic system was not changed by the Macedonian conquerors, or by the Greek migrants who followed behind them, or by the Romans later on, as I have already indicated. There was therefore no "Hellenistic economy"; from the outset there were two, an ancient sector and an Oriental sector.

2 *Class and Status, Free and Unfree Labour*[34]

There are many contexts in which we all speak of "class" vaguely and non-technically, without causing any difficulty in comprehension.[35] That was also the case with Karl Marx himself though in Marxist writing "class" eventually acquired a rather rigid technical sense and a key place in the theory of history. But neither Marx nor Engels ever worked out a properly thought-through definition of class, nor were they sufficiently concerned with the concept in non-capitalist societies. We read, for example, in the opening of the *Communist*

Manifesto of 1848, "The history of all hitherto existing society is the history of class struggles. Freeman and slave, patrician and plebeian, lord and serf, guild-master and journeyman, in a word, oppressor and oppressed, stood in constant opposition to one another. . ."; but in the preface to the second edition (1869) of *The Eighteenth Brumaire* that "in ancient Rome the class struggle took place only within a privileged minority, between the free rich and the free poor, while the great productive mass of the population, the slaves, formed the purely passive pedestal for the combatants".

These two statements would amount to intolerable inconsistency in a writer who was as careful as Marx with his categories and his terminology, unless, as seems to me to be clearly the case, he never really devoted himself to the problem of class relations in pre-capitalist societies. Class structure, Bottomore has recently written, "is a much more complex and ambiguous phenomenon than appears from most of the writings of Marx and Engels, who were greatly influenced in their view by the undoubted salience of class relations in early capitalism, and above all by the irruption into political life of the working-class movement".[36]

In particular, neither slaves were as such members of a single class nor were slave-owners. They varied too greatly in terms of their place in the system of production.[37] Only those slaves who were directly engaged as slave labour in production and those slave-owners who used their slave labour in production can be deemed members of the same class(es). This is not merely a matter of semantics or of Marxist textual criticism; at stake is the conception of ancient society and the ancient economy, for the test I have just stated narrows still further in both time and place the central role of slavery in the ancient economy. Nor is it a mere semantic quibble to refuse to inject the term (and concept) "serfdom" into the ancient world as a label for helots or *penestae* or for the dependent agricultural labour of Hellenistic Asia Minor (called *laoi* in the Greek texts). Serfdom is too closely associated with feudal Europe, and therefore not merely with attachment to the soil but equally with such feudal relations as vassalage and with the legal jurisdiction of the individual landowner, to be torn loose from a social background that did not exist in antiquity in order to maintain a conventional tripartite terminology (slave, serf, free labour).[38] The helots, for example, were ultimately subject to the control of the Spartan state, who could put them to death, impress them into the army or manumit them (hence the geographer Strabo called them "in a way public slaves": 8.5.4); there was nothing, so far as we know, even approximately like the manorial system, with its division into serfs' (or tenants') holdings and the lord's demesne; there were no fiefs, no system of "fines", no private jurisdiction.

All in all, I now appreciate better just how complex and variegated the system of production, and particularly the nature of the labour force, were in antiquity. Two general points which I made—1) that free hired labour was casual and seasonal (pp. 73, 107); 2) that there was no genuine competition or feeling of competition between slave and free labour (pp. 80–81)—are still valid, in my judgment, but they require further analysis and more nuancing.

The relative numbers involved are entirely beyond even guesses, and that creates an initial handicap. However, it is now clear to me that on the land, which occupied the large majority of the population, even the slave-worked larger holdings always required a supplementary force of free men, for elementary economic reasons, most obviously but not exclusively for the harvest. Hence Cato recommended at the beginning of his manual (1.1.3) that one should select a site where, among other considerations, "the labour supply was plentiful". The employment of this supply may have been casual and seasonal but it was none the less indispensable, and that is why I have recently spoken of a symbiosis between free and slave labour.[39] I accept further the argument that much of this rural seasonal labour was that of smallholders seeking to eke out their marginal livelihoods.[40]

The urban situation was somewhat different, at least in the few genuine metropolises which over the years attracted large numbers of migrants, many of whom were unskilled or at best semi-skilled. No doubt many skilled artisans picked up casual work on public projects when the opportunity arose (and when they needed it, which must have been often): the best example comes not from a metropolis but from the great temple-complex at Delos, where the detailed financial records reveal the frequency with which a craftsman turns up from a nearby island for a few days in order to perform a specific piece of work, not to reappear for months or years or even ever again. These men were the parallels to the smallholders taking on such temporary work as harvesting in the countryside. But in Rome, Alexandria, even classical Athens on a much smaller scale, tens of thousands of unskilled and semi-skilled men must have found frequent, though strictly speaking casual, employment in that major urban activity of all pre-industrial societies, the building trade, supplemented by portering, peddling, begging and thieving.[41] Much less of this labour was productive than its rural counterpart and to that extent the notion of a symbiosis with slave labour is less pertinent.

Out of such a labour force it is not to be expected that any positive ideology of work would have emerged. The distinction I have stressed between the man who worked for himself, as an independent farmer or craftsman, and the man who worked for another (e.g. pp. 79–82) remained fundamental and unchallenged throughout antiquity. The distinction is concealed, for example, by an approach that divides work arrangements primarily according to whether or not money changed hands;[42] that leads to a distorted assessment of the place of wage labour in antiquity. The revolutionary slogans, the measure of class consciousness, that we encounter were those of a peasantry, not of a working class. The dozen or so instances of workers' strikes that have been adduced from late antiquity (p. 226n57) turn out, on close examination, not to have been that at all.[43] Hence there was neither a positive ideology of work nor a resentment of slave "competition".[44] In the larger cities, at any rate, and especially in imperial Rome, the basic psychology was reinforced by living conditions, as large numbers of the free poor and many slaves lived and worked side by side in the poorer districts. Thus, when Nero's urban prefect Pedanius Secundus was murdered by one of his slaves in A.D. 61, enforcement of the ancient rule that all his slaves "under the same roof"—four hundred of them—should be put to death was temporarily blocked by a plebeian demonstration (Tacitus, *Annals* 14.42, calls it a *seditio*) until the emperor brought out the troops. No source examines the reasons behind the popular reaction, but it appears likely to have been the simple fact that the plebeian riots were aimed at saving the lives of individuals with whom the plebs (many of them freedmen or descendants of freedmen) associated every day.[45]

What is absent from the record in the Pedanius Secundus story is any criticism of the institution of slavery as such. But, then, there was no such fundamental attack from the side of the slaves either, not even in the rare slave revolts. The three serious revolts—and that is all that there were in antiquity—arose from special circumstances. Otherwise hostile slave reactions were personal—theft, sabotage, personal violence, flight. Although they were common enough, the conclusion is imposed that, not surprisingly, the great majority of slaves accommodated themselves to the system as best they could.[46] There was widespread fear of slaves in sectors of the free population. The Roman law, for instance, could not possibly prevent cohabitation and social intercourse between the free poor and the slaves, but it could prohibit the membership of slaves in benevolent associations (*collegia*) without the express permission of their masters (*Digest* 47.22.3.2), and the satisfactory evidence from the western empire indicates that masters were reluctant to give the necessary approval except in the case of cult associations.[47] The explanation is at hand: it was feared that close personal and social contact in the *collegia* could "infect" the slave-members. However, it does not follow from the existence of fear, no matter how well documented, that it was hostile action by slaves that forced the decline of ancient slavery, as has recently been argued once again at some length (expressly against the account in this volume).[48]

The gap between legality and actual practice was anyway a wide one in the Roman Empire. A century ago Mommsen observed (though insufficient notice was taken of the point) that, with little exception, the individual slaves in the Empire whose origins are specified in literary or epigraphical sources came either from Italy or from provinces *within* the Empire.[49] Such study as there has been since his time has confirmed that finding.[50] There was clearly a super-abundance of imperial enactment prohibiting various forms of "internal enslavement". We know only a portion of that legislation,[51] and virtually nothing about the ability (or desire) of the authorities to enforce it. In any event, whatever the law said, self-sale, the sale of free children and outright kidnapping seem to have been carried on through professional slave-traders on a very large scale. The presence of powerful patrons is implied as a necessary condition.

Impressive new evidence has come to light in the recently discovered (additional) letters of St. Augustine.[52] One (no. 10), dated to about 422 or 423, complains about extensive kidnapping of freeborn children and youths in North Africa, who were shipped overseas as slaves from the port of Hippo. Augustine also says that parents were selling children not only for the twenty-five-year period permitted by law but in perpetuity. We have no other reference to such a law, though there are mysterious hints in some other texts indicating that in the later Empire some exceptions were permitted to the basic (if unenforced) prohibition against such sale.[53] In letter 24 Augustine asks a legal friend about the relevant law in this and comparable situations, but the reply has not been preserved. Much work obviously remains to be done in this area. The starting-point must be that these Augustinian letters reflect something endemic in Roman imperial society, not a new "pre-Vandal" situation.[54]

3 *Exploitation of the Land, Wealth and Profits*

It is generally accepted that the main (and favoured) form of wealth throughout antiquity was the land. It should then follow automatically that exploitation of the land normally involved deployment of the available resources for purposes of self-enrichment or self-advancement in social status and power in a variety of ways, including not only profits in the narrow sense but also, for example, expansion of the manpower under the landowner's personal influence or direct control. That seems to me self-evident, yet I found it necessary to protest (pp. 52–60) against the persistent unwillingness by historians to accept so simple a logic, because they cling to the fallacy that there is no ground between a "subsistence economy" and a full-blown profit-motivated capitalist exploitation. A decade later Whittaker was moved to repeat the same complaint: "The idea that rich landowners were not involved or interested in the profits from the produce of their land . . . is quite simply absurd. 'Business' of this sort, that is, the direct disposal of surpluses and the acquisition of necessities or luxuries (which are, after all, necessities for the rich), whether through the market or not and whether through agents or not, *must be sharply separated from 'living on the profits of buying and selling',* *as Roman legislators tried to define it"* (my italics).[55]

The central difficulty in developing a concrete picture of the complicated, diversified ways in which large landowners exploited their holdings is, notoriously, the almost total silence of the literary and documentary sources on the procedures adopted by the landowners to dispose of their products. Little by little, however, information, or at least hypotheses and probabilities, are being teased out of the inadequate and opaque source-material. At the lower end of the economic spectrum, for instance, it has now emerged that the peasant market became, under certain conditions (notably under the Roman Empire), a source of both income and power to large landowners and to the state.[56] At the upper end, there was not only the sale of commodities on the market but also the use of agricultural wealth as an instrument of patronage and the considerable non-commercial movement of agricultural products in other ways.[57]

For my present purposes, however, it is sufficient to concentrate on the commodity-production aspects of large landholdings, which became central in the classical and immediately post-classical periods of both Greek and Roman history. Most progress in our understanding has been made especially with respect to what has hitherto been treated as a very marginal aspect, namely, the exploitation of clay-beds for the manufacture of pottery, tiles and bricks. Clay does not come to mind "naturally" in an enumeration of the products of the soil, and it is perhaps not too surprising that historians have largely ignored it. Even the Roman bureaucrats and lawyers were uncertain about its status: witness the disagreement among the jurists (*Digest* 8.3.6; 33.7.25.1) as to whether clay-beds counted among the *instrumenta* of an estate for purposes of usufructuary rights or servitudes; or, in the fourth century A.D., after Constantine had introduced the *collatio lustralis*, a tax on *negotiatores*,[58] the repeated efforts of the emperors to narrow the incidence of the tax by exempting the normal business of estate management (*Theodosian Code* 13.1).

However, these are fine-spun lawyers' arguments, meaningful though they may have been in particular contexts, in the face of the growing demonstration that landowners had a considerable concern with their clay resources, whether as direct exploiters or, more probably in the case of *latifundia* owners, as rentiers. The most impressive demonstration so far has emerged from a close analysis of the stamps on Roman bricks of the first two centuries of the Empire, when bricks became the most important single building material and were therefore required in huge quantities.[59] It emerges that the owners of the clay-beds, unlike the personnel in charge of, or joining in, the brick production were largely members of the upper classes, with the emperors increasingly predominant as time went on. In Italy and Sicily, even sanctuaries and cities participated. There are also indications that something comparable was often the case with ceramic production, too—not with the fine painted ware of Athens and elsewhere, the products of a small urban industry, but with the mass-produced amphoras and table ware, manufactured in the millions everywhere in the ancient world. That has been shown by brilliant archaeological work for the north Aegean island of Thasos in the fourth and third centuries B.C., and for the region of Cosa in central Italy in the late Republic and early Empire.[60] And the same has been argued persuasively for the Gallic centres of *terra sigillata*, especially La Graufesenque.[61]

What archaeology cannot show, of course, is the legal and economic relationship between the landowners and the manufacturers of pottery, tiles and bricks. Surprisingly few kiln-sites have even been identified—a truly archaeological activity—and even fewer have been systematically investigated.[62] However, the recent publication of three mid-third-century A.D. papyri from Oxyrhynchus has brought to light one possible relationship between landowners and potters that has, to my knowledge, hitherto been ignored in all the speculations.[63] The papyri are contracts for two-year leases of the potteries on large estates (the phrase used in the text) in the name. The tenants, who identify themselves as "potters who make wine jars", undertake to manufacture annually 15,000, 24,000 and 16,000 four-choes jars, respectively, for which they are to be paid 32 drachmas per 100 in the first two cases, but 36 per 100 in the third. They are also to produce a small number of two- and eight-choes jars, to be paid for in jars of wine or amounts of lentils. The landlords are to provide the potteries, the raw materials and the equipment, the potters only the labour-force (unspecified). And in two of the cases (the unpublished ones) other evidence reinforces the view that the landowners were people of considerable substance.[64]

I do not suggest that the Oxyrhynchus leases represented a common method of putting potteries into production in the Roman world (though I see no way to demonstrate that it was uncommon). But I believe it to be certain, firstly, that there was a considerable variety of "methods", not only in the great centres, Arezzo, Pisa, Puteoli, Lezoux, La Graufesenque, North Africa, but also in the countless small centres of production for purely local distribution; secondly, that all landowners, large and small, who were fortunate enough to have the available raw materials directly or indirectly profited from their exploitation. That was inherent in the very fact of their being landowners.

4 *The Consumer City and Urban Production*[65]

Ancient literature is filled with references to the contrast between the city and the countryside, starting from the sharp pejorative implications of words meaning "rustic". What is absent from that literature, however, is the notion of a fundamental *economic* divide between the two sectors of human society, whether in the harmonious formulation with which Adam Smith opened the third book of his *Wealth of Nations* — "The great commerce of every civilized society is that carried on between the inhabitants of the town and those of the country. . . . We must not . . . imagine that the gain of the town is the loss of the country. The gains of both are mutual and reciprocal . . ."—or in the idea of a fundamental hostility expressed by Marx and Engels in *The German Ideology* (completed by 1846) and repeated by Marx in the first volume of *Capital*—"The foundation of every division of labour which has attained a certain degree of development and has been brought about by the exchange of commodities, is the separation of town from country. One might well say that the whole economic history of society is summed up in this antithesis."[66]

Of course Greeks and Romans were aware of the exchange of commodities between town and country, even of a conflict of interest. Every unlettered peasant encountered such exchanges and such conflict throughout his life. That is of no importance because even the intellectuals failed to erect any theory of the economy or of society, any concepts, upon that base of rudimentary observation. It was not before the eighteenth century that such a development took place, and not before the late nineteenth or the beginning of the twentieth century that the great divide was clearly recognized that had occurred between the ancient city and the late medieval and modern European city. That was the work of Max Weber and Werner Sombart, who were closely associated for many years, preceded by Karl Bücher. The medieval town, wrote the latter, "was not a mere centre of consumption, as were the towns of the Greeks and Romans".[67] Sombart then elaborated and refined the notion: "By a consumption city I mean one which pays for its maintenance (*Lebensunterhalt*) . . . not with its own products, because it does not need to. It derives its maintenance rather on the basis of a legal claim (*Rechtstitel*), such as taxes or rents, without having to deliver return values."[68]

Historians of classical antiquity have normally ignored these views, or, following the lead of Eduard Meyer, they have treated Bücher, Weber and Sombart as ignorant and not very bright trespassers onto a field they were advised to abandon. I trust that I need not repeat what I have already written about Weberian ideal types (or models), and that I need not make the point at any length that he and the others were perfectly aware that the overwhelming majority of the urban population, slaves, aliens and citizens, worked for their livelihood as artisans, unskilled labourers, shopkeepers, professional men. Many—slave or free does not matter in this context—were engaged in making things for sale at home or for export. None of this has ever been seriously in dispute. I point to what I wrote originally about the pottery of Arezzo, the linen garments of Tarsus or the woollens of Patavium (pp. 136–7), although I also accepted more such activity than is warranted. It is now evident, for example, that Marseilles may have been an entrepot for products imported from or exported to the barbarians of the interior (p. 131) in its early "colonial" days but not thereafter.[69] It has also been demonstrated that the supposed woollen industry of Tarentum (Rostovtzeff included it among the "large industrial centres of the ancient world") has not a shred of support in any ancient source.[70]

Much of my analysis, it has recently been said, "rests on the argument from silence and its twin, the generalization from insufficient data".[71] What we seem to be getting in place of the hated argument from silence is, in large doses, what I have elsewhere called the "missing persons argument", that is to say, speculations and assertions about what would be in texts that do not exist. It would be futile to examine this kind of argumentation at any length, but two examples may be permitted in view of the current pervasiveness of the technique. D'Arms began an article on the status of traders in the Roman world by citing the recently discovered personal correspond- ence of an ennobled family from La Rochelle in the early eighteenth century, in which much unhappiness was evident over the fact that the family fortune, properly vested in land, originated in profits from the slave trade. But the Roman evidence, D'Arms continues, "fails us in one particular . . . we do not have even one example, so far as I know, of a Roman senator who, like Depont, deprecated traders but can be shown nevertheless to have trade in his own background"; and he concludes as follows: "If more private, as distinct from literary correspondence, had survived from Rome . . . I feel confident that we should indeed find our Jean Samuel Deponts in ancient Rome."[72]

A more massive and spectacular effort is that of Moeller to create a great woollen industry in Pompeii, based in the first instance on local sheep-raising for which there is no evidence, unless one accepts his claim that Lactarius Mons, a name which implies milk production, was a sheep-breeding region despite the fact that the ancient sources specify cattle. The whole structure of Moeller's argument for the existence of an entrepreneurial export industry controlled and coordinated by the fullers rests on a succession of such guesses and mistakes. For instance, he converts one house into a small factory with some twenty workers on the basis of a graffito in which a man is identified as a weaver. And a large building in which a statue of Eumachia was set up by the fullers becomes, against all archaeological probability, the guild-hall of the fullers and a "cloth exchange where goods in large quantities were sold at auction".[73]

But that is more than enough of such painfully elementary methodological discussion. The model of a "consumer city" and indeed the whole analysis I have attempted of the ancient economy would not be in the least affected or impaired by the discovery of a few more textile workshops in Pompeii or of a few members of the senatorial aristocracy who actively engaged in commerce and manufacture. There can be no dispute over the existence of exceptional men, even of exceptional cities. No historical or sociological model pretends to incorporate all known or possible individual instances. In the absence of meaningful quantitative data, the best that one can do is to judge whether or not a model, a set of concepts, explains the available data more satisfactorily than a competing model. (The still prevalent antiquarian procedure of listing all known discrete "facts" is no method at all.) The model of a consumer city rests not only on the presence of a decisive sector which derived its maintenance from rents and taxes rather than from commercial transactions with an "alien" agricultural sector but also on the restriction of most urban production to petty commodity production, to the production by independent craftsmen of goods retailed for local consumption. Even the quintessential consumer-city, Rome, required large numbers of such men, but normally only for petty commodity production. The critical proposition was put forward by Sombart immediately following the bit I have already quoted defining the consumer-city, when he wrote: "The original, primary city creators were consumers, the derived secondary (tertiary, etc.) creators were producers", and the latter were a dependent element, "whose existence was determined by the share of the consumption fund allowed to them by the consumption class".

That is the issue to which the arguments must be directed. Stated differently, the question is whether or not urban manufacture and trade *generated* wealth in the ancient world to any significant extent or whether they merely took a share of the consumption fund created by the agrarian and mining sectors. That the latter grew considerably, if somewhat unevenly, throughout antiquity is beyond doubt: the mere incorporation of all the territory that eventually constituted the Roman Empire is proof enough. The number of Sombart's secondary and tertiary city creators also grew enormously, though I believe that there came a time, say by the third century and only in the western Empire, when urban commodity production began to suffer some decline, both because a sufficient flight of large landowners occurred from the cities and because the state increasingly withdrew its needs from the market (briefly above, p. 160). That is a suggestion that requires more research than has so far been conducted into the question, and anyway in the present context its significance is chiefly in fixing a time when even the possibility of urban economic growth ceased to exist.[74]

In the end, after all the exceptions, real or imaginary, have been assembled, a number of my general points about urban production have remained untouched by the recent efforts to elevate it to a quasi-modern stature. The first is that there were no guilds in antiquity (p. 138): that has been reaffirmed once again by the most recent study of the Roman *collegia*.[75] The second point follows from the first, namely, if there were no guilds there were *a fortiori* no Guildhalls, no Cloth Halls, and further no Bourses, no Exchanges (pp. 137–8). Occasional attempts to discover them are desperately pathetic, as in the Pompeian "building of Eumachia" already noticed, or in the so-called "Piazzale delle Corporazioni" of Ostia, a typically exuberant archaeologists' name for a building with an uncertain function, that was at most a commercial office building with cell-like rooms.[76] Such general points (and several others to be considered immediately in the next section) seem to me to be fundamental in any attempt to characterize the ancient economy.

5 *Money and Credit*

It is not easy for anyone living in a western capitalist country today to grasp properly the functioning of a money-using society in which money was essentially coined metal and nothing else, in which in particular there was no fiduciary money (which is different from base metal circulating at conventional values, as tokens) and no negotiable paper. Most obviously, any discussion of ancient inflation, notably the supposed inflation of the third and fourth centuries A.D., is essentially defective if it fails to centre on that elementary fact.[77] No less obviously, the money supply depended in large part on the amount of gold and silver available to the issuing authority, and there can be no doubt that the supply was often inadequate for the ongoing needs of the society, let alone for the prospects of economic growth. Even if one were to agree with Lo Cascio in his persistent efforts to argue that the Roman authorities from the last century of the Republic on had a sufficiently "empirical understanding ... of some economic notions" to develop a "monetary policy intended" among other things "to supply the market with adequate means of exchange"[78]—and I am not wholly persuaded—it remains beyond dispute that even Rome suffered an occasional "crisis" attributable to a shortage of coin, however one explains the latter.[79] It is also beyond dispute that, Rome and other imperial states apart, ancient states were faced with chronic shortages except when they had windfalls through conquest or a lucky strike in mining.

However, my concern here is with credit rather than with coin, and specifically with the machinery for credit beyond the lending of coins. In the original edition, I stressed the absence of devices, familiar from the late Middle Ages or from the early modern era, which permitted the *creation* of credit, that is to say, the extension of the society's resources by techniques that permitted lenders or lending institutions to deal with tokens of one sort or another as if they were cash. I noted in particular the lack of negotiable paper, the corresponding absence of bourses or exchanges, and the absence of a public debt in the form of official banknotes or similar fiduciary money (pp. 141–3). The essential role of these institutions and techniques in the growth of the modern economy is too familiar to any economic historian to require documentation, and their absence in antiquity, if that was the case, is as fundamental as the absence of guilds and Guildhalls. No parade of possible exceptions can overcome that basic condition of ancient business practice and finance.

Two massive "anti-primitivist" attacks on my position have now appeared, by Andreau and Thompson, and it is necessary to ask how they have dealt with the question of the creation of credit.[80] It is not worth devoting much space to the familiar "missing persons arguments", in which Thompson specializes while offering his private explanation of the silences of the sources: Athenian "juries did not want to hear the details of estate management".[81] But when both scholars rely heavily on that kind of argument to declare that a significant amount of ancient moneylending was intended for productive use, it is essential to call a halt and insist on the evidence. A recent "catalogue of almost nine hundred loan transactions of all types, drawn from the whole of classical Greece," has produced "perhaps five—excluding maritime loans—which might conceivably be classed as productive".[82] No special pleading, no dispute about the classification of any single transaction in that catalogue, can alter the impact of the arithmetic. For the Hellenistic world and for Rome no such synoptic picture is available, and we are driven to guesses and hunches. Although I cannot state with assurance that the picture of non-productive moneylending was not significantly altered, the evidence that I know argues in that direction.

Thompson appears not to have taken in the point about the creation of credit at all. Andreau registers the absence of public debt but dismisses it in less than a sentence, incorrectly, as a phenomenon restricted to the time of the industrial revolution "and the period which immediately preceded it" (p. 1132). He then argues that banking even in antiquity "had the effect of increasing the global purchasing power available within the framework of a fixed economic quantity of money" because it doubled the amount, on the one hand as money still the property of the depositors and at the same time as money that the bank could lend (p. 1143). That baffles me and I see no alternative but to dismiss it as a curious aberration.[83] The absence of credit-creating instruments and institutions remains as an unshaken foundation of the ancient economy.

Perhaps, before leaving the subject, I might say once again that I do not for a moment dispute that there was a vast amount of moneylending in antiquity, that an unknown and undiscoverable percentage of it took the form of petty usurious loans to the poor in the towns and the countryside, and that the profits of moneylending at interest were a regular part of the income of the upper classes. The point at issue is not that, but the role of moneylending in production and in economic growth, on which my position is almost wholly negative.

6   *Feeding the Cities*

Some ancient cities were compelled to import significant quantities of grain from abroad regularly, most obviously Athens and Rome. The latter was in a class by itself, needing to import (on a conservative modern estimate) at least 150,000 tons of grain annually from the first century B.C. to the third century A.D. (in addition to the supplies for the far-flung Roman armies).[84] Such amounts (and after A.D. 332 the supplies for Constantinople), it has been noted, were "the only example in antiquity of a continuous transport over a long distance of cheap goods in considerable amounts". It "was a very complicated system that could easily be disrupted", yet we should "stress not the apparent deficiencies of the system, but rather the fact that it normally worked fairly well".[85] The grain was obtained partly through rents and taxes in kind and partly by purchase (both private and public) from central Italy, Sicily, Sardinia, North Africa, eventually from Egypt, and in less significant quantities from Gaul and Spain. Most of this enormous supply, at a guess 85 per cent, came by sea (during a sailing season of some seven months) not to Rome itself but to Puteoli in the Bay of Naples before Claudius began to create the port of Ostia, and even thereafter river transit up the Tiber was the final stage. The largest vessels were of the order of 400 to 600 tons, reduced for the Tiber run to about 150 tons. However, there is no way of knowing how much of the transport was in smaller ships, especially on the coastal voyage from Puteoli to the Tiber. In order to encourage shipbuilders during a grain shortage, the emperor Claudius offered various incentives to anyone constructing vessels capable of carrying a minimum of about 70 tons of wheat.[86]

I give these figures only in order to hint concretely at the scale of the effort required to feed the population of the city of Rome. There is no way to quantify the material and the personnel required to move the grain to the ports in the supply regions, to load and unload the ships by hand, to warehouse the grain in Puteoli, Ostia and Rome, to shift the raw corn from warehouse to miller, baker and final distributor.[87] One can only say that the numbers of people involved, in Italy, Sicily, Egypt, North Africa and elsewhere, were large and that the administrative machinery was considerable, all the more so in a basically non-bureaucratic society. Yet, as the measures taken by Claudius to encourage ship-building illustrate, state intervention was very slow to develop and long remained restricted in scope. During the Republic, intervention was a crisis phenomenon. Under the Principate, then, the state created an administrative machinery from early in the reign of Augustus,[88] but the state still preferred "privileges and favourable terms" rather than "compulsory services" until the late third or the fourth century, in an operation that was "something less than *libero commercio* or *laisser faire, laisser passer*" but still far from "*dirigisme*".[89] The comparison in this respect is striking with the only other ancient city about which we know enough, namely, classical Athens, where a relatively large body of officials and stringent regulations requiring Athenian-based merchants and shippers to bring grain to Athens were accompanied by a failure to interfere with the personnel as such, many of whom were metics, not citizens.[90] Athens did not even make use of its tax system to further the food-supply needs, but charged the same harbour duties on imported grain as on any other commodity (p. 164). Of other cities our knowledge is too scrappy to permit any proper assessment: for neither Alexandria nor Carthage, the two cities most comparable to imperial Rome in size, have we any meaningful information on the subject.

It was, I suppose, unavoidable that the corn dole and crisis measures should have occupied the attention of historians far more than the routine problems of feeding the larger cities. Although new evidence is a mere trickle, in the form of inscriptions and papyri which provide marginal and accidental information only, there has been enough recent discussion to require some reexamination of what I wrote originally (pp. 40, 169–71). It remains true that only in Rome itself and later in Constantinople was there a regular, large-scale distribution of grain or eventually bread (and sometimes other foods) by the (Roman) state. What else could one have expected? The wealth of the Roman emperors could not have coped with an extended scheme even remotely comparable to the dole in the city of Rome. Every other known scheme—and their number remains small—was either a privately financed or a municipal one, applied to relatively few people and showing no proof of great longevity.[91] It is impossible to quantify either the total sums available under these various schemes, the majority of which were destined for games, feasts, memorial statues, and so on, rather than for grain or alms distribution, or the numbers of recipients. In imperial Italy, at any rate, the evidence seems clear enough that, apart from benefactions by a few members of the municipal or imperial oligarchies, the sums donated were rather small.[92] How small they sometimes were is illustrated by a recently published mid-second-century A.D. inscription from Tlos in Lycia, recording a gift of 12,500 denarii from a woman named Lalla, which was placed at interest. Out of the income, the city guaranteed to give one denarius on 15th June every year to each of the 1100 names on an existing list of citizens qualified to share in a municipal grain distribution.[93]

When discussing the Roman corn dole originally (pp. 40 and 170–71), I stressed that it was the exception that proves the rule that, before the Christianization of the empire, not even the state cared much for its poor.[94] That it was a real exception seemed to me certain, and it still does. The repeated stress in the modern accounts on the fact that the dole was open to all citizens, without trace of a means test, is misplaced in its implication. The critical question is not one of eligibility but of practice: Who actually drew the free grain-ration in the hundreds of years that it continued to be available (not who had a paper right to it)? The ancient sources are unanimous in their view of the dole as a form of poor relief won by the plebs after considerable struggle.[95] They even tell stories of citizens "cheating" by pseudo-manumissions of their slaves in order to pass some of the costs of their maintenance onto the state. To argue against that testimony, and against elementary common sense, that every senator also had the right to queue up for his ration, or to send a domestic to do so for him, strikes me as pedantic absurdity. When the tribune Clodius Pulcher introduced the regular corn dole in 58 B.C. he established it as a right of citizens, not as charity for the poor. That is interesting symbolically, ideologically, but it does not change the reality as it was seen by his supporters and by successive Roman commentators.[96] The emperors, beginning with Augustus, then quickly saw political advantages to be gained from holding themselves up as the patrons of the free corn ration. But that too does not make the dole any the less a form of poor relief.

One further exception was introduced by Trajan (or conceivably by Nerva) with his so-called *alimenta* programme in Italy. A large sum of money was set aside by the emperor—how much is unknown—for the maintenance of poorer boys (and fewer girls), perhaps to the ages of eighteen and fourteen, respectively. The money was, however, not handed over to the local authorities directly but was siphoned to them through interest payments, of about five per cent, made by larger landowners on loans they took from the original fund of about eight per cent of the value of the charged holdings. The scheme was complex, involving considerable estimation of value, and was in perpetuity, so far as we know, though no

regulations could have prevented economic failure and individual
defaults. Altogether forty-nine towns are today known to have been
involved in the scheme, nearly three quarters of them in the four
central regions of Italy.[97] Although the evidence is entirely
epigraphic and therefore subject to chance, it is now virtually certain
that the scheme never reached all the towns of Italy. We have no idea
how the selection was made, how the children were chosen who were
to benefit, or what percentage they represented of all the free children
in each community.

Whatever the purposes of the scheme, it was restricted to Italy.
The political implications are obvious, but otherwise the purposes
are, perhaps surprisingly, still subject to considerable and inconclu-
sive debate. That on the surface the aim was to provide financial
relief for some of the poor by way of maintenance for their children is
beyond dispute. But Veyne in particular has argued that so much
concern for the poor is incomprehensible without some ulterior
motive, which he finds in the desire to foster the birth rate.[98] I
accepted that originally (p. 40), but now I wonder. Veyne has
guessed that in Veleia, from which we have the most detailed
information, perhaps one child in ten was a beneficiary. That is only
a guess, but it is good enough. What sort of scheme to increase the
birth rate of Italy was it that restricted the beneficiaries to some of the
cities and to only a small percentage of the children? Why did the
emperors resort to such an indirect device rather than the standard
ones of a penalty on bachelors and direct benefits to parents with
more than some specified number of children, well known from other
societies and employed by Augustus early in his reign in Rome?
Veyne's answer to such objections is that governmental demographic
policy has always been blind and that one should not judge Trajan's
aims by the ineffectiveness of the scheme. Perhaps, but I am not
certain that the simple political explanation inherent in the extension
of the emperor's patronage is not better, and I am even less impressed
by the recent revival of an old suggestion that the scheme was
simultaneously aimed at improving Italian agriculture by creating a
land-fund.[99] The notion that what amounted to a tax on the land (the
interest on the loans) would compel landowners to make improve-

ments in order to recover the money, and to do so in perpetuity as the annual payments went on without stop, seems to me wholly unworkable, and again we know that direct brutal methods could be employed when thought desirable, as in Domitian's short-lived attempt to restrict viticulture (p. 244n47).

One final puzzle remains to be considered about the *alimenta*. The last reference to the scheme dates to shortly after the middle of the third century, so that it had a life of at least a century and a half. There is reason to believe that some further imperial capital was injected into it, and there can be no doubt that there were bankruptcies and defaults during the long life of the scheme. But was participation voluntary or compulsory? If the former, were the contributors free to withdraw? It has been vigorously and persuasively argued that both the internal evidence and such little external testimony as we have (notably Pliny, *Letters* 10.55) make compulsion unlikely.[100] I accept the arguments, but I doubt that the alternative has been correctly posed. The image of thousands of prosperous Italian landowners taking on a perpetual financial burden to help maintain poor children for the greater glory of the emperor (let alone to help stimulate the Italian birth rate) seems to me even more contrary to the mentality of the time than the idea of unsullied imperial benevolence to the poor. There are many ways in which to exert "moral" pressure in such a situation other than legislative fiat. Willingness, like sincerity, is a slippery commodity.

A new turn has been given to the discussion of Roman food distribution by the publication in 1972 of a group of papyri from Oxyrhynchus, dating between A.D. 268 and 272, which reveal a monthly corn ration to probably 4000 local householders. The papyri show, says the editor, "that the doles were not a provision for the very poor, but a perquisite of the already privileged middle classes of the cities, *as in Rome*" (my italics).[101] This remarkable conclusion, which makes nonsense of the internal history of Rome from the time of Claudius (and even before), has received some surprising assent, all because some of the machinery for filling vacancies and identifying recipients in the Oxyrhynchus roster seems to have been copied from Roman imperial practice.[102] The interpretation has now been sharply, and I believe decisively, challenged.[103] In any event, all the known references to grain distribution to the end of the empire add up to hardly anything, apart from the continuing exceptions of Rome and Constantinople. Nor were any of the others permanent, though we have no idea when they were introduced or why they were either introduced or abandoned when they were. The "provincial economy", it has rightly been said, "would have had difficulty in surviving an excessive multiplication" of institutions like the grain distribution of Oxyrhynchus.[104] I still prefer to judge the mentality of the later emperors from the practice of Constantinople, the second capital, rather than from what may have been done for a few years by the insignificant Egyptian village of Oxyrhynchus.

7 War and Empire

These twin topics naturally recur in this book (especially pp. 156–61 and 169–76), apart from the special problems of the later Roman Empire (pp. 90–93). Here, too, some aspects, or at least nuances, require reconsideration.

On the central point that there were neither commercial wars nor commercial imperialism, great as the profits of empire may have been, I have no reason to alter my views.[105] It is perhaps worth repeating, in order to prevent any misunderstanding, that I do not propose to minimize the exploitation, public and private, of subject or subordinate peoples, nor do I deny that trade may have benefited from war and empire. The latter, however, was largely an unintended by-product, not essential to the motivation of war and conquest, and certainly the interests of merchants cannot be detected in the thinking of those who made policy decisions. Failure ever to use taxation as a commercial lever, which I noted briefly once or twice, probably deserves more emphasis, as perhaps the most characteristic symptom of this negative point.

As always, there are exceptions, but they are surprisingly few. One is known only from a single satirical half-sentence in Cicero's *Republic* (3.16): "we are the justest of men, who do not allow the people beyond the Alps to plant olives and vines, so that our own olive groves and vineyards are worth more". Cicero provides neither a date nor a context, *and there is no other known measure in Roman history that is comparable.* Doubts have therefore been expressed about the authenticity. However, it is difficult to imagine why Cicero, for all his historical unreliability, should have invented this particular regulation (putting aside all questions of its enforcement or enforceability), and there are now archaeological reasons to place the measure late in the second century B.C.[106] From the last quarter of the second century to the last quarter of the first, possibly as many as 100,000 hectolitres of wine were shipped annually from Italy, chiefly from the Tyrrhenian coast, to Gaul, and that was in addition to the wine supplied to Roman soldiers there.

The chief beneficiaries were of course the larger landowners of Italy rather than independent merchants or shippers. It has further been observed that, substantial though the amount of 100,000 hectolitres is, it represented probably less than one tenth of the wine consumption in the imperial period of the city of Rome alone, and one has the right to ask whether that warranted such an unjust rule (Cicero's own description). The attractive hypothesis has now been offered that for this one century, when the Gallic élite was still in the pre-commodity stage and was proverbially addicted to neat wine consumption (Diodorus 5.26.3), wine served the Romans as a kind of currency in a gift-exchange system for the specific purpose of slave procurement. This unique trade then stopped abruptly when the incorporation of Gaul into the empire ended the legal enslavement of the Gauls and, more or less at the same time, the socio-economic structure of Gaul underwent an internal transformation.[107]

Such curiosities apart, the profits of empire in antiquity are well enough understood today, but the profits of war remain insufficiently examined (and were not adequately dealt with in this book originally).[108] Two distinctions now seem to me fundamental. The first is between small and large states, which are to be distinguished not by quantitative tests but by their ability effectively to deploy military power.[109] Once the ancient world had moved beyond the stage of frequent razzias between neighbouring communities, in which small states could also play their part, the profits of war were restricted to the larger states. And that leads to my second distinction, that between a small number of "conquest-states" and the rest. The former were the aggressive states, who profited from war and empire and who were the stable states of antiquity.[110]

It is as impossible for us to calculate the gross or net profits (or losses) of an ancient war as it was for the actors themselves. When Thucydides reported that the two-year siege of Potidaea cost the Athenian state 2000 talents (2.70.2), he was able to give that figure only because the state had built up a large cash reserve from the tribute paid by subject-states—a very rare phenomenon in antiquity—but he made no attempt even to guess other costs, let alone to set against them the income from booty that went to individuals or to the treasury. Hence, when I wrote (p. 157) that in all the conquests by Roman emperors "the economic element . . . was normally on the debit side", there was a danger that the wrong implication might be drawn. By the time the Empire was founded, space available for conquest was at such a great distance from the centre as to disturb all the traditional cost calculations. An analysis of the economics of war and conquest under the Roman Empire thus becomes entangled with the exceedingly difficult problem of the limits of ancient imperialism, of whether by the death of Augustus, say, Rome had not reached the limits imposed by its technology, manpower, economic and social organization. Certainly the time was to come, in the third and fourth centuries, when the Empire could no longer extend its taxable capacity and therefore could not increase its military force as the new circumstances required. Whether taxation had by then in fact become much more exorbitant (as I wrote earlier, pp. 89–90) or whether, as has now been strongly urged, the difficulty was chiefly one of glaring imbalances and of the weakness of the imperial centre in the face of growing self-assertion by the élite,[111] requires further inquiry. Be that as it may, there can be no disagreement that in the four centuries ending with the death of Augustus, Roman warfare had produced profits, to individuals and to the state, in a great crescendo. So, on an incomparably smaller scale, did the conquests of classical Athens.[112]

The essential point is that to the end of the Republic, and probably even later, Romans assumed that war would bring profits and they made decisions accordingly. Cicero complained about Caesar's invasion of Britain (cited on p. 157) because this time a war was proving insufficiently profitable: not even the captives were good enough (and it is worth remembering that the emperors' wars continued to bring large numbers of captives into the empire as slaves at least as late as the end of the fourth century). However, I give the final word not to a Roman, whose views on such matters we are learning to take for granted, but to Thucydides. In his statement explaining why in the end everyone voted for the Sicilian expedition at the crucial meeting of the Athenian assembly in 415 B.C., Thucydides included the following (6.24): "the great mass of the people, including those serving on the expedition, thought that they would earn money at present and also add a force (i.e. to the empire) that would guarantee permanent pay in the future".

Abbreviations and Short Titles

Andreau, "Banque"—J. Andreau, "La banque antique et l'économie moderne", *Annali* . . . *Pisa*, 3rd ser., 7 (1977) 1125–52

Annales—*Annales: Economies, Sociétés, Civilisations* (earlier *Annales d'histoire économique et sociale*)

ANRW—*Aufstieg und Niedergang der römischen Welt*, ed. H. Temporini

Ausbüttel, *Vereine*—F. M. Ausbüttel, *Untersuchungen zu den Vereinen im Westen des römischen Reiches* (*Frankfurter Althistorische Studien* 11, 1982)

Balland, *Xanthos*—*Fouilles de Xanthos*, vol. 7, ed. A. Balland (1981)

Bogaert, *Banques*—R. Bogaert, *Banques et banquiers dans les cités grecques* (Leiden 1968)

Brunt, *Manpower*—P. A. Brunt, *Italian Manpower 225 B.C.–A.D. 14* (Oxford 1971)

Carrié, "Distributions"—J. M. Carrié, "Les distributions alimentaires dans les cités de l'Empire romain tardif", *MEFRA* 87 (1975) 995–1101

Crook, *Law*—J. A. Crook, *Law and Life at Rome* (London 1967)

De Ste. Croix, *Struggle*—G. E. M. de Ste. Croix, *The Class Struggle in the Ancient Greek World* . . . (London 1981)

Duncan-Jones, *Economy*—R. D. Duncan-Jones, *The Economy of the Roman Empire: Quantitative Studies* (2nd ed. Cambridge 1982)

EcHR—*Economic History Review*

Finley, *E. & S.*—M. I. Finley, *Economy and Society in Ancient Greece*, ed. B. D. Shaw and R. C. Saller (London & New York 1981)

Finley, *Land and Credit*—M. I. Finley, *Studies in Land and Credit in Ancient Athens* (New Brunswick 1952)

Finley, *Roman Property*—*Studies in Roman Property*, ed. M. I. Finley (Cambridge 1976)

Finley, *Slavery*—M. I. Finley, *Ancient Slavery and Modern Ideology* (London & New York 1980)

Finley, "Slavery and Freedom"—M. I. Finley, "Between Slavery and Freedom", *Comparative Studies in Society and History* 6 (1964) 233–49

Finley, *Studies*—M. I. Finley, ed., *Studies in Ancient Society* (London 1974)

Finley, "Technical Innovation"—M. I. Finley, "Technical Innovation and Economic Progress in the Ancient World", *EcHR*, 2nd ser., 18 (1965) 29–45

Frank, *Survey*—T. Frank, ed., *An Economic Survey of Ancient Rome* (6 vols., Baltimore 1933–40)

Frederiksen, "Caesar"—M. W. Frederiksen, "Caesar, Cicero and the Problem of Debt", *JRS* 56 (1966) 128–41

Garnsey, *Labour*—*Non-slave Labour in the Greco-Roman World*, ed. P. Garnsey (Cambridge Philological Society, Supp. vol. 6, 1980)

Garnsey, *Trade*—*Trade in the Ancient Economy*, ed. P. Garnsey et al. (London and Berkeley 1983)

Giardina/Schiavone—*Società romana e produzione schiavistica*, ed. A. Giardina and A. Schiavone (3 vols., Bari 1981)

Heitland, *Agricola*—W. E. Heitland, *Agricola* (Cambridge 1921)

Jones, *LRE*—A. H. M. Jones, *The Later Roman Empire 284–602* (3 vols., Oxford 1964)

JRS—*Journal of Roman Studies*

Kohns, *GGA*—H. G. Kohns, review of this book in *Göttingische gelehrte Anzeiger* 230 (1978) 120–32

Kreissig, Seleukidenreich—H. Kreissig, *Wirtschaft und Gesellschaft im Seleukidenreich* (Berlin 1978)

Kula, *Theory*—W. Kula, *An Economic Theory of the Feudal System* (London 1976)

Liebeschuetz, *Antioch*—J. H. W. G. Liebeschuetz, *Antioch . . . in the Later Roman Empire* (Oxford 1972)

Lo Cascio, "Coinage"—E. Lo Cascio, "State and Coinage in the late Republic and Early Empire", *JRS* 71 (1981) 76–86

MEFRA—*Mélanges de l'École française de Rome. Antiquité*

Ossowski, *Class Structure*—S. Ossowski, *Class Structure in the Social Consciousness*, transl. S. Patterson (London 1963)

PBSR—*Papers of the British School at Rome*

Pritchett, *Military Practices*—W. K. Pritchett, *Ancient Greek Military Practices*, pt. I [*Univ. of California Publications: Classical Studies*, vol. 7 (1971)]

Proceedings . . . Aix—*Proceedings* of the 2nd International Conference of Economic History, Aix-en-Provence 1962, vol. 1. *Trade and Politics in the Ancient World* (Paris and The Hague 1965)

Rostovtzeff, *RE*—M. Rostovtzeff, *The Social and Economic History of the Roman Empire*, 2nd ed. by P. M. Fraser (2 vols., Oxford 1957)

Rougé, *Commerce*—J. Rougé, *Recherches sur l'organisation du commerce maritime en Méditerranée sous l'empire romain* (Paris 1966)

Salvioli, *Capitalisme*—G. Salvioli, *Le capitalisme dans le monde antique*, transl. from the Italian MS by A. Bonnet (Paris 1906). An Italian edition, published in 1929, was not available to me.

Sherwin-White, *Pliny*—A. N. Sherwin-White, *The Letters of Pliny. A Historical and Social Commentary* (Oxford 1966)

Syll.—W. Dittenberger, ed., *Sylloge inscriptionum graecarum*, 3rd ed. by F. Hiller von Gaertringen (4 vols., Leipzig 1915–24)

Thompson, "Entrepreneur"—W. E. Thompson, "The Athenian Entrepreneur", *L'Antiquité classique* 51 (1982) 53–85

Tod, *GHI* II—M. N. Tod, ed., *A Selection of Greek Historical Inscriptions*, vol. 2, 403–323 B.C. (Oxford 1948)

VDI—*Vestnik drevnei istorii*

Veyne, "Alimenta"—P. Veyne, "Les 'alimenta' de Trajan", in *Les empereurs romains de l'Espagne* (Paris, CNRS 1965)

Veyne, "Trimalcion"—P. Veyne, "Vie de Trimalcion", *Annales* 16 (1961) 213–47

Whittaker, "Inflation"—C.R. Whittaker, "Inflation and the Economy in the Fourth Century A.D.", in *Imperial Revenue, Expenditure and Monetary Policy in the Fourth Century*, ed. C. E. King (*British Archaeological Reports*, Intl. Series 76, 1980), pp. 1–22.

ZSS—*Zeitschrift der Savigny-Stiftung für Rechtsgeschichte, Romanistische Abteilung*

Notes

NOTES TO CHAPTER I
(Pages 17–34)

1. *Moral Philosophy* (3rd ed., Glasgow 1764) p. 274.

2. Cf. Aristotle's definition, *Politics* 1278b37–38: "The economic art is rule over children and wife and the household generally." For recent anthropological discussion of the distinction between "family" and "household", see D. R. Bender, "A Refinement of the Concept of Household", *American Anthropologist* 69 (1967) 493–504. The discussion would benefit from a broadening of its horizon to include historical societies as well as the restricted kind of community anthropologists customarily study.

3. See O. Brunner, "Das 'ganze Haus' und die alteuropäische Ökonomik", in his *Neue Wege der Sozialgeschichte* (Göttingen 1956) pp. 33–61, at p. 42 (originally published in the *Zeitschrift für Nationalökonomik* 13 [1950] 114–39). C. Ampolo, "Oikonomia", *Archeologia e storia antica* 1 (1979) 119–30, replaces all previous accounts of the history of the word in the Greek world.

4. Brunner, *ibid.*, and H. L. Stoltenberg, "Zur Geschichte des Wortes Wirtschaft", *Jahrbücher für Nationalökonomik und Statistik* 148 (1938) 556–61.

5. Translations can easily mislead. The best is in French, by P. Chantraine in his edition of the *Oikonomikos* in the Budé series (Paris 1949); see my review in *Classical Philology* 46 (1951) 252–3.

6. See G. Mickwitz, "Economic Rationalism in Graeco-Roman Agriculture", *English Historical Review* 52 (1937) 577–89.

7. *History of Economic Analysis*, ed. E. B. Schumpeter (New York 1954) pp. 9, 54.

8. E. Cannan, *A Review of Economic Theory* (London 1929, reprint 1964) p. 38. Cannan's brief second chapter, "The Name of Economic Theory", provides the essential documentation for my next remarks; cf. the entry "Economy" in the *Oxford English Dictionary*.

9. Dinarchus 1.97 and Polybius 4.26.6, respectively. Elsewhere (4.67.9) Polybius uses the word to mean "military dispositions".

10. Quintilian 1.8.9; 3.3.9. Examples of this usage in later Greek writers (and in English, for that matter) are easily found in a lexicon.

11. This observation was made by Karl Bücher as long ago as 1893; see *Die Entstehung der Volkswirtschaft* (5th ed., Tübingen 1906) p. 114.

12. See Talcott Parsons and Neil J. Smelser, *Economy and Society* (London 1956).

13. See my "Aristotle and Economic Analysis", *Past & Present*, no. 47 (1970) 3–25, reprinted in Finley, *Studies* chap. 2.

14. "Of the Populousness of Ancient Nations", in his *Essays* (London, World's Classics ed., 1903) p. 415.

15. "Der 'Sozialismus' in Hellas", in *Bilder und Studien aus drei Jahrtausenden— Eberhard Goitein zum siebzigsten Geburtstag* (Munich and Leipzig 1923) pp. 15–59, at pp. 52–53.

16. *A History of Economic Thought* (rev. ed., London 1945) p. 373. Roll does not introduce into his definition the element of "scarce resources" that is common in other formulations, but that does not in the least affect my point.

17. Quoted from Cannan, *Review* p. 42.

18. See the review-article by M. Blaug, "Economic Theory and Economic History in Great Britain, 1650–1776", *Past & Present*, no. 28 (1964) 111–16.

19. For Rome, where the evidence about wage rates is even more skimpy than for Greece, the dominance of a conventional, rather than a market-determined, figure is shown by M. H. Crawford, *Roman Republican Coinage* (2 vols., Cambridge 1974) II chap. 6.

20. See G. E. M. de Ste. Croix, "The Estate of Phaenippus (Ps.-Dem. xlii)", in *Ancient Society and Its Institutions: Essays for V. Ehrenberg*, ed. E. Badian (Oxford 1966) pp. 109–14. The desperate lack of quantitative information about Roman property is revealed by Duncan-Jones, *Economy*, Appendix 1.

21. Appian, *Civil War* 1.14.117. There is no greater virtue in the figures given by Velleius Paterculus 2.30.6 (90,000) and Orosius 5.24.2 (70,000) just because they are smaller. Hypothetically, Roman writers could have compiled reasonable slave totals, at least for Italy and other districts, from the census figures, in which such property was itemized. The essential point, however, is that no one ever did, and that, even if anyone had, no reliable count would have been available of the supporters of Spartacus.

22. R. J. Fogel, "The New Economic History, Its Findings and Methods", *EcHR*, 2nd ser., 19 (1966) 642–56, at pp. 652–3.

23. A. N. Whitehead, *Modes of Thought* (New York 1938) p. 195, quoted from the Appendix, "A Note on Statistics and Conservative Historiography", in Barrington Moore, Jr., *Social Origins of Dictatorship and Democracy* (Penguin ed., 1969) p. 520 note 15.

24. "And yet," writes Nicholas Georgescu-Roegen, one of the pioneers of

modern mathematical economics, "there is a limit to what we can do with numbers, as there is to what we can do without them": *Analytical Economics* (Cambridge, Mass., 1966) p. 275.

25. J. Stengers, "L'historien devant l'abondance statistique", *Revue de l'Institut de Sociologie* (1970) 427–58, at p. 450.

26. Quoted from H. Westergaard, *Contribution to the History of Statistics* (London 1932) p. 40.

27. I need not enter into the question, not irrelevant, of the extent to which the unusually extensive records of Ptolemaic Egypt were more often expressions of bureaucratic pretence rather than records of what was actually going on in the country; see P. Vidal-Naquet, *Le bordereau d'ensemencement dans l'Égypte ptolémaïque* (Brussels 1967).

28. *An Essay on the Distribution of Wealth* . . . (London 1831); see Karl Marx, *Theorien über den Mehrwert*, in the edition of his *Werke* published by the Institut für Marxismus–Leninismus, vol. 26 (Berlin 1968) pp. 390–3.

29. See my survey in *Proceedings* . . . *Aix*, pp. 11–35; E. Will, "Trois quarts de siècle de recherches sur l'économie grecque antique", *Annales* 9 (1954) 7–22; E. Lepore, "Economia antica e storiografia moderna (Appunti per un bilancio di generazioni)", in *Ricerche* . . . *in memoria di Corrado Barbagallo*, vol. 1 (Naples 1970) pp. 3–33. Polanyi's relevant publications are conveniently assembled in *Primitive, Archaic and Modern Economies*, ed. G. Dalton (Garden City, N.Y., 1968). Cf. W. Nippel, "Die Heimkehr der Argonauten aus der Südsee", *Chiron* 12 (1982) 1–39.

30. It is instructive to read the discussion between E. Lepore and W. Johannowsky (and other specialists on the Greeks in the west) in *Dialoghi di Archeologia* (1969) 31–82, 175–212.

31. H. Michell, *The Economics of Ancient Greece* (2nd ed., Cambridge 1957). Contrast C. Mossé, *The Ancient World at Work*, transl. Janet Lloyd (London 1969), a revised version of the French original.

32. *A Theory of Economic History* (Oxford 1969) pp. 42–43.

33. A. French, *The Growth of the Athenian Economy* (London 1964) p. 54.

34. Georgescu-Roegen, *Analytical Economics* p. 111. The whole of his Part I is a powerful argument against the applicability to other societies of economic theories and concepts formulated for a capitalist system; see also the beautifully succinct statement on pp. 360–2.

35. G. H. Nadel, "Periodization", in *International Encyclopedia of the Social Sciences* 11 (1968) pp. 581–5, at p. 581.

36. On the inapplicability of the divisions, categories and concepts of western history to the history of China, see A. F. Wright and D. B. ˈde in *Generalization in the Writing of History*, ed. L. Gottschalk (Chicago 1963) pp. 36–65.

37. "Some historians seem to be unable to recognize continuities and distinctions at the same time." That is the opening sentence of a relevant footnote by E. Panofsky, *Meaning in the Visual Arts* (Penguin ed., 1970) p. 26 note 3.

38. See my "Slavery and Freedom"; more generally, the suggestive "dialogue" between J. Gernet and J.-P. Vernant, "L'évolution des idées en Chine et en Grèce du VIe au IIe siècle avant notre ère", *Bulletin de l'Association Guillaume Budé* (1964) 308–25.

39. I have had to state my position briefly and dogmatically, and I cite only A. L. Oppenheim, *Ancient Mesopotamia* (Chicago and London 1964) chap. 2, and "Trade in the Ancient Near East", a paper prepared for the 5th International Congress of Economic History, Leningrad 1970, and published by the Nauka Publishing House (Moscow 1970). Not all specialists on the ancient Near East agree; see e.g. S. L. Utchenko and I. M. Diakonoff, "Social Stratification of Ancient Society", a similarly published paper prepared for the 13th International Historical Congress, Moscow 1970, which has to be read in the light of the current discussion in Marxist circles of the "Asiatic mode of production", the only serious theoretical discussion I know of the problem of classification I have been considering. ("Asiatic" is an unfortunate, historically conditioned and imprecise taxonomic label: it probably embraces, outside the great river-valleys of Asia, Minoan and Mycenaean Greece, the Aztecs and Incas, perhaps the Etruscans, but not the Phoenicians.)

The bibliography has become almost unmanageable; I single out E. J. Hobsbawm's introduction to Karl Marx, *Pre-capitalist Economic Formations*, transl. J. Cohen (London 1964), a volume that contains only an extract of a large neglected German manuscript by Marx; two articles in German by J. Pečírka, in *Eirene* 3 (1964) 147–69, 6 (1967) 141–74, summarizing and discussing the Soviet debate; G. Sofri, "Sul 'modo di produzione asiatico'. Appunti per la storia di una controversia", *Critica storica* 5 (1966) 704–810; H. Kreissig and H. Fischer, "Abgaben und Probleme der Wirtschaftsgeschichte des Altertums in der DDR", *Jahrbuch für Wirtschaftsgeschichte* (1967) I 270–84; I. Hahn, "Die Anfänge der antiken Gesellschaftsformation in Griechenland und das Problem der sogenannten asiatischen Produktionsweise", *ibid.* (1971) II 29–47. The whole of this discussion appears to be unknown to N. Brockmeyer, *Arbeitsorganisation und ökonomisches Denken in der Gutswirtschaft des römischen Reiches* (diss. Bochum 1968), both in his survey of the Marxist literature (pp. 33–70) and in the polemic against Marxist views that pervades his book. For him, as for his teacher Kiechle, "Marxism" appears to be restricted to historians in the Soviet Union and other eastern European countries.

40. *The Decline and Fall of the Roman Empire*, ed. J. B. Bury (London 1900) I 18.

41. The fundamental work on ancient population figures remains that of Julius Beloch, *Die Bevölkerung der griechisch-römischen Welt* (Leipzig 1886); see the conclusion reached after a massive re-examination of one portion of the field by Brunt, *Manpower*.

42. See F. Braudel, *The Mediterranean and the Mediterranean World in the Age of Philip II*, transl. S. Reynolds, vol. 1 (London 1972) pt. 1. E. C. Semple, *The Geography of the Mediterranean Region* (New York 1931) chap. 5, is still useful for its geographical material.

43. Josephus, *Jewish War* 2.385.

44. Among contemporary scholars, Lynn White, Jr., has been most insistent on the implications of heavy soils; see e.g. his *Medieval Technology and Social Change* (London 1962) chap. 2. On the long-range consequences of inland settlement, see now G. W. Fox, *History in Geographic Perspective. The Other France* (New York 1971).

45. A. Déléage, *La capitation du Bas-Empire* [*Annales d l'Est*, no. 14 (1945)] p. 254. Diversity of taxation was also prevalent in the early Empire, for the same reason, but no complete modern study of the subject exists.

46. F. W. Walbank, *The Awful Revolution. The Decline of the Roman Empire in the West* (Liverpool 1969) pp. 20, 31. Cf. "Mit der politischen Einheit verband sich die kulturelle und wirtschaftliche Einheit": S. Lauffer, "Das Wirtschaftsleben im römischen Reich", in *Jenseits von Resignation und Illusion*, ed. H. J. Heydorn and K. Ringshausen (Frankfurt 1971) pp. 135–53, at p. 135.

47. Walbank, *Awful Revolution* pp. 28 and 26, respectively.

48. Rostovtzeff, *RE* p. 69.

49. M. Wheeler, *Rome beyond the Imperial Frontiers* (Penguin ed., 1955) p. 109. The text says "400 square miles", an obvious misprint.

50. For comparable examples, see Rougé, *Commerce* pp. 415–17.

51. Julian, *Misopogon* 368c–369d.

52. The attempt by F. M. Heichelheim, "On Ancient Price Trends from the Early First Millennium B.C. to Heraclius I", *Finanzarchiv* 15 (1955) 498–511, is purely fanciful. The elaborate "price indexes" and other calculations by J. Szilagyi, "Prices and Wages in the Western Provinces of the Roman Empire", *Acta Antiqua* 11 (1963) 325–89, cannot be taken any more seriously: the material is scattered too widely in time and place, and the calculations fail to distinguish sufficiently between peasants and urban workers, for example, besides resting on too many unprovable, and sometimes patently false, assumptions which are not even made explicit. The essential point that "world trade" does not automatically imply a "world market price" was incisively made long ago by K. Riezler, *Über Finanzen und Monopole im alten Griechenland* (Berlin 1907) pp. 54–56.

53. B. J. L. Berry, *Geography of Market Centers and Retail Distribution* (Englewood Cliffs, N.J., 1967) p. 106.

NOTES TO CHAPTER II
(Pages 35–61)

1. Augustus, *Res gestae* 16.1 and Appendix 1.

2. Petronius, *Satyricon* 48.1–3, transl. J. Sullivan (Penguin ed., 1965).

3. See generally Veyne, "Trimalcion".

4. See Wilhelm (Gulielmus) Meyer, *Laudes Inopiae* (diss. Göttingen 1915); R. Visscher, *Das einfache Leben* (Göttingen 1965).

5. For a rapid survey of usage, see H. Hunger, "Φιλανθρωπία. Eine griechische Wortprägung auf ihrem Wege von Aischylos bis Theodoros Metochites", *Anzeiger d. Oesterreichischen Akad. d. Wiss., Phil.-hist. Kl.* 100 (1963) 1–20.

6. See M.-Th. Lenger, "La notion de 'bienfait' (*philanthrōpon*) royal et les ordonnances des rois Lagides", in *Studi in onore di Vincenzo Arangio-Ruiz* (Naples 1953) I 483–99. There is an exact parallel in the Roman *indulgentia principis*; see J. Gaudemet, *Indulgentia Principis* (Publication no. 3, 1962, of the Istituto di storia del diritto, Univ. of Trieste) p. 14.

7. See generally A. R. Hands, *Charities and Social Aids in Greece and Rome* (London 1968), esp. chaps. 3–6; H. Bolkestein, *Wohltätigkeit und Armenpflege im vorchristlichen Altertum* (Utrecht 1939).

8. See R. Duncan-Jones, "The Finances of the Younger Pliny", *PBSR*, n.s. 20 (1965) 177–88, reprinted with revisions in his *Economy*.

9. The fact that modern writers on antiquity sometimes speak of sin is immaterial; see K. Latte, "Schuld und Sünde in der griechischen Religion", *Archiv für Religionswissenschaft* 20 (1920/21) 254–98, reprinted in his *Kleine Schriften* (Munich 1968) pp. 3–35.

10. The best discussion is R. Duncan-Jones, "The Purpose and Organisation of the Alimenta", *PBSR*, n.s. 19 (1964) 123–46, reprinted with revisions in his *Economy*. Despite some valid criticisms by Duncan-Jones, P. Veyne, "La table des Ligures Baebiani et l'institution alimentaire de Trajan", *Mélanges d'archéologie et d'histoire* 70 (1958) 177–241, remains valuable on the narrowly Italian aim of the scheme (esp. 223–41). See also P. Garnsey, "Trajan's Alimenta: Some Problems", *Historia* 17 (1968) 367–81. There were also a few private *alimenta*, of no significance in the total picture. (See now chap. 7, sect. 6.)

11. It is enough to cite Frederiksen, "Caesar".

12. Thorstein Veblen, *The Theory of the Leisure Class* (Modern Library ed., New York 1934) p. 15.

13. Visscher, *Das einfache Leben* p. 31; cf. C. J. Ruijgh, "Enige Griekse adjectiva die 'arm' betekenen", in *Antidoron . . . S. Antoniadis* (Leiden 1957) pp. 13–21.

14. The evidence has been systematically collected by J. Hemelrijk, *Πενία en Πλοῦτος* (diss. Utrecht 1928); J. J. Van Manen, *ΠΕΝΙΑ en ΠΛΟΥΤΟΣ in de periode na Alexander* (diss. Utrecht 1931).

15. Visscher, *Das einfache Leben* pp. 30–31.

16. Quoted from M. L. Clarke, *Classical Education in Britain 1500–1900* (Cambridge 1959) p. 169.

17. B. Dobson, "The Centurionate and Social Mobility during the Principate", in *Recherches sur les structures sociales dans l'antiquité classique*, ed. C. Nicolet (Paris 1970) pp. 99–116.

18. L. Dumont, *Homo Hierarchicus. The Caste System and Its Implications*, transl. M. Sainsbury (London 1970) p. xvii.

19. Veyne, "Trimalcion" pp. 238–9.

20. I exclude caste from consideration for the good reason that castes did not exist in the ancient world; see Dumont, *Homo Hierarchicus*, esp. pp. 21, 215; E. R. Leach, "Introduction: What Should We Mean by Caste?" in *Aspects of Caste in South India, Ceylon and North-west Pakistan*, ed. Leach (Cambridge 1960) pp. 1–10; J. Littlejohn, *Social Stratification: An Introduction* (London 1972) chap. 4. Definitions of caste differ widely, but C. Bouglé's minimal formulation will suffice for my argument. In Dumont's phrasing of it (p. 21), "the caste system divides the whole society into a large number of hereditary groups, distinguished from one another and connected together by three characteristics: *separation* in matters of marriage and contact, whether direct or indirect (food); *division* of labour, each group having, in theory or by tradition, a profession from which their members can depart only within certain limits; and finally *hierarchy*, which ranks the groups as relatively superior or inferior to one another." When ancient historians write "caste", they mean "order".

21. P. A. Brunt, *Social Conflicts in the Roman Republic* (London 1971) p. 47. His chap. 3, "Plebeians versus Patricians, 509–287", is perhaps the best short account of the subject.

22. M. I. Henderson, "The Establishment of the Equester Ordo", *JRS* 53 (1963) 61–72, at p. 61, reprinted in R. Seager, ed., *The Crisis of the Roman Republic* (Cambridge and New York 1969) pp. 69–80. It is unnecessary for me to consider in detail the confused history of the *equites equo publico*, on which see most recently T. P. Wiseman, "The Definition of 'Eques Romanus' in the Late Republic and Early Empire", *Historia* 19 (1970) 67–83.

23. P. A. Brunt, "*Nobilitas* and *Novitas*", *JRS* 72 (1982) 1–17; Keith Hopkins, *Death and Renewal* (Cambridge 1983), chap. 2. On social mobility at this level, see now T. P. Wiseman, *New Men in the Roman Senate 139 B.C.–A.D. 14* (London 1971), a useful work despite the objections I shall make in a note later in this chapter.

24. See K. Hopkins, "Elite Mobility in the Roman Empire", *Past & Present*, no. 32 (1965) 12–26, reprinted in Finley, *Studies* chap. 5; H. Pleket, "Sociale Stratificatie en Sociale Mobiliteit in de Romeinse Keizertijd", *Tijdschrift voor Geschiedenis* 84 (1971) 215–51; M. Reinhold, "Usurpation of Status and Status Symbols in the Roman Empire", *Historia* 20 (1971) 275–302.

25. See Crook, *Law* pp. 37–45.

26. In introducing the volume on social structure cited in note 17, Nicolet records (pp. 11–12) that the original title of the colloquium from which the book emerged, "Ordres et classes dans l'Antiquité", was abandoned because that title would "effectively have eliminated historians of Greece". This decision seems to me to rest on a far too narrow, Roman-law conception of orders.

27. The social and political situation that developed in the Hellenistic age introduces new complications that would require too much space for the restricted objectives of the present discussion. Nor have I thought it necessary

to enter (beyond a passing reference) into the further complication of double citizenship in the Roman Empire.

28. Solon's system is the classic example from antiquity of "an estate structure in which status was not pre-determined by birth": Ossowski, *Class Structure* p. 42.

29. See my "Land, Debt, and the Man of Property in Classical Athens", *Political Science Quarterly* 68 (1953) 249–68, reprinted in Finley, *E. & S.*, chap. 4.

30. There is a vast literature on this point; see briefly Ossowski, *Class Structure* pp. 44–49.

31. See the brilliant analysis in *ibid.*, esp. chap. 5.

32. See P. Vidal-Naquet, "Les esclaves grecs étaient-ils une classe?" in his *Le Chasseur noir* (rev. ed., Paris 1983), pp. 211–21; cf. sect. 2 of chap. 7 below for a more extended discussion.

33. I write very positively, thanks to the definitive studies by P. A. Brunt, "The Equites in the Late Republic", in *Proceedings . . . Aix*, pp. 117–49, with comment by T. R. S. Broughton, pp. 150–62, both reprinted in Seager, *Crisis* pp. 83–130; and C. Nicolet, *L'ordre équestre à l'époque républicaine (312–43 av. J.-C.)* (Paris 1966), on which see Brunt's review in *Annales* 22 (1967) 1090–8.

34. *History and Class Consciousness* (London 1971), pp. 55–9; cf. W. G. Runciman, "Capitalism without Classes . . .", *British J. of Sociology* 34 (1983) 157–81; J.-P. Vernant, *Mythe et société . . .* (Paris 1974), pp. 11–19.

35. See C. Habicht, "Die herrschende Gesellschaft in den hellenistischen Monarchien", *Vierteljahrschrift für Sozial- und Wirtschaftsgeschichte* 45 (1958) 1–16.

36. The Latin is *quorum ordini conveniunt*, but Cicero is surely using *ordo* here in its generic sense, not in the technical sense of an order or estate. I have already indicated that I do not use "status" as the Romans did when they were speaking juridically.

37. Veyne, "Trimalcion" pp. 244–5.

38. *Ibid.*, p. 240.

39. See Ossowski, *Class Structure* chap. 7.

40. See H. G. Pflaum, "Titulature et rang social durant le Haut-Empire", in *Recherches* (cited in note 17) pp. 159–85; P. Arsac, "La dignité sénatoriale au Bas-Empire", *Revue historique de droit français . . .* 4th ser., 47 (1969) 198–243.

41. S. Treggiari, *Roman Freedmen during the Late Republic* (Oxford 1969) pp. 88–89.

42. T. P. Wiseman, "The Potteries of Vibienus and Rufrenus at Arretium", *Mnemosyne*, 4th ser., 16 (1963) 275–83. In *New Men* p. 77, Wiseman says of the *De officiis* passage that the attitude there expressed "was based on . . . the idealized memory of men like L. Cincinnatus . . ., who worked their own small farms and had no need of money. The survival of that ideal, which became obsolete in practice as soon as Rome progressed beyond what was essentially a subsistence economy, was largely due to the opinions and influence of the elder Cato." The idea that either Cato or Cicero was perpetuating an ideal in

which there was "no need of money" is so astonishing that I am at a loss for a reply other than a recommendation to read the works of Cato and Cicero, and to consider the Greek influence on the *De officiis* passage (see e.g. Seneca, *Moral Epistles* 88.21–23); cf. D. Nörr, "Zur sozialen und rechtlichen Bewertung der freien Arbeit in Rom", *ZSS* 82 (1965) 67–105, at pp. 72–79.

43. Frederiksen, "Caesar" p. 131 note 26.

44. In what follows I shall concentrate largely on convention, ignoring such a law as the one passed in 218 B.C. that limited the size of ships a senator could own, in effect to coasting-vessels large enough to carry the products of their own estates. Legal deterrents are on the whole mere details, effective only when the social climate is favourable, and it is the latter which therefore matters.

45. The documentation will be found in the rather chaotic book by G. Billeter, *Geschichte des Zinsfusses im griechisch-römischen Altertum* (Leipzig 1898).

46. See Frederiksen, "Caesar"; J. A. Crook, "A Study in Decoction", *Latomus* 26 (1967) 363–76.

47. *Letters to his Friends* 5.6.2. Cf. his thundering denunciation, *De officiis* 2.78–84, of debt-relief measures, in particular Caesar's, which he calls robbery on the same plane as agrarian laws; he was protecting property, not moneylenders.

48. *Letters to Atticus* 5.4.3; 7.3.11; 7.8.5.

49. See O. E. Schmidt, *Der Briefwechsel des M. Tullius Cicero von seiner Prokonsulat in Cilicien bis zu Caesars Ermordung* (Leipzig 1893) pp. 289–311.

50. See briefly Gelzer, *Nobility* pp. 114–17. Cicero's reference in 54 B.C., *Letters to his Friends* 1.9.18, to Caesar's great *liberalitas* to both himself and his brother, need not refer to the loan of 800,000 sesterces, which cannot be dated but is first attested in 51 B.C. (*Letters to Atticus* 5.5.2), but the word *liberalitas* certainly points away from interest if Cicero is being at all consistent in his usage, e.g. *De officiis* 1.43–44; *Laws* 1.48. The suggestion that Caesar charged interest rests on the elliptical phrase, "the 20,000 and the 800,000", in two letters to Atticus, 5.5.2 and 5.9.2. But 20,000 is puzzling if it is interest (at 2½%) on 800,000; interest rates in antiquity were normally in multiples or fractions of twelve, i.e. at so much per month.

51. The main texts are Cicero, *Letters to Atticus* 5.21; 6.1; see the brief account by E. Badian, *Roman Imperialism in the Late Republic* (2nd ed., Oxford 1968) pp. 84–87.

52. On the matters discussed here, see A. Bürge, "Vertrag und personale Abhängigkeit in Rom der späten Republik und der frühen Kaiserzeit", *ZSS* 97 (1980) 105–56, esp. pp. 114–38.

53. W. V. Harris, *War and Imperialism in Republican Rome* (Oxford 1979), pp. 68–104; Badian, *Imperialism*, chap. 5–6; A. H. M. Jones, *The Roman Economy*, ed. P. A. Brunt (Oxford 1974), pp. 114–22. (See further chap. 7, sect. 7.)

54. See Brunt, *Manpower*, pp. 301–5.

55. In the standard work by Lily Ross Taylor, *Party Politics in the Age of Caesar* (Berkeley and Los Angeles 1949), the following entry in the index,

"Bribery, see Elections, Jurors, Malpractice", encompasses everything that is said on the financial aspects, and that is hardly anything. Cf. D. Stockton, *Cicero, A Political Biography* (London 1971) p. 240, about Brutus's loan to the Salaminians: "The whole business stank of corruption."

56. A century later, when large fortunes were becoming steadily larger, the young Pliny, not one of the very richest senators but far from the poorest, had an annual income estimated to have been in the neighbourhood of 2,000,000 sesterces; see Duncan-Jones, "The Finances of Pliny". Cicero, incidentally, deposited his Cilician earnings with the tax-farmers in Ephesus and eventually had them confiscated by Pompey's agents; see Schmidt, *Briefwechsel* pp. 185–9.

57. Pritchett, *Military Practices* p. 85.

58. I. Shatzman, "The Roman General's Authority over Booty", *Historia* 21 (1972) 177–205.

59. Tacitus, *Annals* 13.42; Dio 61.10.3.

60. Crook, *Law* p. 90.

61. K.-H. Below, *Der Arzt im römischen Recht* (Munich 1953) pp. 7–21; cf. K. Visky, "La qualifica della medicina e dell' architettura nelle fonti del diritto romano", *Iura* 10 (1959) 24–66.

62. These possibilities are soberly stated by Broughton, in Seager, *Crisis* pp. 119–21.

63. Rougé, *Commerce* p. 311.

64. Brunt, in Seager, *Crisis* p. 94.

65. Broughton, *ibid.* pp. 118, 129.

66. Tenney Frank, *An Economic History of Rome* (2nd ed., London 1927) pp. 230–1. Roman jurists debated whether clay-pits were to be counted among the *instrumenta* of a farm and whether they could be subjects of a usufruct: *Digest* 8.3.6; 33.7.25.1.

67. Rostovtzeff, *RE* pp. 176–7.

68. "The Economic Life of the Towns of the Roman Empire", in his *The Roman Economy*, chap. 2.

69. *Ibid.* pp. 183–4.

70. Broughton, in Seager, *Crisis* pp. 129–30.

71. Cicero, *Letters to Atticus* 1.17.9, is instructive.

72. See briefly J. Pečírka, "A Note on Aristotle's Conception of Citizenship and the Role of Foreigners in Fourth Century Athens", *Eirene* 6 (1967) 23–26.

NOTES TO CHAPTER III
(Pages 62–94)

1. See Y. Garlan, "Les esclaves grecs en temps de guerre", in *Actes du Colloque d'histoire sociale*, Univ. of Besançon 1970 (Paris 1972) pp. 29–62.

2. The Roman *peculium* is discussed in every textbook of Roman law; on Athens, see E. L. Kazakevich, "Were οἱ χωρὶς οἰκοῦντες Slaves?", *VDI* (1960) no. 3, pp. 23–42, and "Slave Agents in Athens", *ibid.* (1961) no. 3, pp. 3–21 (both in Russian); L. Gernet, "Aspects du droit athénien de l'esclavage", in his *Droit et société dans la Grèce ancienne* (reprint, Paris 1964) pp. 151–72, at pp. 159–64 (originally published in *Archives d'histoire du droit oriental* 5 [1956] 159–87).

3. The full significance of the *peculium* in the assessment of ancient slavery has not been properly expressed, largely, I believe, because of over-concentration on the juridical aspect. An important early exception was E. Ciccotti, *Il tramonto della schiavitù nel mondo antico* (repr. Turin 1977) pt. II, chap. 9, who then weakened his argument by linking the slave with a *peculium* functionally to wage labour. E. M. Shtaerman, "Slaves and Freedmen in the Social Struggles at the End of the Republic", *VDI* (1962) no. 1, pp. 24–45 (in Russian), is clear about the distinction but fails to draw many of the implications because of her narrow focus, indicated by the title of her article. For a useful analogy, see H. Rosovsky, "The Serf Entrepreneur in Russia", *Explorations in Entrepreneurial History* 6 (1954) 207–33.

4. See e.g. *Theodosian Code* 5.17.1: *coloni* who seek to flee "should be put in irons like slaves, so that they may be compelled by a servile penalty to perform the duties appropriate to them as free men"; Justinian's *Code* 11.53.1: *coloni* and *inquilini* shall be "slaves of the land, not by tie of the tax but under the name and title of *coloni*".

5. A serf may not be easy to define precisely, but his status is describable only in terms of his personal relations to his lord, governed by customary rules about rights and obligations and marked, in particular, by the latter's full juridical authority (in the strict sense); see e.g. Marc Bloch, in *Cambridge Economic History*, vol. 1, ed. M. M. Postan (2nd ed., Cambridge 1966) pp. 253–4. Helots cannot be located in such terms. Any reader who chances upon my introductory chapter to D. Daiches and A. Thorlby, ed., *Literature and Western Civilization*, vol. 1 (London: Aldus Books 1972), may be puzzled by "helots (serfs)" on p. 30. The explanation is that the word "serfs" was added, without my knowledge, after I had approved the final copy for the printer.

6. The history of the interrelationship between the work regime and the consciousness of time is itself revealing. I know of no study pertaining to antiquity; for modern history, see E. P. Thompson, "Time, Work-Discipline, and Industrial Capitalism", *Past & Present*, no. 38 (1967) 56–97, with extensive bibliography.

7. See J. A. C. Thomas, "'Locatio' and 'operae'", *Bulletino dell' Istituto di diritto romano* 64 (1961) 231–47; J. Macqueron, *Le travail des hommes libres dans l'antiquité romaine* (cyclostyled "Cours de Pandectes 1954–5", Aix-en-Provence) pp. 25–29.

8. Cf. the legendary story told by Herodotus (8.37) about the founders of the Macedonian royal dynasty.

9. See "Debt-Bondage and the Problem of Slavery" in Finley, *E. & S.*, chap. 9.

10. For a brief theoretical analysis in a modern framework, see Ossowski, *Class Structure* pp. 92–96. This is an approach I first developed in "Servile Statuses of Ancient Greece", *Revue internationale des droits de l'antiquité*, 3rd ser., 7 (1960) 165–89, and "Slavery and Freedom".

11. Nor did intellectuals of servile origin produce any anti-slavery ideas, or indeed any ideas that distinguished them from their free-born counterparts; see Shtaerman, "Slaves and Freedmen" pp. 34–35.

12. D. M. Pippidi, "Le problème de la main-d'œuvre agricole dans les colonies grecques de la Mer Noire", in *Problèmes de la terre en Grèce ancienne*, ed. Finley (Paris and The Hague 1973) chap. 3, is decisive on this last point.

13. See my "Debt-Bondage"; Frederiksen, "Caesar" p. 129; W. L. Westermann, "Enslaved Persons Who Are Free", *American Journal of Philology* 59 (1938) 1–30, at pp. 9–18.

14. Caesar. *Civil War* 1.34.2; cf. 1.56.3.

15. N. D. Fustel de Coulanges, "Le colonat romain", in his *Recherches sur quelques problèmes d'histoire* (Paris 1885) pp. 15–24. The source references are Pliny, *Letters* 9.37; Columella, *De re rustica* 1.3.12; Varro, *De re rustica* 1.17.2; cf. Sallust, *Catiline* 33.1.

16. I myself overlooked Fustel de Coulanges when I wrote "Debt-Bondage"; now I should write p. 159 with difference nuances. See now my "Private Farm Tenancy in Roman Italy before Diocletian", in Finley, *Roman Property*, chap. 6.

17. The labour force on the land in the Hellenistic and Roman east needs thorough re-examination. The available literature is shot through with irrelevancies, loose terminology and concepts, and unwarranted "quantitative" assertions (e.g. the supposed preponderance of free independent peasants). The following bibliography is very selective: M. Rostowzew, *Studien zur Geschichte des römischen Kolonates* (*Archiv für Papyrusforschung*, Beiheft 1, 1910) and *The Social & Economic History of the Hellenistic World*, corr. ed. (3 vols., Oxford 1953), where the relevant discussion is scattered and subject to correction on the matter of temple-estates in Asia Minor (not central to my purposes), on which see T. R. S. Broughton, "New Evidence on Temple-Estates in Asia Minor", in *Studies . . . in Honor of Allan Chester Johnson*, ed. P. R. Coleman-Norton (Princeton 1951) pp. 236–50, and T. Zawadzki, "Quelques remarques sur l'étendue de l'accroissement des domaines des grands temples en Asie Mineure", *Eos* 46 (1952/3) 83–96, both with further references; Zawadzki, *Problems of the Social and Agrarian Structure in Asia Minor in the Hellenistic Age*, published by the Historical Commission of the Poznan Society of Friends of Science, vol. 16, no. 3 (1952) in Polish, with English summary, pp. 67–77; Westermann, "Enslaved Persons"; E. Bikerman, *Institutions des Séleucides* (Paris 1938) pp. 172–185; H. Kreissig, "Hellenistische Grundbesitzverhältnisse im oströmischen Kleinasien", *Jahrbuch für Wirtschaftsgeschichte* (1967) I 200–6; Liebeschuetz, *Antioch* pp. 61–73. The exceptional situation in Judaea after the Maccabees put

an end to Hellenistic tenures (but not to debt bondage) is significant in reverse: Kreissig, "Die landwirtschaftliche Situation in Palästina vor dem judäischen Krieg", *Acta Antiqua* 17 (1969) 223–54. (See now chap. 7, *n* 11.)

18. See S. Gsell, "Esclaves ruraux dans l'Afrique romaine", in *Mélanges Gustave Glotz* (2 vols., Paris 1932) I 397–415. It was a Carthaginian, Mago, whom Roman writers called the "father of husbandry"; his work, in 28 books, was translated into Latin by order of the Senate (Columella 1.1.13). The labour situation in Gaul, Spain and the rest of North Africa is still open to discussion. My view is that agricultural slavery was far more common than most modern writers allow; for one thing, I see no other way to explain the very large farm-building complexes of imperial Gaul. (I have changed my position on this subject: see chap. 7, sect. 1 below.)

19. On 20,000, see A. H. M. Jones, *Athenian Democracy* (Oxford 1957) pp. 76–79; 400,000, a figure appearing in Athenaeus VI 272c, still has its defenders despite the devastating critique by W. L. Westermann, "Athenaeus and the Slaves of Athens", *Harvard Studies in Classical Philology*, supp. vol. (1941) 451–70; see the survey of recent literature by L. Gallo in *Annali . . . Pisa*, 3rd ser., 9 (1979) 1595–1605.

20. The slave population of Italy may have been twice that of adult male citizens at the death of Caesar: Brunt, *Manpower*, chap. 10.

21. See K. M. Stampp, *The Peculiar Institution: Slavery in the Ante-Bellum South* (New York 1956) pp. 29–30.

22. Plutarch, *Caesar* 15.3; Appian, *Celtica* 1.2. See also the data tabulated by Pritchett, *Military Practices* pp. 78–79, and generally P. Ducrey, *Le traitement des prisonniers de guerre dans la Grèce antique* (Paris 1968), esp. pp. 74–92, 131–9, 255–7; H. Volkmann, *Die Massenversklavungen der Einwohner eroberten Städte in der hellenistisch-römischen Zeit* [Akad. der Wissenschaften und der Literatur, Mainz, *Abhandlungen der geistes- und sozialwissenschaftliche Klasse* (1961) no. 3], the latter to be used with caution: see my review in *Gnomon* 39 (1967) 521–2.

23. Notably by Westermann, "Athenaeus".

24. S. Lauffer, *Die Bergwerkssklaven von Laureion* [Mainz *Abhandlungen* (1955) no. 15, (1956) no. 11] II 904–12. As many as 40,000 slaves were regularly employed in the silver mines of Carthagena in Spain in the early second century B.C. according to Polybius (quoted by Strabo 3.2.10).

25. Strictly speaking, the 120 were the property of Cephalus's sons, Lysias and Polemarchus, also metics, confiscated by the Thirty Tyrants in 404 B.C., and a few were presumably domestics, not shield-makers: Lysias 12.19.

26. L. R. Taylor, "Freedom and Freeborn in the Epitaphs of Imperial Rome", *American Journal of Philology* 82 (1961) 113–32.

27. On the restrictions on the freedom of free gold miners in Dacia, see A. Berger, "A Labor Contract of A.D. 164", *Classical Philology* 43 (1948) 231–242; cf. Macqueron, *Travail* pp. 202–26.

28. In Athens, casual labour "shaped up" daily at a particular spot near the Agora: see A. Fuks, "Κολωνὸς μίσθιος: Labour Exchange in Classical

Athens", *Eranos* 49 (1951) 171–3. I shall be reminded of the third-century funeral monument from Maktar in central Tunisia (*Corpus Inscriptionum Latinarum* VIII 11824), memorializing a farm labourer who ended his life as a local senator. I pay my respects to the defunct, but until a few more such epitaphs are discovered, I shall remain unpersuaded by the attention this "Harvester inscription" receives in modern accounts, including such not uncommon nonsense as that it "bears proud testimony to the material and spiritual rewards of that life of toil and frugality idealized in Virgil's *Georgics*": G. Steiner, "Farming", in *The Muses at Work*, ed. C. Roebuck (Cambridge, Mass., 1969) pp. 148–170, at pp. 169–70.

29. Demosthenes 27.19,26; 28.12. For further Greek evidence see my *Land and Credit* pp. 66–68.

30. There is no disagreement about Arezzo and Lezoux: see G. Pucci, "La produzione della ceramica aretina", *Dialoghi di archeologia* 7 (1973) 255–93; F. Kiechle, *Sklavenarbeit und technische Fortschritt im römischen Reich* (Wiesbaden 1969) pp. 67–99; generally, W. L. Westermann, "Industrial Slavery in Roman Italy", *Journal of Economic History* 2 (1942) 149–63. The pattern in La Graufesenque appears to have been more complex; see R. Marichal in *Comptes rendus de l'Acad. des Inscriptions . . .* (1971) 188–208. Even if it should turn out that there were some enterprises in antiquity employing hired free labour, that could not significantly alter the pattern so unanimously witnessed by the sources at our disposal.

31. A. H. M. Jones, "The Caste System in the Later Roman Empire", *Eirene* 8 (1970) 79–96, at p. 83. The best account of the imperial factories remains that of A. W. Persson, *Staat und Manufaktur im römischen Reiche* (*Skriften . . . Vetenskaps-Societeten Lund*, no. 3, 1923) pp. 68–81, apparently unknown to N. Charbonnel, "La condition des ouvriers dans les ateliers impériaux au IVe et Ve siècles", *Travaux et recherches de la Faculté de Droit de Paris*, Série "Sciences historiques", 1 (1964) 61–93.

32. Perhaps the best Greek evidence is provided by the temple records at Delos, analyzed by G. Glotz, "Les salaires à Délos", *Journal des Savants* 11 (1913) 206–15, 251–60; and P. H. Davis, "The Delos Building Accounts", *Bulletin de correspondance hellénique* 61 (1937) 109–35. See also A. Burford, *The Greek Temple Builders at Epidauros* (Liverpool 1969), esp. pp. 191–206; "The Economics of Greek Temple Building", *Proceedings of the Cambridge Philological Society*, n.s. 11 (1965) 21–34. No comparably detailed data are available from Rome. Some exceptions must be acknowledged, one of which (from Athens) will be considered later in this chapter.

33. See Crook, *Law* pp. 191–8. In Roman law a free man who fought wild beasts in the arena for pay suffered *infamia*, but not one who did so for sport: *Digest* 3.1.1.6. That is precisely the distinction I have been stressing in another sphere, commonly overlooked by historians, as in the following passage from Frank, *Survey V* 235–6: "That free builders continued to make their livelihood in the capital is proved by the unusually large and active *collegium fabrum tignuariorum*. . . . From a study of the membership lists it seems likely that these 1000–1500 free or freed *fabri* were successful carpenters who controlled the

services of numerous slaves. . . . It is probable, then, that in public works large numbers of *free laborers* were employed" (my italics).

34. *"Panem et circenses* was the formula . . . on which they relied to keep the underlying population from imagining vain remedies for their own hard case": T. Veblen, *Essays in Our Changing Order* (reprint, New York 1954) p. 450. He added, characteristically: "in the matter of *circenses* . . . there has been change and improvement during these intervening centuries . . .; since it is the common man who is relieved of afterthought, it is only reasonable that the common man should pay the cost." The demonstration that the Roman plebs could not have "spent the greater part of its time at the races, the theatre and gladiatorial shows" is beside the point: J. P. V. D. Balsdon *"Panem et circenses"*, in *Hommages* . . . *Renard* II (Brussels 1969), pp. 57–60; cf. A. Cameron, *Bread and Circuses* (Inaug. Lecture, King's College, London 1973); J. Le Gall, "Rome ville de fainéants?", *Revue des études latines* 49 (1971) 266–77.

35. Frontinus, *On the Aqueducts of the City of Rome* 96–118. On the important role of slaves in the building trades generally, the sparse evidence will be found in H. J. Loane, *Industry and Commerce of the City of Rome (50 B.C.–200 A.D.)* (Baltimore 1938) pp. 79–86.

36. Lucian, *Apology* 10; see D. Nörr, "Zur sozialen und rechtlichen Bewertung der freien Arbeit in Rom", *ZSS* 82 (1965) 67–105, at pp. 75–76.

37. Westermann, "Industrial Slavery" p. 158.

38. E.g. A. M. Duff, *Freedmen in the Early Roman Empire* (reprint, Cambridge 1958) p. 11: an "uneven struggle against more astute Orientals".

39. M. L. Gordon, "The Freedman's Son in Municipal Life", *JRS* 21 (1931) 65–77, based on more than 1000 texts.

40. Lines 56–57 of a letter of Claudius, first published by H. I. Bell, *Jews and Christians in Egypt* (1924), most recently in the *Corpus Papyrorum Judaicarum*, ed. V. A. Tcherikower and A. Fuks, vol. 2 (Cambridge, Mass., 1960) no. 153.

41. Lines 59–60 and 99–101, respectively, of a long Greek inscription published by J. H. Oliver, *Marcus Aurelius: Aspects of Civic and Cultural Policy in the East (Hesperia*, Suppl. 13, 1970).

42. J. Day, "Agriculture in the Life of Pompeii", *Yale Classical Studies* 3 (1932) 166–208, at pp. 178–9 (his estimates of acreage rest on too flimsy a base). Some literary and epigraphical texts are collected by Shtaerman, "Slaves and Freedmen" pp. 26–27, and S. Treggiari, *Roman Freedmen during the Late Republic* (Oxford 1969) pp. 106–10, but neither attempts to evaluate the evidence.

43. See Veyne, "Trimalcion" pp. 230–1, who calls them an "aborted class".

44. J. H. Plumb, *The Growth of Political Stability in England 1675–1725* (Penguin ed., 1969) pp. 21–22.

45. Most reminiscent of Stolz was Zenon, manager of the great estate of Apollonius under Ptolemy II, and it has now become evident that he was unusual and in the end a failure; see the articles by J. Bingen and D. J. Crawford in *Problèmes de la terre*, ed. Finley, chaps. 11–12.

46. Catullus 23.1; 24.5, 8, 10.

47. *Orations* 31.11; see Jones, *LRE* p. 851.

48. *Ibid.*, p. 647.

49. For the data, see J. H. Randall, Jr., "The Erechtheum Workmen", *American Journal of Archaeology* 57 (1953) 199–210.

50. The rate might come out different for the men paid on piecework, if we knew how to calculate it.

51. The classic text is Appian, *Civil Wars* 1.9–11.

52. See Shtaerman, "Slaves and Freedmen" pp. 25–26, 36, 41–43.

53. *Eastern Tour* (1771) IV 361, quoted from R. H. Tawney, *Religion and the Rise of Capitalism* (Penguin ed., 1947) p. 224.

54. K. Hopkins, "Slavery in Classical Antiquity", in *Caste and Race: Comparative Approaches*, ed. A. de Reuck and J. Knight (London 1967) pp. 166–77, at pp. 170–1.

55. Brunt, *Manpower* chap. 19.

56. For second-century allotments, see Livy 35.40; 39.44,55; 40.29; 42.4. On the complicated evidence for Caesar's measure, see Brunt, *Manpower* pp. 312–15. Presumably the recipients of such small allotments were expected to supplement their crops by pasture on common land or seasonal work on larger neighbouring estates. Be that as it may, such pitiful holdings are reliably attested, the poor prospects of the recipients predictable.

57. The "Harvester inscription" commented on in note 28 above has its counterpart in this field in the repeated evocation of a "bakers' strike" supposedly recorded in a fragmentary inscription from Ephesus, probably of the late second century, published by W. H. Buckler, "Labour Disputes in the Province of Asia", in *Anatolian Studies Presented to Sir William Ramsay* (Manchester 1923) pp. 27–50, at pp. 29–33, conveniently reproduced by T. R. S. Broughton, in Frank, *Survey* IV 847–8. This isolated, incomplete and far from lucid text gives no clue to the reasons for the bakers' "seditiousness", no basis for assuming collective economic grievances or demands of a guild character. Rostovtzeff's paragraphs (*RE* pp. 178–9) on Roman Asia Minor, "where the workmen had ceased to be serfs but had not become citizens of the cities", engaged in "real professional strikes" and organized "genuine attempts at social revolution", are imaginative fiction.

58. See J.-P. Vernant, *Mythe et pensée chez les Grecs* (Paris 1965) pt. 4; F. M. De Robertis, *Lavoro e lavoratori nel mondo romano* (Bari 1963) pp. 9–14; cf. the opening pages of H. Altevogt, *Labor improbus* (Münster 1952); B. Effe, "Labor improbus — ein Grundgedanke der Georgica in der Sicht des Manilius", *Gymnasium* 78 (1971) 393–9.

59. See Marie Delcourt, *Héphaistos ou la légende du magicien* [*Bibliothèque de la Fac. de philosophie et lettres*, Liège, no. 146 (1957)]. The attempt by H. Philipp, *Tektonon Daidalos. Der bildende Künstler und sein Werk im vorplatonischen Schrifttum* (Berlin 1968) chap. 3, to argue otherwise (without any reference to Delcourt) is unpersuasive special pleading. It is perhaps necessary to add that the outburst of coins depicting Hephaestus in Asia Minor during the Roman imperial

period, chiefly from the chaotic years 235–270, is to be linked with the Achilles legend, not with local cults of Hephaestus; see F. Brommer, "Die kleinasiatischen Münzen mit Hephaistos", *Chiron* 2 (1972) 531–44.

60. Shtaerman, "Slaves and Freedmen", comes down firmly on this point despite her positive assessment (pp. 31–33) of the "bonds" between free and slave in the *collegia*. It is a pity that we know nothing more about the unusual case of the revolt of Aristonicus in Asia Minor in 132 or 131 B.C. than that "he quickly assembled a multitude of poor men and slaves (*douloi*) whom he won over by a promise of freedom and whom he called Heliopolitans" (Strabo 14.1.38); see most recently J. C. Dumont, "A propos d'Aristonicos", *Eirene* 5 (1966) 189–96, and briefly my "Utopianism Ancient and Modern", in *The Critical Spirit. Essays in Honor of Herbert Marcuse*, ed. K. A. Wolff and B. Moore, Jr. (Boston 1967) pp. 3–20, at pp. 10–12, reprinted in my *Use and Abuse of History* (London 1975), chap. 11. By *douloi* Strabo probably referred to dependent labour other than chattel slaves, but that is not significant in the present context.

61. Petronius, *Satyricon* 69.3; 75.11, etc.; cf. Veyne, "Trimalcion" pp. 218–219.

62. For example, at Morgantina in the second Sicilian revolt: Diodorus 36.3; see my *Ancient Sicily* (rev. ed., London 1979) chap. 11.

63. See Garlan, "Esclaves en guerre" pp. 45–48.

64. E.g. Max Weber, "Die soziale Gründe des Untergangs der antiken Kultur", in his *Gesammelte Aufsätze zur Sozial- und Wirtschaftsgeschichte* (Tübingen 1924) pp. 289–311, at pp. 299–300; Salvioli, *Capitalisme* pp. 250–3; E. M. Schtajerman, *Die Krise der Sklavenhalterordnung im Westen des römischen Reiches*, transl. from the Russian by W. Seyfarth (Berlin 1964) pp. 34–35, 69 and elsewhere.

65. Of the large and growing body of literature, it is enough to mention the articles printed in R. W. Fogel and S. L. Engerman, ed., *The Reinterpretation of American Economic History* (New York 1971) pt. 7, with the critique by N. G. Butlin, *Ante-bellum Slavery—A Critique of a Debate* (Australian National Univ., Canberra, 1971); E. D. Genovese, *The Political Economy of Slavery* (New York 1965) pt. 2; the methodologically weak, but nonetheless useful, work of R. S. Starobin, *Industrial Slavery in the Old South* (New York 1970), esp. chap. 5; M. Moohr, "The Economic Impact of Slave Emancipation in British Guiana, 1832–1852", *EcHR*, 2nd ser., 25 (1972) 588–607, who concludes; "Had planters and public officials ... been completely successful in their attempts to keep the colony's former slaves landless, emancipation would have resulted in an economy which would have been difficult to distinguish from its pre-emancipation counterpart." Acknowledgement should be made of the pioneering study of C. A. Yeo, "The Economics of Roman and American Slavery", *Finanzarchiv*, n.F., 13 (1952) 445–85, though the American analysis is now antiquated and some of the argument is faulty.

66. Schtajerman, *Krise* pp. 90–91.

67. The medieval evidence, admittedly thin but also very consistent, is tabulated by B. H. Slicher van Bath, *Yield Ratios, 810–1820* [*A.A.G. Bijdragen*, no. 10 (1963)]; cf. his *The Agrarian History of Western Europe, A.D. 500–1850* (London 1963) pp. 18–20 and the table on pp. 328–33. Slicher van Bath has no Italian figures earlier than the eighteenth century, and that complicates an already difficult comparison, given the state of both the ancient and the medieval evidence. Furthermore, yield ratios alone are far from an adequate index of agricultural production; see e.g. P. F. Brandon, "Cereal Yields on the Sussex Estate of Battle Abbey during the Later Middle Ages", *EcHR*, 2nd ser., 25 (1972) 403–20. But that is all we have from antiquity (and not enough even of that) except for Ptolemaic and Roman Egypt, which are out of consideration. At least, there is no evidence known to me that supports the view I am contesting.

68. See my "Technical Innovation" p. 43. On the considerable technical achievements (without innovation) of the Romans in the Spanish mines, see P. R. Lewis and G. D. B. Jones, "Roman Gold-mining in North-west Spain", *JRS* 60 (1970) 169–85.

69. A. Fishlow and R. W. Fogel, "Quantitative Economic History: An Interim Evaluation", *Journal of Economic History* 31 (1971) 15–42, at p. 27.

70. An excellent collection of these texts has been made by E. M. Shtaerman, "The 'Slave Question' in the Roman Empire", *VDI* (1965) no. 1, pp. 62–81. At one point (p. 66) she seems to say that fear of revolt posed serious *economic* questions, but her material leads her to abandon this idea in the rest of the article.

71. Ammianus 31.4–6; see E. A. Thompson, *The Visigoths in the Time of Ulfila* (Oxford 1966) pp. 39–42.

72. *Theodosian Code* 10.10.25; 5.7.2; 5.6.3, respectively.

73. *Colonus* originally meant "farmer", "rustic", then also "tenant", but I shall restrict my use to its late sense of "tied tenant". See K.-P. Johne et al., *Die Kolonen in Italien und den westlichen Provinzen des römischen Reiches* (Berlin 1983), to the end of the second century; for Italy, the English version of *Colonus*, by P. W. de Neeve (Amsterdam 1984). Free landowning peasants also remained in existence, but there is no way even to guess their proportion. I suggest that historians tend to exaggerate it, for example with respect to the peasants about whom Libanius spoke so vehemently in his 47th oration.

74. For a discussion of this point, with some detail and bibliography, see sect. 2 of chap. 7 below.

75. See W. L. Westermann, *The Slave Systems of Greek and Roman Antiquity* (Philadelphia 1955) pp. 32–33 (central Greece after 150 B.C., when the slave trade was largely diverted to Italy); I. Biezunska-Malowist, "Les esclaves nés dans la maison du maître . . . en Égypte romaine", *Studii Clasice* 3 (1962) 147–162, and "La procréation des esclaves comme source de l'esclavage" (with M. Malowist), in *Mélanges offerts à K. Michalowski* (Warsaw 1966) pp. 275–80.

76. See generally P. Garnsey, *Social Status and Legal Privilege in the Roman Empire* (Oxford 1970); on punishments, his "Why Penal Laws Became Harsher: the Roman Case", *Natural Law Forum* 13 (1968) 141–62, at pp. 147–52.

77. *Corpus Inscriptionum Latinarum* VIII 10570; text and translation are given by R. M. Haywood, in Frank, *Survey* IV 96–98.

78. Rostowzew, *Kolonat* pp. 370–3.

79. Garnsey, *Legal Privilege* p. 274.

80. The sparse evidence on early Christian attitudes has most recently been examined at interminable length by H. Gültzow, *Christentum und Sklaverei in den ersten drei Jahrhunderten* (Bonn 1969).

81. Cf. the attitude of Stoics and Christians to punishment generally: Garnsey, "Penal Laws" pp. 154–6.

82. See D. B. Davis, *The Problem of Slavery in Western Culture* (Ithaca 1966) chaps. 1–3.

83. See E. A. Thompson, "Peasant Revolts in Late Roman Gaul and Spain". *Past & Present*, no. 2 (1952) 11–23, reprinted in Finley, *Studies* chap. 14. The destruction visible archaeologically in southern Gaul of the late fourth century may be the work of the Bacaudae; see Fouet, *Villa de Montmaurin* p. 311.

84. Rostovtzeff, *RE* p. 514.

85. Jones, *LRE* p. 469; cf. his "Over-Taxation and the Decline of the Roman Empire", *Antiquity* 33 (1959) 39–43. (But see chap. 7, sect. 7.)

86. There is no reason to reject, for example, the picture in *Panegyrici latini* 5.5–6 of the devastation of Burgundy in 269–70.

87. See A. L. Rivet, "Social and Economic Aspects", in *The Roman Villa in Britain*, ed. Rivet (London 1969) pp. 173–216, at pp. 189–98; cf. Erik Gren, *Kleinasien und der Ostbalkan in der wirtschaftlichen Entwicklung der römischen Kaiserzeit* [*Uppsala Universitets Årsskrift* (1941) no. 9] pp. 135–49. Grain from Britain was also shipped to the armies on the Rhine: Ammianus 18.2.3; Libanius, *Orations* 18.83.

88. Ammianus, 16.5.15; cf. Salvian, *On the Government of God* 4.30–31; 5.35.

89. *Ibid.* 5.25, 38–45.

90. See briefly A. Grenier, "Aux origines de l'histoire rurale: la conquête du sol français", *Annales* 2 (1930) 26–47, at pp. 40–41.

91. Fustel de Coulanges, "Colonat", gave an elegant demonstration (esp. pp. 92, 119) from the law codes that practice preceded legislation. Max Weber made the same point, independently so far as I can tell: *Die römische Agrargeschichte* (Stuttgart 1891) p. 219.

92. See the fundamental study of Ernst Levy, "Von römischen Precarium zur germanischen Landleihe", *ZSS* 66 (1948) 1–30, at pp. 17–25.

93. Even e.g. in North Africa: H. D'Escurac-Doisy, "Notes sur le phénomène associatif dans le monde paysan à l'époque du Haut-Empire", *Antiquités Africaines* 1 (1961) 59–71.

94. P. Collinet, "Le colonat dans l'empire romain", *Recueils de la Société Jean Bodin* 2 (1937) 85–122; on regional variations, see also J. Percival, "Seigneurial Aspects of Late Roman Estate Management", *English Historical Review* 84 (1969) 449–73.

95. Both the availability and the neglect of untapped sources of information are documented by I. Hahn, "Freie Arbeit und Sklavenarbeit in der spätantiken Stadt", *Annales Univ.* . . . *Budapestiensis, Sectio historica* 5 (1961) 23–39, on which my brief account is largely based, and W. Seyfarth, *Soziale Fragen der spätrömischen Kaiserzeit im Spiegel der Theodosianus* (Berlin 1963) pp. 104–27. On the riots in the city of Rome, see H. P. Kohns, *Versorgungskrisen und Hungerrevolten in spätantiken Rom* (Bonn 1961); for a somewhat earlier period, C. R. Whittaker, "The Revolt of Papirius Dionysius A.D. 190", *Historia* 13 (1964) 348–69.

NOTES TO CHAPTER IV
(Pages 95–122)

1. Tertullian, *Apologeticum* 13.6, called direct taxes "marks of bondage" (*notae captivitatis*).

2. How exceptional this was (and is) can be seen from the theme of political subjection that runs through *Peasants and Peasant Societies*, ed. T. Shanin (Penguin 1971).

3. Heitland, *Agricola* pp. 226 and 200–1, respectively (echoing Lucretius 3.1060–70). This book remains the fullest presentation of the Graeco-Roman literary sources on the subject. The aristocrats of Antioch provide a late, eastern analogy; see Liebeschuetz, *Antioch* p. 51.

4. Xenophon's account, *Hellenica* 5.2.5–7, of the Spartan dismantling of Mantinea in Arcadia in 385 B.C. provides a suggestive example.

5. The source is Dionysius of Halicarnassus, *On the Orations of Lysias* 32 (often published as the "argument" to Lysias 34). I have elsewhere demonstrated the impossibility of making any reliable calculation of Athenian landholding units from the available evidence: *Land and Credit* pp. 56–60.

6. I exclude the innumerable bits and pieces of information in the Greek papyri of Hellenistic and Roman Egypt, reflecting an untypical land regime about which a little will be said shortly.

7. Supposedly the best ancient source as far as calculations are concerned, Columella, has now been demolished by Duncan-Jones in chap. 2 of his *Economy*. Attempts such as that of René Martin, "Pline le Jeune et les problèmes économiques de son temps", *Revue des études anciennes* 69 (1967) 62–97, to translate recorded money-figures of estates into acreage on the basis of a mythical (and anyway irrelevant) average selling price of 1000 sesterces per *jugerum* must be rejected out of hand.

8. See D. J. Crawford, *Kerkeosiris* (Cambridge 1971).

9. C. Préaux, *L'économie royale des Lagides* (Brussels 1939) pp. 17–20.

10. The calculations, reasonably well founded, are those of Jones, *LRE* pp. 780–4. The basic study of the Apion estates in E. R. Hardy, Jr., *The Large Estates of Byzantine Egypt* (New York 1931); for the more recent bibliography, see D. Bonneau, "L'administration de l'irrigation dans les grandes domaines d'Égypte...", and J. Fikhman, "On the Structure of the Egyptian Large Estate in the Sixth Century", in the *Proceedings* of the XIIth International Congress of Papyrology (Toronto 1970) pp. 43–60 and 123–32, respectively.

11. *Syll.* 141. Here and elsewhere in this discussion I am compelled to qualify the figures because of the vagaries of Greek measurements. This text is quite specific—three *plethra* of vineland—and a *plethron* was 100 × 100 Greek feet. But the Greek foot was not stable.

12. On the Buselos family, see J. K. Davies, *Athenian Propertied Families 600–300 B.C.* (Oxford 1971) no. 2921. For other Athenian examples (and the impossibility of going beyond mere examples), see my *Land and Credit* pp. 56–60; for other Greek examples, A. Jardé, *Les céréales dans l'antiquité grecque* (Paris 1925) pp. 118–22.

13. For what follows, see P. Graindor, *Un milliardaire antique, Hérode Atticus et sa famille* (Cairo 1930; repr. New York 1979).

14. It is revealing that Rostovtzeff, *RE* pp. 149–50, exhibits Herodes as one of the prize specimens of "the wealth which was concentrated in the hands of city *bourgeoisie*".

15. A brief summary of the evidence will be found in John Day, *An Economic History of Athens under Roman Domination* (New York 1942) pp. 235–6.

16. U. Kahrstedt, *Das wirtschaftliche Gesicht Griechenlands in der Kaiserzeit* (Bern 1954) pp. 47–48.

17. I say this with confidence despite the undeniable uncertainty of the recorded census figures; the most recent discussion is Brunt, *Manpower* pp. 77–81.

18. Caesar, *Civil War* 3.4.4 and 1.17, respectively.

19. The data have to be assembled from the Greek and Latin lives of Melania and from Palladius, *Lausiac History*. There is a good modern edition of the Greek life by D. Gorce (Paris 1962).

20. See e.g. S. Applebaum, in *The Agrarian History of England and Wales*, vol. I ii, ed. H. P. R. Finberg (Cambridge 1972) pp. 230–1; G. Fouet, *La villa gallo-romaine de Montmaurin (Haute-Garonne)* [*Gallia*, supp. 20 (1969)] pp. 304–12.

21. J. O. Tjader, *Die nichtliterarischen lateinischen Papyri Italiens aus der Zeit 445–700* (Lund 1955) no. 1.

22. Graeco-Roman pagan temples were not large landowners, except in some eastern provinces; see the articles by Broughton and Zawadzki cited in chap. 3, note 17.

23. Plutarch, *Marius* 34.1–2. Cf. Cicero's allegation, in his speech for Sextus Roscius (20–21), that Sulla's freedman Crysogonus acquired ten of

Roscius' estates in the Tiber Valley worth six million sesterces for a mere two thousand.

24. See M. Jaczynowska, "The Economic Differentiation of the Roman Nobility at the End of the Republic", *Historia* 11 (1962) 486–99.

25. On luxurious private building, an excellent pointer, see J. H. D'Arms, *Romans on the Bay of Naples* (Cambridge, Mass., 1970); Axel Boëthius, *The Golden House of Nero* (Ann Arbor 1960).

26. See chap. 2 at note 10 and the references there. What follows is based on the careful computation by Duncan-Jones.

27. The figures are given in his short poem, *De herediolo* ("On My Little Inheritance"); see the analysis by M. K. Hopkins, "Social Mobility in the Later Roman Empire: the Evidence of Ausonius", *Classical Quarterly*, n.s. 11 (1961) 239–49, at pp. 240–3.

28. See e.g. R. P. Duncan–Jones, "Some Configurations of Landholding in the Roman Empire", in Finley, *Roman Property*, chap. 2; A. H. M. Jones, "Census Records of the Later Roman Empire", *JRS* 41 (1953) 49–64, reprinted in his *Roman Economy*, chap. 10.

29. J. S. Saul and R. Woods, in Shanin, *Peasants* p. 105. The editor, in his introduction (pp. 14–15) and again pp. 240–5, also includes "specific traditional culture" and "the underdog position". No doubt they commonly are "basic facets" but, as I have already stressed, the classical Graeco-Roman peasant stood apart in these respects, falling rather within Shanin's class of "analytically marginal groups".

30. A. Galeski, *ibid.* p. 122.

31. On the earlier veteran settlements, see Brunt, *Manpower* pp. 294–7. The two fourth-century texts are *Theodosian Code* 7.20.3, 8.

32. See I. Biezunska-Malowist, "Die Expositio von Kindern als Quelle der Sklavenbeschaffung im griechisch-römischen Ägypten", *Jahrbuch für Wirtschaftsgeschichte* (1971) II 129–33.

33. S. H. Franklin, *The European Peasantry: the Final Phase* (London 1969) chap. 2. For what it is worth, note that even a fourth-century B.C. Athenian orator dismisses a fourteen-acre farm as a small one: Isaeus 5.22.

34. Franklin, *Peasantry* pp. 1 and 19. Cf. N. Georgescu-Roegen, *Analytical Economics* (Cambridge, Mass., 1966) p. 371: "In the 1930's, studies originating in several countries with large peasantries revealed the astounding fact that a substantial proportion of the population could disappear without the slightest decrease in the national product."

35. See M. Crawford, "Money and Exchange in the Roman World", *JRS* 60 (1970) 40–48, esp. pp. 43–45.

36. I ignore such marginal regions as the infertile hills of northern Syria, where an olive monoculture developed in the Roman Empire, by peasants whose status is uncertain: G. Tchalenko, *Villages antiques de la Syrie du nord* (3 vols., Paris 1953).

37. See the figures in D. J. Crawford, *Kerkeosiris* pp. 129–31.

38. The destructive effects of military service on the peasantry is one of the main themes of Brunt, *Manpower*; see his summary remarks, pp. 130, 155.

39. The best known case is the land belonging to two temples in Heraclea in southern Italy; see most recently A. Uguzzoni and F. Ghinatti, *Le tavole greche di Eraclea* [Istituto di Storia Antica, Univ. of Pavia, *Pubblicazioni* no. 7 (1968)].

40. K. D. White, *Roman Farming* (London 1970) p. 452; see the review by P. A. Brunt, *JRS* 62 (1972) 153–8. Cf. Jardé, *Céréales* p. 194: "Greek agriculture in general, and the cultivation of grain in particular, were scarcely modified in historical times. It is through an illusion . . . that some have depicted Greek agronomy as being in a state of perpetual progress."

41. I have tried to develop this analysis in "Technical Innovation". Cf. H. W. Pleket, "Technology and Society in the Graeco-Roman World", *Acta Historiae Neerlandica* 2 (1967) 1–25; "Technology in the Greco-Roman World: A General Report", *Talanta* 5 (1973) 6–47.

42. I. Goncharov, *Oblomov*, transl. D. Magerschack (Penguin 1954) pp. 128–9.

43. On the inadequacy of the accounting technique, see G. Mickwitz, "Economic Rationalism in Graeco-Roman Agriculture", *English Historical Review* 52 (1937) 577–89, and "Zum Problem der Betriebsführung in der antiken Wirtschaft", *Vierteljahrschrift für Sozial- und Wirtschaftsgeschichte* 32 (1939) 1–25; G. E. M. de Ste. Croix, "Greek and Roman Accounting", in *Studies in the History of Accounting*, ed. A. C. Littleton and B. S. Yamey (London 1956) pp. 14–74.

44. See also Varro, *De re rustica* 1.22.1; Pliny, *Natural History* 18.40.

45. Gromatici veteres, ed. C. Lachmann (Berlin 1848) p. 53.

46. Fouet, *Villa de Montmaurin* pp. 32, 43–46, 291. The estate at Chiragan may have been seven or eight times as extensive, with housing for some 500 people; the one at Anthée in the province of Namur, Belgium, included a large villa and twenty other buildings, some obviously industrial, within a walled enclosure of about thirty acres: Grenier, *Manuel* II ii, pp. 843–58, 888–97. Very recent aerial photography in the Somme basin in the north of France has revealed hundreds of large, hitherto unknown and unexpected, villas spaced two or more kilometers apart, apparently concentrated on wheat production and sheep farming: R. Agache, *Détection aérienne de vestiges protohistoriques gallo-romains et médiévaux* . . . [*Bulletin de la Société de Préhistoire du Nord*, No. special 7 (1970)] chap. 4 and the maps on plates 185–6. For the larger estates in Britain, see Applebaum, in *Agrarian History* pp. 240–4, 266–7. The word "villa" has lost all specificity as used by archaeologists and historians (and already had among the Romans: Varro, *De re rustica* 3.2), but its meaning is unequivocal in the present context.

47. See D. Adamesteanu, "Due problemi topografici del retroterra gelese" [Accademia nazionale dei Lincei, *Rendiconti della Classe di scienze morali*, 8th ser., 10 (1955)] 198–210; P. Orlandini, "Lo scavo del thesmophorion di

Bitalemi e il culto delle divinità ctonie a Gela", *Kokalos* 12 (1966) 8–35; Finley, *Ancient Sicily* (rev. ed., London 1979), pp. 159–61.

48. The key passages are *Oration for Aulus Caecina* 11, 21, 94, and *Oration for Sextus Roscius* 20. Cicero repeatedly refers to the single farm as a *fundus* (e.g. *On Oratory* 1.58.249), a technical term for a unit of exploitation; see A. Steinwenter, *Fundus cum instrumento* [Akad. d. Wissenschaften in Wien, Phil.-hist. Klasse, *Sitzungsberichte* 221, no. 1 (1942)] pp. 10–24. I cannot resist one more example, the widely scattered estates of perhaps the richest family in fourth-century A.D. Antioch; see Liebeschuetz, *Antioch* p. 42 and note 2.

49. E. Feder, "*Latifundia* and Agricultural Labour in Latin America", in Shanin, *Peasants* pp. 83–97, at p. 88.

50. See the evidence assembled by A. G. Drachmann, *Ancient Oil Mills and Presses* (Copenhagen 1932).

51. I have no hesitation in using *latifundia* loosely for "large estates", as I believe the Romans themselves did, despite the attempts to find a technical meaning for the term, e.g. by K. D. White, "Latifundia", *Bulletin* of the London Institute of Classical Studies 14 (1967) 62–79; or by René Martin, "Pline le Jeune", and repeatedly in *Recherches sur les agronomes latins et leurs conceptions économiques et sociales* (Paris 1970), on the basis of unfounded calculations of size (see above, note 7). The too often quoted dictum of the elder Pliny (*Natural History* 18.35) that "the *latifundia* have destroyed Italy" is no more than moralizing archaism (cf. the contemporary Seneca, *On Benefits* 7.10.5, where the word *latifundia* happens not to be used), a lamentation for the lost Roman yeomanry and the simpler good old days. I can find nothing in the texts to suggest that there was serious discussion of a choice between intensive large-scale exploitation and more fragmented units. Unlike Martin, "Pline le Jeune" p. 67, I do not consider the younger Pliny's hesitation about risking two estates under the same weather hazards to be a serious discussion.

52. Horace's Sabine farm, a gift from Maecenas, was subdivided into one sector he exploited directly, with a permanent staff of eight slaves under a slave-bailiff, and five other sectors leased to tenants; see briefly Heitland, *Agricola* pp. 215–16. The estate provided Horace with a sufficient income on which to live in Rome properly, though, by contemporary standards of high society, modestly. He was not even a gentleman farmer, and it is a strange aberration of Rostovtzeff, *RE* p. 59, to write that Horace "belonged therefore to the same category of landowners as the veterans".

53. See J. H. Kent, "The Temple Estates of Delos, Rheneia, and Mykonos", *Hesperia* 17 (1948) 243–338.

54. See P. A. David, "The Mechanization of Reaping in the Ante-Bellum Midwest", in *Industrialization in Two Systems: Essays ... Alexander Gerschenkron* (New York 1966) pp. 3–39, reprinted in B. W. Fogel and S. L. Engerman, ed., *The Reinterpretation of American Economic History* (New York 1971) pp. 214–27. Much of the current controversy over the ancient "Gallic reaper" seems to me to overlook the implications of the notion of a threshold point; see K. D. White, "The Economics of the Gallo-Roman Harvesting Machines", in *Hommages à*

Marcel Renard 2 (Brussels 1969) pp. 804–9; *Agricultural Implements of the Roman World* (Cambridge 1967) chap. 10.

55. Sherwin-White, *Pliny* p. 258.

56. The best English translation of Pliny's *Letters*, by Betty Radice in both Penguin Classics and the Loeb Classical Library, renders the key sentences of 3.19 as follows: "It is true that nearly all my *capital* is in land, but I have some *investments* and it will not be difficult to borrow. I can always have money from my mother-in-law, whose *capital* I am able to use as freely as my own." (The words I have italicized may be compared with the more literal translation proposed in my text.) Sherwin-White's commentary, *Pliny* p. 259, "He can pay off a large part of the price by calling in his loans, and can later pay off whatever he needs to borrow out of income savings", is fanciful and incomprehensible.

57. See Mickwitz, "Betriebsführung" pp. 21–22. It is surprising that Mickwitz, who made such excellent comparative use of Hanseatic and Renaissance Italian material, failed to look at American sources and therefore believed that the mere presence of slaves precluded the concept of amortization.

58. The main text is Demosthenes 27.9–11, but it is necessary to study the two orations, nos. 27 and 28, fully in order to appreciate all the implications. For the various misguided attempts to convert Demosthenes' accounts into acceptable modern business procedures, see F. Oertel, "Zur Frage der attischen Grossindustrie", *Rheinisches Museum* 79 (1930) 230–52; J. Korver, "Demosthenes gegen Aphobos", *Mnemosyne*, 3rd ser., 10 (1941/2) 8–22.

59. See Duncan-Jones, *Economy*, chap. 2, and below, chap. 7, sect. 1.

60. I must be explicit about the basis for my next few paragraphs. It is scarcely credible that there has been no systematic study (and hardly any study at all) of the buying and selling of land in antiquity, apart from the law of sale, which has only marginal interest. I feel fully confident only about Athens, because of my *Land and Credit*; for the rest, I rely on long familiarity with the sources and on what one can glean, chiefly in a negative way, from such works as Frank, *Survey*; Heitland, *Agricola*; G. Billeter, *Geschichte des Zinsfusses im griechisch-römischen Altertum* (Leipzig 1898); E. Ziebarth, *Das griechische Vereinswesen* (Leipzig 1896); F. Poland, *Geschichte des griechischen Vereinswesens* (Leipzig 1903); J. Waltzing, *Étude historique sur les corporations professionelles chez les Romains* (2 vols., Louvain 1895–6); Jones, *LRE*.

61. I quote from H. Sieveking, "Loans, Personal", in *Encyclopaedia of the Social Sciences* 9 (1933) pp. 561–5, at p. 561, in order to draw attention to this valuable brief analysis of the economic, social and historical role of the personal or consumer's loan.

62. F. M. Heichelheim, *An Ancient Economic History*, transl. Joyce Stevens, vol. 2 (Leiden 1964) pp. 66–67.

63. The Liddell-Scott-Jones lexicon translated προπώλης as "one who buys for another or negotiates a sale, a broker". Despite the fact that this was shown to be false by J. Partsch, *Griechisches Bürgschaftsrecht* (Leipzig and Berlin 1909),

and by others subsequently, the error was not corrected in the 1968 supplement. The correct translation is "warrantor".

64. See e.g. Brunt, *Manpower*, Appendix 8.

65. Translated by Betty Radice (Penguin 1963). Again (as in note 56 above) I have replaced her words "invest" and "capital", with their inescapable modern overtones, this time by the literal "concentrate" and "patrimony". For a similar reason I have written "increasing the amount available for sale" instead of Mrs. Radice's "bringing more into the market".

66. That is the explanation e.g. of Heitland, *Agricola* p. 274; correctly explained by Sherwin-White, *Pliny* pp. 379–80. Marcus Aurelius made a second attempt, but reduced the compulsory Italian fraction to one quarter of a senator's total patrimony: *Historia Augusta, Marcus* 11.8.

67. Brunt, *Manpower* p. 297.

68. The source material is assembled by E. J. Jonkers, *Economische en sociale toestanden in het Romeinsche Rijk blijkende uit het Corpus Juris* (Wageningen 1933) chap. 1.

69. The most famous Greek example appears in Xenophon, *Oikonomikos* 20.22, famous because it is cited so regularly that one drifts into the illusion that this case of a single Athenian gentleman, possibly fictitious, was a universal Greek phenomenon. See e.g. the account by Claude Mossé, *La fin de la démocratie athénienne* (Paris 1962), pp. 35–67, of land speculation in Athens in the fourth century B.C. Crassus' 500-slave "fire department" is equally unique and very likely equally fictitious: B. W. Frier, *Landlords and Tenants in Imperial Rome* (Princeton 1980), pp. 32–4. On urban property as a source of income among the Romans, see in addition P. Garnsey, "Urban Property Investment", in Finley, *Roman Property*, chap. 7.

70. C. Clark and M. Haswell, *The Economics of Subsistence Agriculture* (4th ed., London 1970) p. 164.

NOTES TO CHAPTER V
(Pages 123–149)

1. The most explicit statement appears briefly in 4.1.5, but the theme recurs with some frequency; see A. N. Sherwin-White, *Racial Prejudice in Imperial Rome* (Cambridge 1967) pp. 1–13.

2. R. F. Pahl, in R. J. Chorley and P. Haggett, ed., *Models in Geography* (London 1967) p. 237; cf. H. J. Gans, "Urbanism and Suburbanism as Ways of Life: A Re-evaluation of Definitions", in A. M. Rose, ed., *Human Behavior and Social Processes* (London 1962) pp. 625–48, esp. pp. 643–4. See generally W. Sombart, *Der moderne Kapitalismus*, vol. I i (5th ed., Munich and Leipzig 1922) chap. 9.

3. N. J. G. Pounds, "The Urbanization of the Classical World", *Annals of the Amer. Assn. of Geographers* 59 (1969) 135–57, has attempted to draw a

"functional" distinction between ancient cities and villages, and he correctly stresses the continuing "agricultural function" of the former in the great majority of cases. However, he is satisfied with an aesthetic-architectural canon, ignoring the political dimension, and his attempt to estimate size of population, primarily from areas and, for classical Greece, from the amount of tribute paid to Athens, is methodologically indefensible. On the administrative and archaeological aspects of Greek towns, the most complete and most sophisticated work is Roland Martin, *L'Urbanisme dans la Grèce ancienne* (Paris 1956); cf. R. E. Wycherley, *How the Greeks Built Cities* (2nd ed., London 1962).

4. M. Weber, "Agrarverhältnisse im Altertum", in his *Gesammelte Aufsätze zur Sozial- und Wirtschaftsgeschichte* (Tübingen 1924) pp. 1–288, at p. 13 (cf. p. 6).

5. It is enough to cite Plato, *Republic* 370E–371A; Aristotle, *Politics* 1327a25–31.

6. See Jones *LRE* pp. 841–2 and generally chap. 21; Duncan-Jones, *Economy*, Appendix 17. Cf. Cato, *De agricultura* 22.3, more than 400 years earlier, on the cost of transporting an olive-press by oxen.

7. The evidence is most fully summarized by A. M. Burford, "Heavy Transport in Classical Antiquity", *EcHR*, 2nd ser., 13 (1960) 1–18.

8. See L. Bonnard, *La navigation intérieure de la Gaule à l'époque gallo-romaine* (Paris 1913); cf. A. Grenier, *Manuel d'archéologie gallo-romaine*, vol. II ii (Paris 1934) chaps. 12–13; Y. Burnand, "Un aspect de la géographie des transports dans la Narbonnaise rhodanienne: les nautes de l'Ardèche et de l'Ouvèze", *Revue archéologique de Narbonnaise* 4 (1971) 149–58.

9. See F. G. Moore, "Three Canal Projects, Roman and Byzantine", *American Journal of Archaeology* 54 (1950) 97–111; Sherwin-White, *Pliny* pp. 621–625 (who incorrectly gives the distance as eighteen miles).

10. See I. Hodder and M. Hassall, "The Non-Random Spacing of Romano-British Walled Towns", *Man* 6 (1971) 391–407, at p. 404, the only attempt known to me to examine an ancient region in the light of modern central-place theory, on which see B. J. L. Berry, *The Geography of Market Centers and Retail Distribution* (Englewood Cliffs, N.J., 1967); Chorley and Haggett, *Models*, chap. 9. The important critique of this theory by J. E. Vance, Jr., *The Merchant's World: the Geography of Wholesaling* (Englewood Cliffs, N.J., 1970), seems to me to be of little relevance to the ancient economy, as his few inexpert remarks on the subject betray.

11. B. J. Garner, in Chorley and Haggett, *Models* p. 304.

12. F. Benoit, "L'usine de meunerie hydraulique de Barbegal (Arles)", *Revue archéologique*, 6th ser., 15 (1940) 18–80. Cf. Libanius' praise (*Orations* 18.83) of the emperor Julian for having restored the lower Rhine as a highway up which corn from Britain reached the armies.

13. See R. Meiggs, *Roman Ostia* (2nd ed., Oxford 1973) chap. 3.

14. Polybius 1.20–21; see J. H. Thiel, *A History of Roman Sea-Power before the Second Punic War* (Amsterdam 1954).

15. L. Friedländer, *Darstellungen aus der Sittengeschichte Roms*, 10th ed. by G. Wissowa (reprint, Aalen 1964) II 50–76.

16. Polybius 31.7.10–12; see F. S. Gruen in *Classical Quarterly* 25 (1975) 58–81 for the background.

17. Aristotle, *Politics* 1291b24, says only that Chios was an example of a mercantile city (along with Aegina), but that the slave trade was the key seems to me to follow from Thucydides' statement (8.40.2) that Chios had the most numerous slaves in Greece after Sparta and from the curious tradition, going back at least to the fourth-century B.C. historian Theopompus, a native of the island, that the Chiots were the first Greeks to buy slaves (Athenaeus 6.264C–266F).

18. See E. Lepore, "Strutture della colonizzazione focea in Occidente", *Parola del Passato* 25 (1970) 19–54.

19. A. W. Gomme, "Traders and Manufacturers in Greece", in his *Essays in Greek History and Literature* (Oxford 1937) pp. 42–66, at p. 45.

20. That the two Pliny texts have led to tedious modern attempts at economic analysis is irrelevant; for example, E. H. Warmington, *The Commerce between the Roman Empire and India* (Cambridge 1928) pp. 272–318. See now P. Veyne, "Rome devant la prétendue fuite de l'or: Mercantilisme ou politique disciplinaire?", *Annales* 34 (1979) 211–44.

21. Berry, *Market Centers* p. 3. The evidence underlying the rest of this paragraph is fully presented by E. Erxleben, "Das Verhältnis des Handels zum Produktionsfaktoren in Attica im 5. und 4. Jahrhundert v.u.Z.", *Klio* 57 (1975) 365–98, which ends with a surprisingly limp conclusion.

22. H. Michell, *The Economics of Ancient Greece* (2nd ed., Cambridge 1957) p. 285.

23. *Inscriptiones Graecae* II² 1100; a revised text and translation will be found in J. H. Oliver, *The Ruling Power* [*Transactions of the Amer. Philosophical Society*, n.s., vol. 43 (1953) pt. 4] pp. 960–3.

24. In the text I have italicized the words, "from important urban communities", to underscore the irrelevance, in the present context, of such a wine-producing region as the Roman province of Baetica in southern Spain. The much discussed Italian wine trade of the late Roman Republic and the Empire is also largely irrelevant here. Most Italian wines were shipped to Rome, a fabulous consumer of wine, to other Italian cities and to Roman armies in the north, as in Pannonia until it began to produce enough on its own. They were therefore not a foreign export balancing imports in the sense now under consideration. L. Casson, "The Grain Trade of the Hellenistic World", *Transactions of the Amer. Philological Assn.* 85 (1954) 168–87, a useful collection of data, is so obsessed with balance of trade that he leaves the patently false impression that wine exports, assisted by such miscellaneous products as honey, fuller's earth and cheese, could be seriously, if not wholly, balanced against a grain trade which, on his own assessment, at one time "employed an organized fleet that . . . did not see a peer until the days of steam". (Cf. chap. 7, sect. 7.)

25. I have examined this aspect of the passage, with its stress on quality rather than on quantity of production, in "Technical Innovation" and in "Aristotle and Economic Analysis", *Past & Present*, no. 47 (1970) 3–25.

26. It is astonishing that Pounds, "Urbanization" p. 144, misreads the passage in the *Cyropaedia* to say that larger cities had "functions clearly related . . . to needs felt far beyond their own territorial limits". That is not in the text and is incomprehensible in the context. The quotation from Aelius Aristides (*To Rome* 61) which Pounds then introduces has nothing to do with the subject.

27. *Inscriptiones Graecae* XII Supp., no. 347.

28. The evidence for sheep-raising in the region is collected by G. E. F. Chilver, *Cisalpine Gaul* (Oxford 1941) pp. 163–7; but see Brunt, *Manpower* pp. 181–2.

29. The full quotation is given in chap. 1 at note 14.

30. It would be a great waste of effort to go through the list of ancient cities elevated by one or another modern historian to the rank of international industrial centre, but Capua perhaps deserves to be singled out because it has become something of a favourite. The most important city in Campania from early times, it naturally served as a main, but not the only, centre of production for equipment required by the landowners of the region (Cato, *De agricultura* 135). It also produced fine bronzes for export, notably to the northern frontiers, archaeologically attested in substantial but not spectacular numbers, requiring no larger scale of operations than other examples of modern overstatement I mentioned at the end of chap. 1. But still more is claimed. "That much of the ordinary Roman bronze-ware was made in Capua cannot seriously be questioned": M. W. Frederiksen, "Republican Capua: A Social and Economic Study", *PBSR* 27 (1959) 80–130, at p. 109. That is incredible—Rome had its own bronze industry—and nothing in Frederiksen's long account offers any plausible evidence in support.

31. Martin, *Urbanisme* p. 34.

32. Weber, "Agrarverhältnisse" p. 257; cf. his *Wirtschaftsgeschichte*, ed. S. Hellman and M. Palyi (Munich and Leipzig 1923) *passim* (via the detailed table of contents), an English translation of which, by F. H. Knight, is available under the title, *General Economic History* (Collier Books ed., New York 1961).

33. G. Mickwitz, *Die Kartellfunktion der Zünfte* . . . [Societas Scientiarum Fennica, *Commentationes Humanarum Litterarum* VIII 3 (1936)] chap. 5, is fundamental.

34. Berry, *Market Centers* p. 93. On periodic markets in different regions of the Roman empire, see R. MacMullen, "Market-days in the Roman Empire", *Phoenix* 24 (1970) 333–41.

35. G. W. Fox, *History in Geographic Perspective* (New York 1971), has some suggestive comments on this point, especially in chap. 3.

36. Examples are given by Bogaert, *Banques* pp. 336, 368–70.

37. See my "Land, Debt, and the Man of Property in Classical Athens",

Political Science Quarterly 68 (1953) 249–68; cf. Bogaert, *Banques* pp. 352–5; Rougé, *Commerce*, pt. III, chaps. 2 and 7.

38. B. J. Fogel and S. L. Engerman, ed., *The Reinterpretation of American Economic History* (New York 1971) p. 441.

39. Bogaert, *Banques* pp. 356–7. The two examples are Demosthenes 40.52 and Lysias; frag. 38.1, the latter certainly suspect.

40. *Ibid.* p. 355; Bogaert, "Banquiers, courtiers et prêts maritimes à Athènes et à Alexandrie", *Chronique d'Égypte* 40 (1965) 140–56. There is only one mutilated papyrus dealing with a maritime loan and very little direct Roman evidence: Rougé, *Commerce*, pt. III, chap. 2. See further chap. 7, sect. 5 below.

41. This is the implication in the material examined by Rougé, *ibid.* I say "apparently" because Rougé's method is impressionistic, not quantitative.

42. Cicero, *Letters to Atticus* 7.18.4; 9.9.4; 10.11.2; 10.14.1, all from the first half of 49 B.C., the Caesarian crisis mentioned immediately below in my text; Dio Cassius 51.21.5 (cf. Suetonius, *Augustus* 41.1–2).

43. C. Nicolet, "Les variations des prix et la 'théorie quantitative de la monnaie' à Rome, de Cicéron à Pline l'Ancien", *Annales* 26 (1971) 1203–27, at p. 1225. The phrase in inverted commas in the title and much of the earlier part of the discussion tend to make too much "theory" of rudimentary common sense, as Nicolet in effect concedes in the sentence I have quoted; cf. the comments of M. H. Crawford that follow immediately in the *Annales* (pp. 1228–1233) under the title, "Le problème des liquidités dans l'antiquité classique". An interesting, easily overlooked discussion of the impact of coin shortages is that of J. M. Kelly, *Roman Litigation* (Oxford 1966) chap. 3.

44. *Syll.* 364. The text, an Italian translation and a brief commentary, with full bibliography, will be found in D. Asheri, "Leggi greche sul problema dei debiti", *Studi classici e orientali* 18 (1969) 5–122, at pp. 42–47 and Appendix II.

45. The fullest account is that of Frederiksen, "Caesar".

46. See the account of the crisis by C. Rodewald, *Money in the Age of Tiberius* (Manchester 1976), and chap. 7, sect. 5. below.

47. M. H. Crawford, "Money and Exchange in the Roman World", *JRS* 60 (1970) 40–48, at p. 46.

48. See the summary in the opening pages of chap. 7 of Crook, *Law*.

49. See Rougé, *Commerce* pp. 420–1 (the word "fixity" is his, p. 491). Characteristically, Rougé says there were many "agent" networks, an adjective that he justifies only by one or two examples. The tone of Pseudo-Demosthenes 56 in describing the agents posted in Rhodes by Cleomenes, Alexander's governor in Egypt, implies a novel practice, and that is one reason for my saying "since the end of the fourth century B.C."

50. That is demonstrated, in my view, by the special pleading with which Rougé, *ibid.* pp. 423–34, tries to argue the contrary. He overlooks the significance of the fact that his one plausible example consists of merchants engaged in a governmental operation, the imperial *annona*.

51. I follow closely the argument of my "Technical Innovation".

52. See O. Davies, *Roman Mines in Europe* (Oxford 1935) p. 24.

53. The references are Pliny, *Natural History* 36.195; Petronius, *Satyricon* 51; Dio Cassius 57.21.7.

NOTES TO CHAPTER VI
(Pages 150–176)

1. N. Lewis, "*Leitourgia* and Related Terms", *Greek, Roman and Byzantine Studies* 3 (1960) 175–84; 6 (1965) 226–30.

2. J. K. Davies, "Demosthenes on Liturgies: A Note", *Journal of Hellenic Studies* 87 (1967) 33–40.

3. See A. H. M. Jones, "The Caste System in the Later Roman Empire", *Eirene* 8 (1970) 79–96; S. Dill, *Roman Society in the Last Century of the Western Empire* (2nd ed., London 1921) pp. 248–70.

4. E.g. J. Vogt, *The Decline of Rome*, transl. J. Sondheimer (London and New York 1967) pp. 27–28.

5. See Jones, *LRE* pp. 827–9.

6. The most detailed analysis (for the African provinces and Italy) will be found in Duncan-Jones, *Economy* chaps. 3–4.

7. See T. Pekáry, *Untersuchungen zu den römischen Reichsstrassen* (Bonn 1968) chap. 3, with corrections, chiefly for the Republican period by T. P. Wiseman, in *PBSR* 38 (1970) 140–52; W. Eck, *Die staatliche Organisation Italiens in der hohen Kaiserzeit* (Munich 1979), pp. 69–79.

8. See P. Garnsey, "Aspects of the Decline of the Urban Aristocracy in the Empire", in *Aufstieg und Niedergang der römischen Welt*, ed. H. Temporini II 1 (Berlin 1974) pp. 229–52.

9. Quoted from Lukacs; see chap. 2 at note 34.

10. S. Lauffer, "Das Wirtschaftsleben im römischen Reich", in *Jenseits von Resignation und Illusion*, ed. H. J. Heydorn and K. Ringshausen (Frankfurt 1971) pp. 135–53, at p. 137.

11. This was proved long ago by J. J. Hatzfeld, *Les trafiquants italiens dans l'Orient hellénistique* (Paris 1919). A. J. N. Wilson, *Emigration from Italy in the Republican Age of Rome* (Manchester and New York 1966), devotes two chapters (7–8) to an unsuccessful attempt to refute Hatzfeld's conclusions. His argument, largely hypothetical, rests on a false conception of the Roman economy and value-system, taken over from Rostovtzeff: "Roman citizens were probably the better placed, so far as capital was concerned, for overseas trade" (p. 88). His further attempt to re-assign individuals to "nationalities" from their names, which is all we can go by, is largely special pleading, with another certainly false central hypothesis: "It is most unlikely that the pioneer, or pioneering group, to whom each family [trading in the east] must go back, was not free"

14

(p. 107). Yet even he agrees (p. 102) that in the action of the Roman government establishing Delos as a free port, no special privileges were given to Italians ("Romans").

12. Strabo 14.5.2 came as close as he dared to a frank statement of the position; cf. Cicero, *De imperio Pompeii* 32–33, 54; Plutarch, *Pompey* 25.1.

13. Justin 9.1–2, repeated by Orosius 3.13.1–4, probably based on the contemporary historian Theopompus; see A. Momigliano, "Della spedizione scitica di Filippo . . .", *Athenaeum*, n.s. 11 (1933) 336–59.

14. Tenney Frank, *An Economic History of Rome* (2nd ed., London 1927) pp. 114–18, saw this clearly, though, characteristically, he proceeded to criticize the Romans for being "blinded to the economic point of view" (p. 125).

15. E. J. Bickerman, reviewing the first edition (which has never been corrected on this point) of H. Bengtson, *Griechische Geschichte*, in *American Journal of Philology* 74 (1953) 96. Cf. Ed. Will, *Le monde grec et l'Orient*, vol. 1 (Paris 1972) pp. 201–11.

16. Rougé. *Commerce* pp. 465–6.

17. *Ibid.* pp. 443–9. The fullest account is S. J. De Laet, *Portorium*, published by the University of Ghent (Brugge 1949).

18. A. H. M. Jones, in the *Proceedings* of the Third International Conference of Economic History, Munich 1965, vol. 3, *The Ancient Empires and the Economy* (Paris and The Hague 1969) p. 97 (repr. in his *Roman Economy*, chap. 6.).

19. The fundamental study of the *annona* is still D. van Berchem, "L'annone militaire dans l'empire romain au IIIe siècle", *Mémoires de la Société nationale des antiquaires de France*, 8th ser., 10 (1937) 117–202.

20. On the progressive withdrawal of the army from the private economy, see R. MacMullen, *Soldier and Civilian in the Later Roman Empire* (Cambridge, Mass., 1963) chap. 2; Erik Gren, *Kleinasien und der Ostbalkan in der wirtschaftlichen Entwicklung der römischen Kaiserzeit* [*Uppsala Universitets Årsskrift* (1941) no. 9] chap. 4. Nor should the use of soldiers on roads, bridges and canals be overlooked.

21. See Salvioli, *Capitalisme* pp. 118–25.

22. On the Roman-Carthaginian treaties, see F. W. Walbank, *A Historical Commentary on Polybius*, vol. 1 (1957) pp. 337–56, and my *Aspects of Antiquity* (Penguin ed., 1972) chap. 9.

23. What follows is based largely on P. Gauthier, *Symbola. Les étrangers et la justice dans les cités grecques* [*Annales de l'Est*, no. 42 (1972)].

24. In the *Politics* (1280a38) Aristotle calls them "agreements about imports". On these passages, see Gauthier, *Symbola* pp. 90–93.

25. The chief evidence comes from Demosthenes' 20th oration (*Against Leptines*) and an inscription, *Syll.* 206 (Tod, *GHI* II 167).

26. See Gauthier, *Symbola* pp. 149–55, 198–201; L. Gernet, "Sur les actions commerciales en droit athénien", *Revue des études grecques* 51 (1938) 1–44, re-

printed in his *Droit et société dans la Grèce ancienne* (reprint, Paris 1964) pp. 173–200.

27. The evidence presented by Gauthier, *Symbola*, seems to me to impose this conclusion, though he himself makes it in a whisper (p. 204 note 20).

28. Note, however, the comment by Y. Garlan, "Les esclaves grecs en temps de guerre", in *Actes du Colloque d'histoire sociale*, Univ. of Besançon 1970 (Paris 1972) pp. 29–62, at p. 49, on the proposal in the *Poroi* (6.41–42), apparently unique among Greek writers, that the state-owned slaves be enrolled in the infantry.

29. D. Whitehead, *The Ideology of the Athenian Metic* (Cambridge Philological Soc., Supp. vol. 4, 1977), replaces all previous accounts.

30. I am unaware of any systematic study of this documentation.

31. Ps.-Demosthenes 59.27 is decisive, at least for Athens.

32. The evidence is assembled by F. M. Heichelheim, "Monopole", in *Paulys Real-Enzyklopädie der klassischen Altertumswissenschaft* 16 (1933) 147–99.

33. On coin supply see C. G. Starr, *Athenian Coinage 480–449 B.C.* (Oxford 1970), esp. pp. 64–70; Bogaert, *Banques* pp. 328–9; Frederiksen, "Caesar" pp. 132–3; M. Crawford, "Money and Exchange in the Roman World", *JRS* 60 (1970) 40–48, at pp. 46–7, "La problème des liquidités dans l'antiquité classique", *Annales* 26 (1971) 1228–33, at pp. 1231–2. (See also chap. 7, sect. 5.)

34. J. M. Keynes, *A Treatise on Money* (2 vols., London 1930) I 12.

35. See the elaborate calculations of R. Bogaert, "Le cours du statère de Cyzique au Ve et IVe siècles avant J.-C.", *L'Antiquité classique* 32 (1963) 85–119, with discussion in 34 (1965) 199–213, and by S. K. Eddy, in *Museum Notes* 16 (1970) 13–22.

36. It is sufficient to note the pathetically few instances that could be mustered by T. Reinach, "L'anarchie monétaire et ses remèdes chez les anciens Grecs", *Mémoires de l'Acad. des Inscriptions et Belles Lettres* 38 (1911) 351–64. The joint coinages of regional leagues are no exception; as Reinach says (p. 353), this not very important, purely political phenomenon merely enlarged the territorial base of the "anarchy" slightly.

37. See the tables in Bogaert, "Cours du statère" pp. 105 and 114.

38. Xenophon's boast (*Poroi* 3.2) about the preference for Athenian coins receives surprising confirmation from Egypt. Early in the fourth century, the non-coining Egyptians required a steady supply of coins with which to pay Greek mercenaries and they met their need by minting Athenian coins: J. W. Curtis, "Coinage of Pharaonic Egypt", *Journal of Egyptian Archaeology* 43 (1957) 71–76. But there is much we do not understand on this topic and ought to investigate. A lengthy Athenian inscription, published by R. S. Stroud in *Hesperia* 43 (1974) 157–88, announces measures taken by the Athenian state in 375/4 B.C. to penalize traders refusing to accept "owls" offered in payment for goods in the Athenian markets. The text gives no reason why this astonishing regulation was necessary, and I am unable to offer even a guess.

39. *Syll.* 218; see J. Hasebroek, in *Philologische Wochenschrift* 46 (1926) 368–72.

40. See Starr, *Athenian Coinage* chap. 4; Finley, in *Proceedings* . . *Aix* pp. 22–25. The most exhaustive account of the evidence and the modern discussion is E. Erxleben, "Das Münzgesetz des delisch-attischen Seebundes", *Archiv für Papyrusforschung* 19 (1969) 91–139; 20 (1970) 66–132; 21 (1971) 145–62, but I do not find his arguments for a late date, in the second half of the 420s, convincing, much less his offhand conclusion that the decree was part of "Cleon's disastrous policy . . . lacking all reasonable proportion".

41. See L. Gernet, "L'approvisionnement d'Athènes en blé au Ve et au IVe siècles", in *Mélanges d'histoire ancienne* [*Bibliothèque de la Faculté des Lettres, Univ. de Paris* 25 (1909)] chap. 4.

42. See H. Bolkestein, *Wohltätigkeit und Armenpflege im vorchristlichen Altertum* (Utrecht 1939) pp. 251–57, 364–78.

43. Ps.-Demosthenes 34.37–39 gives an idea of the situation in Athens then.

44. *Supplementum epigraphicum graecum* IX 2.

45. There was then a formal purge of the citizen roster, following charges that many ineligible residents took a share of the Pharaonic gift (Plutarch, *Pericles* 37). For other gifts of grain to Athens see Bolkestein, *Wohltätigkeit* pp. 260–2; on the principle of sharing out community goods, *ibid.* pp. 269–73, and K. Latte, "Kollektivbesitz und Staatsschatz im Griechenland", *Nachrichten d. Akad. d. Wissenschaften in Göttingen, Phil.-hist. Kl.* (1946/47) 64–75, reprinted in his *Kleine Schriften* (Munich 1968) pp. 294–312.

46. See D. van Berchem, *Les distributions de blé et d'argent à la plèbe romaine sous l'Empire* (Geneva 1939).

47. Concern for grain production in the interest of the Roman consumer is obviously reflected in Domitian's edict of A.D. 92 prohibiting the extension of vineyards in Italy and ordering destruction of half the vineyards in the provinces. That is stated explicitly by the contemporary (or near contemporary) sources, Statius, *Silvae* 4.3.11–12, and Suetonius, *Domitian* 7.2, the former adding a sumptuary note. Modern historians who persist in citing this edict as a measure designed to protect Italian wine production against provincial competition ignore logic and the explicit assertions of the ancient authorities, and fail to note that the measure was anyway an isolated one, worse still, that it was rescinded by Domitian himself (Suetonius 7.2; 14.5). The attempt by Rostovtzeff, *R E* p. 202, to argue otherwise is desperate: he fails to mention the two statements of Suetonius on the abrogation of the edict.

48. See Liebeschuetz, *Antioch* pp. 126–52.

49. Herodotus 4.153, read in conjunction with an inscription, *Supplementum Epigraphicum Graecum* IX 3, on the early Greek colonization of Cyrene, leaves no doubt about the element of compulsion; nor, for Rome's so-called "Latin colonies", at least, does Cicero, *Oration for Aulus Caecina* 98.

50. For the Greek evidence, see Pritchett, *Military Practices* chaps. 1–2.

51. The Athenian evidence is summarized by R. S. Stroud, "Theozotides and the Athenian Orphans", *Hesperia* 40 (1971) 280–301, at pp. 288–90. The

new inscription published by Stroud gives the text of a decree, probably in 402, providing for maintenance on the same basis as war orphans of the sons of a small number of men killed in the fighting that overthrew the Thirty Tyrants and restored democracy. The decree explicitly restricts even this benefit to the legitimate sons of citizens.

52. A. H. M. Jones, *Athenian Democracy* (Oxford 1957) pp. 5–10, conflates the two questions of the fifth-century introduction of the costly democratic machinery and of its survival in the fourth century.

53. See briefly Claude Mossé, *La fin de la démocratie athénienne* (Paris 1962) pp. 303–13.

54. Larsen, in Frank, *Survey* IV 341.

NOTES TO CHAPTER VII
(Pages 177–207)

1. Kula, *Theory* 95–100.

2. See e.g. J. G. D. Clark, "Traffic in Stone Axes and Adze Blades", *EcHR*, 2nd ser., 18 (1965) 1–28.

3. The phrase ("eine einheitliche grosse Wirtschaftsraum") is that of Kohns, *GGA* 125.

4. Kohns, *GGA* 126, seems to think that the possibility is realistic.

5. Duncan-Jones, *Economy* 63, 120; cf. the appendices (8 and 10) giving the pitiful list of recorded wheat and slave prices (including some fictitious ones) from Rome and Italy.

6. See further sect. 6 below.

7. See the account by Karl Polanyi, *The Livelihood of Man*, ed. H. W. Pearson (New York 1977), pp. 240–51.

8. See Lysias 22 for the situation at Athens early in the fourth century B.C. That was also the situation in Antioch in A.D. 362–363, exacerbated by a drought, which induced Julian to intervene (above, pp. 33–4). I do not understand why Kohns, *GGA* 126–7, and others whom he cites refuse to accept Julian's account while they read him a lesson in "economic liberalism", attributing the shortages of 363 to the emperor's own "miscalculated" remedial measures.

9. I have discussed at length in chap. 3 my reasons for calling certain regions of classical antiquity "slave societies" in certain periods, but that is obviously a different notion from the "slave mode of production": cf. Finley, *Slavery*, and *Opus* 1.

10. See Y. Garlan, "Le travail libre en Grèce ancienne", in Garnsey, *Labour*, chap. 2.

11. See now above all Kreissig, *Seleukidenreich*; cf. K. W. Welwei, "Abhängige Landbevölkerungen auf 'Tempelterritorien' im hellenistischen

Kleinasien und Syrien", *Ancient Society* 10 (1979) 97–118; P. Debord, "Populations rurales de l'Anatolie Greco-Romaine", *Atti del Centro ricerche e documentazione sull' antichità classica* 8 (1976–77) 43–68 (who effectively removes in advance the arguments in the other direction by de Ste. Croix, *Struggle* 151–7); and the sections on Asia Minor and Egypt in T. V. Blavatskaya et al., ed., *Die Sklaverei im hellenistischen Staaten im 3.–1. Jh. v. Chr.* (Wiesbaden 1972; orig. published in Russian in 1969). This does not require acceptance of the notion of an Asiatic mode of production, which has come under attack in recent Marxist literature; therefore add to the bibliography in 214*n*39: P. Anderson, *Lineages of the Absolutist State* (London 1974), pp. 462–549; S. P. Dunn, *The Fall and Rise of the Asiatic Mode of Production* (London and Boston 1982). A massive account (450 pp.) of the development of the ideas of Marx and Engels on the subject is now given by L. Krader, *The Asiatic Mode of Production* (Assen 1975).

12. What I wrote on pp. 112 and 223*n*18 is therefore to be withdrawn. See in particular C. R. Whittaker, "Rural Labour in Three Roman Provinces", in Garnsey, *Labour*, chap. 9, and "Land and Labour in North Africa", *Klio* 60 (1978) 331–62, with bibliography; A. Daubigney, "Reconnaissance des formes de la dépendance gauloise", *Dialogues d'histoire ancienne* 5 (1979) 145–90.

13. See e.g. I. Glodariu, "Die Landwirtschaft im römischen Dakien", in *ANRW* II 6 (1975), pp. 950–89.

14. Marx, *Grundrisse* 513.

15. American slavery is the ground for the objection raised by R. Banaji to the whole notion of social formation: "Modes of Production in a Materialist Conception of History", *Capital & Class* (1977) no. 3, pp. 1–44, esp. pp. 30–31, first published in a shorter version in *Journal of Peasant Studies* 3 (1976) 299–320. The reply by J. Martin in the latter journal, 4 (1977) 190–93, is not persuasive.

16. For a clear, succinct statement of Marx's own (varied) uses of the phrase "mode of production" see G. A. Cohen, *Karl Marx's Theory of History* (Oxford 1978), pp. 79–84.

17. I. Wallerstein, *The Capitalist World-economy* (Oxford 1979), p. 15; on p. 138 he calls it a "spongy term".

18. See in *Opus* 1 (1982) the end of the article by Giardina (pp. 142–5) and briefly Whittaker (pp. 175–6).

19. See briefly Finley in *Opus* 1 (1982) 208–10. C. Wickham, "The Other Transition: from the Ancient World to Feudalism", *Past and Present* 103 (1984) 3–36, has tried to get round the difficulty by an eccentric conception of mode of production that I find incomprehensible.

20. A. Carandini, "Columella's Vineyards and the Rationality of the Roman Economy", *Opus* 2 (1983) 177–204; cf. E. Fentress, *ibid.* 161–75; M. Corbier, in Giardina/Schiavone I (1981) 427–44.

21. I know Kula's work only from the English translation made from an Italian translation of the Polish original (1962), and therefore cannot be certain that Kula wrote precisely what I have quoted. In any event, as Momigliano noticed in *Rivista storica italiana* (87, 1975, 168), Kula never interested himself in

the ancient world. His model was based explicitly on one by W. A. Lewis, "Economic Development with Unlimited Supplies of Labour", *Manchester School* . . . 22 (1954) 139–91, and anyone who takes the trouble to read the latter will quickly appreciate the pointlessness of Carandini's exercise.

22. See the basic study of ancient accounting procedures, ignored by Carandini: G. E. M. de Ste. Croix, "Greek and Roman Accounting", in *Studies in the History of Accounting*, ed. A. C. Littleton and B. S. Yamey (London 1956), pp. 14–74.

23. Kula, *Theory* 36–37; cf. 174–5 (with *n* 10). Writing about medieval English manorial accounting, M. E. Levett noted that "where seigneurial dues were heavy, an account which shows a large total balance might readily cover a net loss on the demesne": "The Financial Organization of the Manor", *EcHR* 1 (1927) 65–86, at p. 69. Cf. M. Confino, *Domaines et seigneurs en Russie vers la fin du XVIIIe siècle* (Paris 1963), pp. 170–76.

24. See especially Andreau, "Banque"; cf. A. Carandini, *L'anatomia della scimmia* (Turin 1979), pp. 209–15.

25. A prior point to be determined, of course, is whether a text reveals a misunderstanding by its author or invites one by historians today; for example, two famous short passages in Pliny's *Natural History* (6.26.101; 12.41.84) commonly taken to indicate massive "bleeding" of gold from the Roman Empire to the east, but on which see now P. Veyne, "Rome devant la prétendue fuite de l'or . . .", *Annales* 34 (1979) 211–44.

26. *Socio-Economic Models in Geography*, ed. R. J. Chorley and P. Haggett (abridged paperback ed., London 1968), p. 22; cf. Kula, *Theory*, chap. 2.

27. M. Weber, *Gesammelte Aufsätze zur Wissenschaftslehre*, ed. J. Winckelmann (5th ed., Tubingen 1982), p. 191.

28. Hopkins has presented his model in different forms on three occasions, with some variations in the nuances; the fullest is in "Taxes in the Roman Empire (200 B.C.—A.D. 400)", *JRS* 70 (1980) 101–25, but see also his "Economic Growth and Towns in Classical Antiquity", in *Towns in Societies*, ed. P. Abrams and E. A. Wrigley (Cambridge 1978), pp. 35–77, and his introduction to Garnsey, *Trade*.

29. T. Pekáry, "Zur Bedeutung des Handels in der Antike", in *Aspekte der historischen Forschung in Frankreich und Deutschland*, ed. G. A. Ritter and R. Vierhaus (Göttingen 1981), pp. 30–39. He had already made the point at length about shortage of coin in *Les "dévaluations" à Rome*, no. 2, publ. by the École française de Rome (1980), pp. 103–20, in a colloquium (Gdansk 1978), in which he was challenged by several participants who misunderstood the central point he was making, as Lévêque noted (p. 119).

30. C. R. Whittaker, in a "multi-review" of this book in *Europa* 5 (1982) 75–90, at p. 87.

31. J. F. Oates, in *ibid.*, p. 77.

32. See along the same lines H. Kreissig, "Versuch einer Konzeption der hellenistischen Epoche", *Jahrbuch für Wirtschaftsgeschichte* (1982) no. 1, 153–60.

33. Oates (cited in *n* 31 above) says about my chap. 2 that "consideration of the social and political ideas of Menander's *Dyscolus* would seriously undercut the idea of the universality of Finley's conceptualization". He fails to specify but I assume that he has in mind the two final scenes, in the first of which the misanthropic farmer Cnemon, who thinks that he is dying, undergoes a sudden change of character, adopts Gorgias, his own daughter's half-brother, makes all his property over to the former and requests him to set half aside as a dowry for his sister, followed by a scene in which a rich townsman relents and agrees to his son's marrying the same daughter, with a rich gift. The text here is full of such sentiments as "so long as you possess your money, father, you ought to use it generously yourself, and put it at everyone's disposal, and make as many people rich as you possibly can" (lines 805–8 in the loose translation by Philip Vellacott in the Penguin edition). But such minority ethical notes respecting wealth and its use can be found as far back as Pindar, Old Comedy and Euripides (documented in detail in the edition of the play by E. W. Handley, London 1965), and there is no reason to hold their appearance in Menander to reflect new economic thinking. Of political ideas I can find no trace.

34. The bibliography of the past twelve or fifteen years is almost unmanageable, especially on slavery. Enough of it will be found in my *Slavery*, with a long survey in chap. 1 of the "ideological history" of the subject; in *Opus* 1, no. 1 (1982), devoted entirely to a discussion of that book held in Rome in 1981; and in Y. Garlan, *Les esclaves en Grèce ancienne* (Paris 1982). See also M. Morabita, *Les réalités d'esclavage d'après le Digeste* (*Annales Besançon* 254, 1981), which is half a computer print-out.

35. I have myself done so in *Politics in the Ancient World* (Cambridge 1983) and explained (pp. 10–12) why that was not inconsistent with my rejection in the present book of class as a useful category in the analysis of the ancient economy.

36. T. E. Bottomore, "Class", in *A Dictionary of Marxist Thought*, ed. Bottomore et al. (Oxford 1983), pp. 74–7. De Ste. Croix, *Struggle* 61, takes another way out: he dismisses as "isolated remarks which are of trivial importance" all statements by Marx that do not coincide with what de Ste. Croix holds to be the only correct interpretation. That leaves him in the remarkable position of asserting that in the preface to the second edition of the *Eighteenth Brumaire*, the passage I have quoted above shows that Marx "could forget the antithesis formulated near the end of that book."

37. This is briefly but sharply stated by Kreissig, *Seleukidenreich* 8–9. De Ste. Croix makes a throwaway concession of the point, essentially unimportant, he insists (pp. 44–5), but he ignores Kreissig's position here as well as later in his assault (pp. 63–5) on Vidal-Naquet's unimpeachable demonstration (reference in 218*n*32) that Graeco-Roman slaves did not constitute a class in a Marxist sense.

38. There is something a bit comic about the unbending Marxist's indignation at my "unreasonable" refusal to accept an "internationally agreed definition" of serfdom (by which he means the 1926 Slavery Convention of the League of Nations): de Ste. Croix, *Struggle* 137–8.

39. Finley, *Slavery* 77–8.

40. See Garnsey, *Labour*, chap. 6 (Garnsey) and 8 (Skydsgaard).

41. See now above all P. A. Brunt, "Free Labour and Public Works at Rome", *JRS* 70 (1980) 81–100, though he strains too much to make some of his points; cf. G. Rickman, *Roman Granaries and Store Buildings* (Cambridge 1971), pp. 8–11, on the portering requirements of the granaries of Ostia and Rome.

42. E.g. M. Corbier, "Salaires et salariat sous le Haut-Empire", in *Les "dévaluations" à Rome*, no. 2 (cited in n29), pp. 61–101.

43. A. Giardina, "Lavoro e storia sociale: antagonismi e alleanze dell' ellenismo al tardoantico", *Opus* 1 (1982) 115–46.

44. The contrary has recently been argued by G. Nenci, "Il problema della concorenza fra mandopera libera e servile nelle Grecia classica", *Index* 8 (1978/9) 121–31, but it is noteworthy that the argument is wholly abstract and hypothetical in an attempt to overcome the silence of the ancient sources, a silence that I should rather interpret as an accurate reflection of the reality.

45. See Finley, *Slavery* 102–3, with bibliography.

46. For all this, see Finley, *Slavery* 103–17.

47. See Ausbüttel, *Vereine* 40–42. The eastern half of the empire appears to have been no different, from Greek times on: F. Poland, *Geschichte der griechischen Vereinswesen* (Leipzig 1909), pp. 328–9.

48. P. Dockès, *Medieval Slavery and Liberation*, trans. A. Goldhammer (London 1982), chap. 4. However, Dockès can produce no evidence other than his inference from the fear and from the harsh measures taken against fugitives and the like, of what he calls the "inner dialectic of the class struggle", in the first intance of slaves against slaveowners.

49. T. Mommsen, "Bürgerliches und peregrinisches Freiheitsschutz im römischen Staat", in his *Juristische Schriften* 3 (Berlin 1907), pp. 1–20 (originally published in 1885).

50. See briefly Finley, *Slavery* 128–9, and now in detail W. V. Harris, "Towards a Study of the Roman Slave Trade", in *The Seaborne Commerce of Ancient Rome*, ed. J. H. D'Arms and E. C. Kopff (*Memoirs of the American Academy in Rome* 36, 1980), pp. 117–40.

51. See W. W. Buckland, *The Roman Law of Slavery* (Cambridge 1908), chap. 18.

52. *Corpus Scriptorum Ecclesiasticorum Latinorum* 88 (Vienna 1981). A valuable summary of the letters, with commentary and reference to related Augustinian material, is provided by H. Chadwick in *Journal of Theological Studies* 34 (1983) 425–52.

53. See M. Humbert, "Enfants à louer ou à vendre: Augustin et l'autorité parentale", in a colloquium on the letters published by Etudes Augustiniennes (Paris 1983), pp. 189–204.

54. See the important protest in this direction (against a developing trend to

speak of the "recrudescence of slavery" in the fourth century) by P. A. Février, in *ibid.*, pp. 101–15.

55. Whittaker in Garnsey, *Trade* 173. The reference to Roman legislation is to *Theodosian Code*, 13.1.13.

56. See B. D. Shaw, "Rural Markets in North Africa and the Political Economy of the Roman Empire", *Antiquités africaines* 17 (1981) 37–83, a considerably expanded version of a previous article with a similar title in *Research in Economic Anthropology* 2 (1979) 91–117.

57. See especially Whittaker in Garnsey, *Trade*, chap. 13 for the period of the later Roman Empire.

58. A. H. M. Jones, *The Roman Economy*, ed. P. A. Brunt (Oxford 1974), chap. 2 (originally published in 1955), remains fundamental.

59. See especially T. Helen, *Organization of Roman Brick Production in the First and Second Centuries A.D.* (Helsinki 1975); cf. P. Setälä, *Private Domini in Roman Brick Stamps of the Empire* (Helsinki 1977). I do not understand why J. Andreau, in reviewing Helen's book in *Annales* 37 (1982) 923–5, throws so much cold water on the analysis while conceding that Helen had opened a discussion of economic aspects of the industry that had scarcely been noticed previously. Contrast the positive reception of the work by D. P. S. Peacock, *Pottery in the Roman World* (London and New York 1982), pp. 133–5.

60. Y. Garlan, "Greek Amphorae and Trade", in Garnsey, *Trade* 34–5; D. Manacorda, "Produzione agricola, produzione ceramica e proprietari nell' ager Cosanus nel I a.C.", in Giardina/Schiavone II 3–54, esp. pp. 47–9.

61. C. Delplace, "Les potiers dans la société et l'économie de l'Italie et de la Gaule au ire siècle av. et au ire siècle ap. J.-C.", *Ktema* 3 (1978) 55–76, at pp. 73–6, with explicit rejection of the point of view of Wiseman criticized above, p. 52 and *n*42.

62. D. P. S. Peacock, "Recent Discoveries of Roman Amphora Kilns in Italy", *Antiquaries Journal* 57 (1977) 262–9, with bibliography; cf. A. Hesnard and C. Lemoine, "Les amphores du Cécube et du Falcone", *MEFRA* 93 (1981) 243–95.

63. H. Cockle, "Pottery Manufacture in Roman Egypt: a New Papyrus", *JRS* 71 (1981) 87–95. Strictly speaking, only one of the papyri has been published; the others are mentioned in the article only in the case of variants. The two not published are for the lease of one third and one fourth of a pottery, respectively, and one must assume, with the editor, that the remainders were leased in documents that have not survived. I have adjusted the figures accordingly.

64. I have omitted some details and possible further complications. It is disturbing that the practice has been ignored though knowledge of it has long been available, if not in such detail, from several other Egyptian pottery leases. Two, of the sixth century A.D., are leases for fractions of a pottery, one fourteenth in one case, one third in the other, for ten years and for the lessee's lifetime, respectively: P. Lond. III 994 (p. 259) and P. Cairo Masp. I 67110.

65. This section rests largely on my "The Ancient City: From Fustel de Cou-langes to Max Weber and Beyond", *Comparative Studies in Society and History* 19 (1977) 305–27, reprinted in Finley, *E & S.*, chap. 1. P. Leveau, "La ville antique et l'organization de l'espace rurale", *Annales* 38 (1983) 920–42, finds the concept of a consumer-city too "recondite", but I do not believe his approach to be incompatible with mine.

66. Quoted from the Penguin translation (1976) by Ben Fowkes, p. 472. In *The German Ideology*, instead of "antithesis" we read "clash of interests" between town and country.

67. K. Bücher, *Die Entstehung des Volkswirtschafts* (5th ed., Tübingen 1906), p. 371.

68. W. Sombart, *Der moderne Kapitalismus* (2nd ed., Munich and Leipzig 1916) I 142.

69. See C. Goudineau, "Marseilles, Rome and Gaul from the Third to the First Century B.C.", in Garnsey, *Trade* 76–86.

70. J.-P. Morel, "La laine de Tarente", *Ktema* 3 (1978) 93–110.

71. W. E. Thompson, "Entrepreneur" 54.

72. J. H. D'Arms, "M. I. Rostovtzeff and M. I. Finley: The Status of Traders in the Roman World", in *Ancient and Modern: Essays in Honor of G. E. Else* (Ann Arbor 1977), pp. 159–79. The two quotations in my text appear on pp. 163 and 179. The article has been reprinted in large part as chap. 1 of D'Arms, *Commerce and Social Standing in Ancient Rome* (Cambridge, Mass., 1981), on which see the review by P. Garnsey in *Classical Philology* 79 (1984) 85–8.

73. W. O. Moeller, *The Wool Trade of Ancient Pompeii* (Leiden 1976). The quotation about the building of Eumachia appears on p. 162. My critique is taken from the devastating analysis in the forthcoming book, *The Economy and Society of Pompeii* by W. S. Jongman, who was kind enough to provide me with an advance copy of the relevant section.

74. I considered this development in the context of the decline of ancient slavery in late antiquity: *Slavery* 139–41. C. R. Whittaker has since discussed the possibility on two occasions. As I understand his hesitation, it rests on uncertainty about the extent and significance of the decline (given the unsatisfactory state of the research), not on a denial of its existence: see Whittaker in Garnsey, *Trade* 174–7, and his fundamental article, "Inflation" 9–12.

75. Ausbüttel, *Vereine*, esp. chap. 3. Unfortunately, Ausbüttel reports without comment too many allegations and guesses by modern scholars, no matter how unfounded and how little he is himself influenced by them, e.g. his brief note (97n72) about Moeller's "allegation" that the magistrates in Pompeii protected the water rights of members of the fullers' association, for which there is no warrant.

76. The "building of Eumachia" was never rebuilt after the earthquake of A.D. 62; see H. Eschebach, *Pompeji* (Leipzig 1978), p. 293. Eschebach accepts

the Moeller account without question, and appears unruffled by the failure to rebuild this supposed guild-hall and cloth exchange in seventeen years. The Ostian *piazzale* has been offered as a candidate by M. Frederiksen in his review of this book in *JRS* 65 (1975) 170, but see R. Meiggs, *Ostia* (2nd ed., Oxford 1973), pp. 283–8, on the difficulties in interpreting the remains.

77. See especially Whittaker, "Inflation".

78. Lo Cascio, "Coinage" 76 (the money supply is discussed at pp. 82–6); cf. his long review in the *Annali* of the Ist. Italiano di Numismatica 25 (1978) 241–61 of C. Rodewald, *Money in the Age of Tiberius* (Manchester 1976).

79. See now Rodewald and the review by Lo Cascio, cited in the previous note.

80. Andreau, "Banque"; Thompson, "Entrepreneur", and his earlier "A View of Athenian Banking", *Museum Helveticum* 36 (1979) 224–41. Thompson seems unaware of Andreau's article.

81. "Entrepreneur" 58. I cannot refrain from one example of the quality of his economic thinking: ". . . but this assumes that they [Athenian bankers] acted conservatively. Yet we know that some of them went bankrupt" ("Banking" p. 235*n*69).

82. P. Millett, "Maritime Loans and the Structure of Credit in Fourth-century Athens", in Garnsey, *Trade* 36–52, at p. 43. The evidence for this calculation will be presented in the volume Millett is now preparing. I had suggested (p. 141) that the exceptional character of maritime loans in this respect and in the extremely high rate of interest involved can be explained by the insurance character of that form of moneylending. Millett (p. 44) has expressed doubts but I do not find his reasoning convincing.

83. As it was rightly and briefly dismissed by Lo Cascio, "Coinage" 77*n*3.

84. Garnsey, *Trade* 118.

85. E. Tengström, *Bread for the People* (*Skrifter* of the Swedish Institute of Rome 12, 1974), pp. 7, 93. Despite the title, the book is about the city of Rome in the fourth century A.D. and is based on a close philological analysis of relevant sections of the *Theodosian Code*. Carandini would claim as another example the North African ceramic ware from the second century to the seventh: "Pottery and the African Economy", in Garnsey, *Trade* 145–62. However, that trade was in no sense indispensable, whereas the city of Rome would have starved without the prodigious annual corn import.

86. All these figures are taken from P. Pomey and A. Tchernia, "Le tonnage maximum des navires de commerce Romains", *Archaeonautica* 2 (1978) 233–51, esp. pp. 237–43.

87. The fullest collection of evidence is now G. Rickman, *The Corn Supply of Ancient Rome* (Oxford 1980).

88. See now H. Pavis d'Escurac, *La préfecture de l'annone* (*Bibl. des Écoles fr. d'Athènes et de Rome* 226, 1976).

89. Garnsey, *Trade* 128.

90. See most recently P. Gauthier, "De Lysias à Aristote (Ath. Pol., 51, 4)...", *Revue historique de droit français* 59 (1981) 5–28.

91. Carrié, "Distributions" 1070–1100.

92. See J. Andreau, "Fondations privées et rapports sociaux en Italie romaine (Ire—IIIe siècles)", *Ktema* 2 (1977) 157–209. An excellent example of the range of benefactions is offered by the career of Opramoas, a wealthy mid-second-century benefactor from Lycia, known only epigraphically: see Balland, *Xanthos*, chap. 7. I am grateful to Peter Garnsey for directing my attention to this publication and to the inscription cited in the following note.

93. The inscription is no. 1 in the group published by C. Naour in *Zeitschrift für Papyrologie und Epigraphik* 24 (1977) 265–90.

94. See the broad outlines in the section entitled "De la générosité antique à la charité chrétienne", in E. Patlagean, *Pauvreté économique et pauvreté sociale à Byzance 4e–7e siècles* (Paris and The Hague 1977), pp. 181–96.

95. See the survey in H. Schneider, *Wirtschaft und Politik* (Erlangen 1974), pp. 361–91.

96. On Clodius, see the important discussion by W. Nippel, "Die *plebs urbana* und die Rolle der Gewalt in der späten römischen Republik", in *Vom Elend der Handarbeit*, ed. H. Mommsen, and E. Schulze (Stuttgart 1981), pp. 70–92, esp. 81–90. As Paul Veyne has phrased it in Veyne, "Alimenta" 166, "Pratiquement ce sont les pauvres qui sont visés...; eux seuls bénéficient des lois agraires, et touchent le blé fourni comme tribut par les provinces.... Cependant, jusqu'à l'époque chrétienne le langage continuera à dissoudre la catégorie sociale des pauvres dans l'universalité civique de la loi."

97. See Duncan-Jones, *Economy*, App. 5. On various administrative aspects, see also W. Eck, *Die staatliche Organisation Italiens in der hohen Kaiserzeit* (Munich 1979), chap. 5.

98. See P. Veyne, *Le pain et le cirque* (Paris 1976), pp. 647–58, and Veyne, "Alimenta".

99. E. Lo Cascio, "Gli alimenta, l'agricoltura italica e l'approvigionamento di Roma", *Rendiconti . . . Lincei*, 8th ser., 33 (1978) 311–54.

100. See especially Garnsey, cited 216n10, and Veyne, "Alimenta".

101. J. R. Rea, ed., *The Oxyrhynchus Papyri* XL, p. 8.

102. The most enthusiastic support has come from E. G. Turner, "Oxyrhynchus and Rome", *Harvard Studies in Classical Philology* 79 (1979) 1–24, at pp. 16–24; see also Balland, *Xanthos* 215–21, and, surprisingly, Carrié, "Distributions", whose own discussion for the most part ignores the shaky foundation laid by Rea. On the machinery, see now C. Nicolet, "Tessères frumentaires et tessères de vote", in *Mélanges . . . Heurgon* (École française de Rome 1976) II 694–716.

103. R. J. Rowland, Jr., "The 'Very Poor' and the Grain Dole at Rome and Oxyrhynchus", *Zeitschrift für Papyrologie und Epigraphik* 21 (1976) 60–72.

104. Carrié, "Distributions" 1096.

105. I have subsequently developed the conceptual analysis more fully in "Colonies—an Attempt at a Typology", *Transactions of the Royal Historical Society*, 5th ser., 26 (1976) 167–88; "Empire in the Greco-Roman World", *Greece and Rome*, 2nd ser., 25 (1978) 1–15, reprinted in *Review* 2 (1978) 55–68.

106. I follow A. Tchernia, "Italian Wine in Gaul at the End of the Republic", in Garnsey, *Trade* 87–104.

107. Tchernia, *ibid.*; A. Daubigney, "Relations marchandes méditerranéennes et procès des rapports de dépendance (*magu-* et ambactes) en Gaule protohistorique", in Colloque de Cortone (1981), published (1983) by the École française de Rome under the title, *Modes de contact et processus de transformation dans les sociétés anciennes*.

108. I here follow my "Soziale Modelle zur antiken Geschichte. II. Krieg und Herrschaft", *Historische Zeitschrift* 259 (1984) 286–308.

109. For Greece, see M. Amit, *Great and Small Poleis* (Brussels 1973).

110. This is a central theme of my *Politics in the Ancient World* (Cambridge 1983).

111. Whittaker, "Inflation" 7–15.

112. See my "The Fifth-Century Athenian Empire: A Balance Sheet", in *Imperialism in the Ancient World*, ed. P. D. A. Garnsey and C. R. Whittaker (Cambridge 1978), chap. 5, reprinted in Finley, *E. & S.*, chap. 3.

Index